Library of
Davidson College

# A PROSPECT OF LIBERAL DEMOCRACY

A Prospect of Liberal Democracy

Edited by William S. Livingston

The University of Texas Bicentennial Committee – Austin

International Standard Book Number 0-292-76454-5 (cloth)
0-292-76455-3 (paper)
Library of Congress Catalog Card Number 79-63171
Copyright © 1979 by the University of Texas Press
All rights reserved
Printed in the United States of America

Distributed by: University of Texas Press
P.O. Box 7819
Austin, Texas 78712

Contents

	Preface	vii
	List of Contributors	viii
1.	Introduction. Liberal Democracy: The Heritage of the Declaration and the Constitution WILLIAM S. LIVINGSTON	3
2.	Two Hundred Years of Liberal Democracy: A Beginning in Revolution and Independence WILLIAM H. GOETZMANN	18
3.	Liberal Democracy and the Image of America OSCAR HANDLIN	43
4.	Liberal Democracy in the United States ROBERT A. DAHL	57
5.	Liberal Democracy in Britain JO GRIMOND	73
6.	Liberal Democracy in India B. K. NEHRU	92
7.	Liberal Democracy in Southern Africa TONY HONORÉ	109
8.	Liberal Democracy in Mexico STANLEY R. ROSS	139
9.	Liberal Democracy in Japan ROBERT E. WARD	161
10.	Liberal Democracy in Israel ABBA EBAN	184

11. Liberal Democracy in Western Europe 199
GIOVANNI SARTORI
12. The Strengths of Liberal Democracy 215
SAMUEL H. BEER

Preface

The essays in this book were originally delivered as lectures in the University of Texas Bicentennial Lecture Program. Many people have had a hand in developing both the lecture series and the book, and I should like to record my gratitude for their labor and their interested concern.

The group that did the original planning included Stanley Ross, William Goetzmann, Walt Rostow, and myself. Ross, who was then Vice-President and Provost, put together the necessary financial backing through grants from the Moody Foundation and the Texas College Bicentennial Program and from funds made available by President Lorene Rogers. The administration of the program—planning topics and schedules, selecting speakers, arranging the lectures and broadcasts—was made easier, indeed possible, by the help of an advisory committee consisting of Ross, Elspeth Rostow, and Harry Middleton—to whom I am profoundly grateful. I am also indebted in quite varied ways for the assistance of Roger Louis, Ruth Smith, William Hays, Gerhard Fonken, and Thomas Dvorak. Virginia Sevier transcribed tapes, typed manuscripts, and conducted all the correspondence connected with the project.

And my wife helped in countless ways, not least by playing hostess to the series of distinguished essayists whose work is here presented.

W. S. L.

Austin
December 1, 1978

List of Contributors

SAMUEL H. BEER. Eaton Professor of the Science of Government, Harvard University. Author: *The City of Reason* (1949), *Treasury Control* (1956), *British Politics in the Collectivist Age* (1965); co-author: *Patterns of Government* (1958, 1962, 1973). Former National Chairman of Americans for Democratic Action. Former President, American Political Science Association.

ROBERT A. DAHL. Sterling Professor of Political Science, Yale University. Guggenheim Fellow. Trustee, Center for Advanced Study in the Behavioral Sciences. Member, National Academy of Sciences. Author: *A Preface to Democratic Theory* (1956), *Who Governs?* (1961), *Political Oppositions in Western Democracies* (1966), *Polyarchy, Participation, and Opposition* (1971). Former President, American Political Science Association.

ABBA EBAN. Member of the Knesset of Israel. Sometime member of the Israeli Cabinet, including service as Foreign Minister and Deputy Prime Minister. Formerly Ambassador to the United States and Representative to the United Nations.

WILLIAM H. GOETZMANN. Professor of History and Stiles Professor of American Studies, The University of Texas at Austin. Fulbright Lecturer, Cambridge University. Guggenheim Fellow. Pulitzer Prize in History. Author: *Army Exploration in the American West* (1959), *Exploration and Empire* (1966), *When the Eagle Screamed* (1966). Former President, American Studies Association.

Rt. Hon. JO GRIMOND, M.P. Member for Orkney and Shetland since 1950. Leader of the Liberal Party, 1956–67 and again in 1977.

Barrister of the Middle Temple. Formerly Rector of the University of Edinburgh and the University of Aberdeen, Chancellor of the University of Kent. Author: *The Liberal Future* (1959), *The Liberal Challenge* (1963), *The Referendum* (1975).

OSCAR HANDLIN. Carl H. Pforzheimer University Professor, Harvard University. Formerly Director of the Center for the Study of the History of Liberty in America. Pulitzer Prize in History. Author: *The Uprooted* (1950), *Al Smith and His America* (1958), *Children of the Uprooted* (1963), *Facing Life: Youth and the Family in American History* (1971).

TONY HONORÉ. Fellow of All Souls College and Regius Professor of Civil Law, Oxford University. Educated in South Africa and at Oxford. Rhodes Scholar. Author: *The South African Law of Obligations* (1954), *The South African Law of Property* (1958), *Causation in the Law* (1959), *Gaius* (1962), *The South African Law of Trusts* (1976), *Tribonian* (1978), *Sex Law* (1978).

WILLIAM S. LIVINGSTON. Professor of Government, Acting Vice-President and Dean of Graduate Studies. The University of Texas at Austin. Ford Foundation Fellow. Guggenheim Fellow. Formerly Editor-in-Chief, *The Journal of Politics*. Author: *Federalism and Constitutional Change* (1956); *Federalism in the Commonwealth* (1963); co-editor, *Australia, New Zealand, and the Pacific Islands since the First World War* (1979). Former President, the Southern Political Science Association and the Southwestern Social Science Association.

B. K. NEHRU. Educated University of Allahabad, London School of Economics, Oxford University. Barrister of the Inner Temple. Served the Government of India as Secretary of the Department of Economic Affairs and as Governor of several Indian states. Formerly Executive Director of the World Bank, Indian Ambassador to the United States, and High Commissioner to the United Kingdom.

STANLEY R. ROSS. Professor of History, formerly Vice-President and Provost, The University of Texas at Austin. Author: *Francisco I. Madero: Apostle of Mexican Democracy* (1955, 1977), *Historia Documental de México* (1964); editor, *Is the Mexican Revolution Dead?* (1966, 1975), *Fuentes de la Historia Contemporánea de México: Peri-*

ódicos y Revistas (1966–67). Former Chairman, Conference on Latin American History.

GIOVANNI SARTORI. Albert Schweitzer Professor in the Humanities, Columbia University. Formerly Professor of Political Science, Stanford University, and Professor of Political Science and Director of the Institute of Political Science at the University of Florence. Former editor, *Rivista Italiana di Scienze Politica*. Visiting Professor at Harvard and Yale Universities. Author: *Democrazia e Definizioni* (1957), *Democratic Theory* (1962, 1979), *Il Parlamento Italiano* (1963), *Parties and Party Systems* (1976).

ROBERT E. WARD. Professor of Political Science and Director of the Center for Research in International Studies, Stanford University. Fulbright Fellow. NSF Senior Fellow. Chairman of the Board, Social Science Research Council. Author: *Japan's Political System* (1967, 1978); co-author: *Political Modernization in Japan and Turkey* (1964), *Political Development in Modern Japan* (1968), *Allied Occupation of Japan, 1945–1952* (1974).

A PROSPECT OF LIBERAL DEMOCRACY

WILLIAM S. LIVINGSTON

1. Introduction
Liberal Democracy: The Heritage of the Declaration and the Constitution

This book had its origins in some conversations at the University of Texas back in 1975. Half a dozen people were pondering the question how the University might contribute most usefully to the commemoration of the nation's birthday—not merely of the Declaration of Independence but of the Philadelphia Constitution as well. The problem was to determine just what it was that those events represented and what message they had really conveyed to their own age and to posterity. On reflection that message seemed clear enough. It was complex, it was contentious, it was highly contemporary; but it had to do with freedom and with self-government. It spoke to that difficult and uncomfortable combination of principles that has come to be called liberal democracy. That, it seemed to us, was the message of those events.

Thus liberal democracy was to be our theme, as it had been the theme of other Americans in 1776 and 1787. The Declaration articulated its ideology; the Constitution elaborated its institutions. Together they contributed an idea and a polity both to America and to the world. Their message was stated in ringing phrases that served not only their contemporary purposes but other purposes in other times and places. The question was, did it still serve the present generation two hundred years later, and was it capable of serving others yet to come?

We decided we should try to find out. We would ask a group of distinguished students (and practitioners) of liberal democracy to consider its present condition and its future prospects, to assess its utility and viability in the light of its history and the pressures bearing in upon it in the various regions of the world. We would communicate the response to as many people as we could—first as lectures to a live audience, second through later broadcasts on radio and television by tape recordings, and third through publication of the lectures in book form.

And that is what we have done. The lectures were delivered in Austin at scattered intervals over a period of eighteen months in 1976 and 1977. Each of the authors has had an opportunity to revise his manuscript, and some have done so extensively. We have not tried to conceal the fact, however, that these essays were first delivered orally as lectures before a live audience. No doubt we could have excised the distinguishing marks, but the meaning would have been no different and some of the flavor might have been lost.

The lecturers—now authors—come from various walks of academic and public life; they represent a rich diversity of experience and points of view. Indeed it is that very diversity that gives the book a special flavor and strength. It combines the ideas of working politicians and the ruminations of academics. Historians and diplomats, political scientists and politicians, march through its pages, each discoursing on the problem as it appears from his perspective and in his part of the world.

Most of the lecturers were asked to address themselves to a common theme, namely the present state and future prospects of liberal democracy in a particular part of the world. The reader will quickly discover, however, that despite that common theme and despite a certain similarity of titles, the lectures vary greatly in approach and argument. Indeed they differ to some extent in their definition of liberal democracy, for we made no attempt to prescribe a standard definition. In some of the essays there is no definition at all, in some there is one for liberalism and one for democracy, but in all there is a common understanding about the phenomenon under discussion, and there seems to be no incompatibility among the several essayists' assumptions concerning its meaning. After all, we all know what liberal democracy is—don't we?

It is no exaggeration to say that the political history of the western world since the seventeenth century can be portrayed in the rise and transformation of liberalism. Indeed Mr. Beer's essay comes close to doing that very thing, though indirectly and as part of a different enterprise. It is important to emphasize, however, that over all those years "liberalism" has been transformed. Indeed the doctrine that first emerged was not liberalism (and it certainly was not so called) but the rule of law, a conception of the constitutional order that placed restraints on government and offered protection to the liberties of the subject. It was fundamentally a British conception, and though it did concern itself with liberty, it was manifested primarily in what Beer calls "government by discussion." It was only in the late eighteenth and early nineteenth centuries, after it had been joined with other notions—in England with nonconformity, natural law, and laisser faire; on the continent with rationalism and egalitarianism—that it assumed the shape and label of liberalism. By then it was a complex doctrine, difficult to rationalize satisfactorily and still more difficult to embody in human institutions. But it had a far-reaching and profoundly exciting appeal, and, as both Oscar Handlin and William Goetzmann make clear, that appeal found its strongest voice and most compelling model in America.

But liberalism was to become still more complex with the evolution of democracy in the nineteenth century, for the two were put in the same harness and expected to run together. We still expect them to run together, and that is the source of many of the problems to which this book is addressed. Liberalism and democracy represent two quite different purposes and yield two quite different rules of order and action. One has to do with freedom, the other with self-government; where they meet is in their common concern for the dignity and status of individual citizens. But they are now inseparably linked, in both theory and practice, and have been for a century and more. Thus it is both convenient and true for us to speak of "liberal democracy."

More than one of the essayists in this volume make the point that democracy cannot function unless certain freedoms are assured, and that there can therefore be no other democracy than liberal democracy. No doubt that is so, but the reverse is far from true, for history produced liberalism long before it produced democracy. Liberalism and democracy sometimes supplement and strengthen each other but sometimes they do not. Ultimately they are not in harmony but in tension, and each pushed to its limits may make the other impossible. Too great an assertion of individual liberty may defeat the will of the people. An unfettered commitment to majority rule may defeat the liberties of the citizen. Liberal democracy is based on conflict and balance, and on the capacity of the political system to avoid pressing either principle to its extreme. Liberal democracy only illustrates again, often quite pointedly and poignantly, the age-old problem that lies at the heart of any polity, that of reconciling effectiveness with responsibility and order with liberty.

The tensions and troubles of the system were exacerbated by the transformation of liberalism in the late nineteenth and early twentieth centuries. What had once been a doctrine emphasizing freedom from government interference became a doctrine that government should assume greater and greater responsibility for the social and economic welfare of its citizens. The motivating forces of the change may be traced to Benthamite utilitarianism, the growth of trade unions, and the revulsion of reformers at the conditions engendered by industrialization and laisser faire. The search for individual security which had first taken the form of a defense against the arbitrary powers of princes and parliaments now reacted to new and different threats and mounted a defense against the whims of the trade cycle, the squalor of urban life, and the indifference of laisser-faire governments. Liberalism ceased to be individualist and became collectivist, and "liberals" came to be identified with the expansion of government services, government functions, and government budgets.

The original combination of liberalism and democracy caused tensions enough. The new liberalism not only changed and enhanced those tensions, but led to an alteration of democracy as well. In the wake of the distresses and dissents that marked many democracies in the mid-twentieth century, there appeared a demand for a fuller participation in the democratic process by all groups, all ages, all peoples, a democracy of universality and participation. Representation was to be representation by cross section rather than by agency, and democratic decision making was somehow to be returned to "the people." Democracy was now to

Introduction 7

be participatory. While the new summons to participation recalled the nostalgia of the town meeting, it also recalled the excesses of jacobinism. And it placed new burdens on liberal democracy and raised new questions about its viability.

The question of its viability cannot be easily or safely ignored. Those who predict its demise or regard its passing with either gloom or glee are legion. We are concerned here, however, not with those who have always been *hostile* to it[1] but with its friends and supporters who think it is no longer working, is about to collapse, or has already done so. But even those are not of one mind. Just as there is no uniformity of understanding about democracy's experience, so there is no uniformity of view about democracy's prospects.

The gloomiest, and in some ways the most trenchant, appraisal comes from those who observe that the demands on democracy have increased at the same time that its decision processes have become more cumbersome, and conclude that democracy is in consequence overloaded and less effective. A recent symposium in *The Public Interest*[2] raised some embarrassing questions along these lines and gave some answers that were far from reassuring. The participants noted a decline in respect for the established institutions of school and family, an erosion of patriotism, a diminished acceptance of the utility of the national community. The world, some said, has rejected America's model of liberal democracy, which now seems to have but little relevance to the needs of the future. Mr. Handlin in the present volume might well breathe "amen." Samuel Huntington, both in *The Public Interest* and in that remarkable volume prepared for the Trilateral Commission called *The Crisis of Democracy*,[3] has argued that a series of developments: the burgeoning of egalitarianism, the growth of public-interest lobby groups, the expanded participation of minorities, the impulses to explore, to dissent, to deny—many of them legitimate and even late—have overloaded the democratic process and distorted the balance between liberalism and democracy. The editor of the report concludes, "The demands on democratic government grow, while the capacity of democratic government stagnates. This, it would appear, is the central dilemma of the governability of democracy."[4] Mr. Sartori in his essay in the present volume reaches somewhat the same conclusions, though he reaches them by quite a different route.

There is no doubt that this adds up to a serious problem. But there is certainly no agreement on the solution. Mr. Robert Nisbet[5] sees these developments as constituting one of the periodic crises of authority that have plagued the western state system. The legitimacy of the centralized state has been eroded and the solution, he believes, lies in a new pluralism of authority—a revival of intermediate powers between the citizen and the state: school, family, voluntary associations, neighborhoods, and interest groups. Mr. Theodore Lowi,[6] on the other hand, says the crisis of authority has been produced by that very pluralism that Nisbet prescribes. Interest-group liberalism, he argues, is based on some impossible assumptions about free group competition and consensus on the rules of the game. Despite its faith that the public good will emerge from the clash of private interests, it permits public power to be parceled out to special interests and it excludes large groups from the benefits of society. Lowi prescribes a more highly centralized administration, an independent bureaucratic elite, a stronger federal regulatory power—the very things Nisbet says have proved their ineffectiveness and have produced the erosion of authority.

A different kind of assessment, but one that is equally gloomy, is that delivered by Senator, and erstwhile Ambassador to the United Nations, Patrick Moynihan. On many occasions and in many forums,[7] Mr. Moynihan has pointed to the diminishing number of liberal democracies that are left in the world—something like two dozen at most. The Third World has been taught that autocratic socialism is likely to be more useful than liberal democracy, and even those new nations that have attempted initially to develop their own democracies have been forced by ideology or circumstance to abandon the attempt. In the twentieth century, he fears, liberal democracy has the same kind of character and future as monarchy in the nineteenth. It is "a holdover form of government, one which persists in isolated or peculiar places here and there, and may even serve well enough for special circumstances, but which has simply no relevance to the future. It is where the world was not where it is going."[8]

Given the variety and intensity of these forebodings about the prospects of liberal democracy, the careful scrutiny embodied in the present essays assumes even greater importance. But a question like "What is the future of democracy?" is never susceptible of a simple answer, even when it is posed in simple terms. It is the variety of approaches to that question, and the complexity of its content, that are reflected in these essays. What emerges is a careful and cautious appreciation, neither cheerily optimistic nor determinedly gloomy.

Mr. Goetzmann, after a shrewd and comprehensive chronicle of democracy in America, concludes that in the postwar world "liberal democracy faces overwhelming challenges, not the least of which is the almost complete obscuring of the individual in a computerized maze." And yet, he believes, we are mastering these threats, and at least in its essentials "liberal democracy is alive and well in this land." Mr. Dahl is less confident. America has undertaken a series of historic commitments: to a constitutional order, to democracy and polyarchy, to a private, corporate economy, to social and economic justice, and to a world order. The difficulty is that these commitments may be impossible of fulfillment, not least because they are not all compatible with one another. To preserve our system, he says, we must improve the mechanisms through which it operates, make sure the president is responsive to Congress and the people, and elect better men to the presidency. The hopes for these improvements are dim, he thinks, and he is thus not optimistic for democracy in America. Neither is Mr. Handlin. His argument is that the image of America and the image of liberal democracy have been closely intertwined from the beginning. Each played its role as the new hope of mankind, and as that hope was disappointed by the exigencies of politics, a disillusionment both with America and with liberal democracy ensued. Handlin traces a melancholy decline in the image of America in the past century, and a corresponding disenchantment with its political system, for the foes of America have also been the foes of liberal democracy.

The essays on other countries are also diverse, and the analysis varies considerably between the industrial and the developing areas. Mr. Grimond argues that liberal democracy in Britain has always presupposed two systems at work: the rule of law and the market economy—working together with a third fundamental, namely a widespread concern for the general interest. But the growth of bureaucracy, the decline of party, and the surge of special interests have imperilled liberal democracy, and the basic problem now is whether the nation can undertake the reforms necessary to save it. He ends with an appeal, "Let us learn from history," rather than a prediction, but his conclusion is at least guardedly hopeful. To Mr. Sartori the future of liberal democracy is very grim indeed, at least in Europe. There the self-regulating mechanisms that continuously restore the balance of society have given way under the pressures of socialism, technology, class politics, and ideology, with the consequence that liberal democracy is directly threatened, not merely with rejection but with an incapacity to function. He thinks the United States may still have time to escape the overloading of demands and the expansion of participation that threaten the viability of the system in Italy and France, but it cannot remain complacent, for there is evidence of a coming "Europeanization" of American democracy.

In examining the prospects in Japan, Mr. Ward very carefully assesses the forces that threaten liberal democracy: economic slowdown, reduced confidence in political leadership, the absence of any literary advocacy—and also those that sustain it: the strength of the liberal democratic governing party, the lack of any real alternatives, and the widespread acceptance of the constitutional system. There are reasons for optimism about the future, he concludes, but they are "as much an act of faith as the product of dispassionate scholarly analysis." As for India, Mr. Nehru is unequivocally optimistic, and the experience of the Emergency has if anything strengthened his confidence. Liberal democracy in India has always operated under serious strains, engendered in part by her colonial past and in part by her parlous economic condition. The Emergency was a reaction to an increasing chaos itself produced by an ingrained disrespect for authority reaching back to British rule. But, he says, there is a nearly unanimous agreement that "India cannot be governed except democratically." The chief threat—and the only thing that could destroy democracy—is the economic problem, but even that is likely to be mastered. The nature of the threat to democracy in Israel is partly economic but principally political. Her commitment to liberal democracy, says Mr. Eban, can be taken for granted, but whether she can maintain her system depends entirely on the power relations in the world around her. "Peace is the issue, not only for the survival of a liberal and democratic Israel but for the survival of Israel itself." If Israel can achieve peace and maintain some measure of economic stability, liberal democracy is safe.

Mr. Ross's careful chronicle of the successes and failures of the Mexican revolution shows clearly how difficult it is to harness democracy to a single-party system. The party provides a channel for political expression for a variety of interests, but serves also as a device for disciplining those groups and co-opting their leadership. Mexico enjoys a considerable measure of freedom but the system is static, and Mr. Ross considers it "unlikely that greater democracy will come to Mexico in the near future." The same is true of Southern Africa, though for entirely different reasons. In one of the most remarkable essays in the book, Mr. Honoré attempts to appraise the prospects for liberal democracy in one of the world's most tormented regions. He argues that there is a substantial democracy—even liberal democracy—within the white community, but that the white community in the Republic will not voluntarily concede black majority rule. We are witnessing the overture to a tragedy in which African and Afrikaner are set on a collision course, leaving the English, the colored, and the Indian to scramble as best they can. On the whole the prospect is gloomy, for "the elements of a revolutionary situation are slowly assembling," but on the other hand the clash is not inevitable; both "tribes" possess the political skill to avoid it if only they can mobilize the political will.

Mr. Beer's concluding essay on the origin and prospects of liberal democracy might as easily have served as an introduction. It is as much retrospective as prospective, and therein lies its richness. He defines liberal democracy as "government by discussion" and finds its basic model in seventeenth-century England. It was not a product of capitalism or of the Protestant Reformation. It was strictly a political development and it came about largely by accident ("the nearest run thing you ever saw") but it survived because of its own repeatedly demonstrated strength. Today it is confined to a small and shrinking portion of mankind, and many observers find its prospects dim. Yet Mr. Beer retains a certain confidence, and that is another reason why his essay has been used as a conclusion. Liberal democracy has passed and survived many a crucial test. Nations that have abandoned it have returned to try it again, and if it faces serious problems, it has faced them before. It has shown a great capacity for survival in the past and Mr. Beer suspects it has not lost that capacity.

These essays do not tell us all we need to know about liberal democracy, nor do they view its future with the same degree of confidence—or despair. But they do shed light on it from widely varying viewpoints, and taken all together they afford us a broad and fascinating prospect of its future course.

The variety should not surprise us, if only because the essayists come from different countries and conditions. But apart from diversity of perspectives and expectations, liberal democracy is inescapably plagued by internal contradictions—rights, duties, equality, majority rule, constitutional limitations—to such an extent than an emphasis on one aspect produces *pari passu* a depreciation of another, and the same core of liberal democratic theory may provide the basis for entirely different theoretical or institutional results.[9] A familiar way of viewing these inner tensions is to see them as a contest between liberty and equality, or as a recent shift in emphasis from one to another. Democracy, says one distinguished student of these things, "has persistently strengthened its equalitarian impulse, encroaching on liberty in reaching for equality."[10] Others see the conflict as emerging from the combination of freedom in the sense of the capitalist market place and freedom in the sense of equal opportunity to realize capabilities.[11] Others would describe "the malady of democratic states as a derangement in the relation between the mass of the people and the government."[12] The tradition of civility, says Walter Lippmann, requires the executive to do the proposing and the representative body to do the disposing. When mass opinion, too often selfish and ill informed, comes to dominate the decision-making process, government inevitably adopts mistaken and even deadly policies.

We cannot ignore the variety—or contrariety—of these interpretations. Each of them has its legitimacy, for the experience upon which they draw is itself variegated. It may be suggested, however, that the variety embodied in the present essays may be brought into better perspective if we go back to first principles and ask ourselves, just what are the requisites of liberal democracy? Not what are the principles it incorporates, but what are the conditions necessary to its functioning? Conceding readily that this exercise has been attempted before, and with results that differ widely in substance and detail, we may none the less suggest (with some confidence and much modesty) that there are two essential conditions and one overriding external circumstance necessary to the effective working of liberal democracy.

The first essential is the existence and maintenance of a substantial consensus on the fundamental principles of the system, on the legitimacy and desirability of liberal democracy itself. Not an agreement on policy matters (though doubtless that would be useful) but an agreement on the rules of the game and a general acceptance of the idea that if the rules are followed, the policy outcome itself is legitimate. Only with that kind of consensus is it possible for politics to concern itself with issues of policy rather than with questions of régime.

The second essential is the assurance of a minimum satisfaction of economic needs. This is a purely pragmatic criterion impossible to state precisely; but if the resources of a society are too lean to afford a minimum level of satisfaction to the citizenry, then politics becomes grimmer and less tolerant. If men are starving and without hope, political issues are both exigent and mortal; there is no patience, no long run, no concession to principle. Liberalism becomes illusory and democracy impossible.

The third essential, what I called the "overriding external circumstance," is simply that the power relations among nations—in particular those among the great powers—be such as to permit the effective operation of liberal democracy in the countries affected by those power relations.

Now if we examine the present essays with these requisites in mind, the character of the threats to democracy becomes clearer. In the developed industrial nations the growing incapacity of the system may be ascribed to an increasing breakdown in the consensus that is necessary to sustain it. In Japan, in Britain, and in Italy, these essays suggest that the viability of democracy is imperiled by reduced confidence in political leadership, a decline of the established parties, the growth of class politics, the divorce of technology from values, and the ever-burgeoning demands of special interests. If the sense of community gives way to a competitive anomie, then the political system that can tolerate even sharp and bitter differences because it rests on a consensus about the rules must yield to one in which all questions are open to contest—even questions about the régime itself.

In the developing nations the problems of democracy are more directly economic. In country after country, in the first exultation of independence, an attempt has been made to create a system that was democratic and sometimes liberal, but in country after country the attempt has failed. The nascent democracy, buffeted by hunger, instability, and squalor, has given way to the charismatic president or the military coup d'état. Economics is not the only problem of the developing nations, but it is the key to the viability of democracy. The achievement of freedom is loaded with expectations of the good life, and when those hopes are disappointed, the load on liberal democracy is more than it can bear. In Mr. Eban's words, "It is in the gap of disillusion between institutional liberation and economic servitude that liberal democracy has fallen into decline."

Senator Moynihan mourns the passing of liberal democracy and demonstrates its demise by noting the diminishing number of states that embrace it. I think that contention rather misses the point. Liberal democracy is a political luxury that not all nations can afford. What has happened in the twentieth century—particularly in the wake of decolonization—is that many states have tried it without possessing the conditions requisite for its success. Surely an equally interesting question is why did so many of them want to try it? The answer is that liberal democracy stood for something good, something they wanted, something worth trying in the hope of emulating those states—usually ex-colonial powers—where it seemed to work. And the attempt was made, even in the face of the bitter ethnic divisions that defeated national identity and the bitter poverty that left neither time nor patience for democracy.

In many of these nations the economic problem was compounded by the absence of any real consensus. Harsh divisions of race, language, religion, and tribal structure rendered impossible the task of creating a national will or interest. Liberal democracy was doomed from the start. But one must not suppose that economic underdevelopment and the lack of consensus always go hand in hand. India is underdeveloped by anybody's calculus, but Mr. Nehru insists most strongly that the consensus supporting democracy is strong and widespread. Israel, though scarcely underdeveloped in the customary sense, nevertheless faces a monumental economic problem, and yet the democratic consensus is clear and unequivocal.

This brings us to the third condition, namely that the external power relations permit the functioning of democracy. The essential importance of this factor is made clear by Mr. Honoré's assessment of the future prospects of South Africa. There the economic problem is manageable and the consensus among the white citizens is unmistakable. The danger comes from the millions of have-nots and from the looming threat of interference by outside powers. Mr. Eban's essay makes an even stronger argument on this point in regard to Israel. The objective conditions within the country are not of themselves enough. Israel must have peace in the region, an acknowledgement of her right to exist, and for the foreseeable future she must have a continuing infusion of outside aid if she is to sustain her economy.

Thus if we are to achieve a general view—a prospect—of liberal democracy, we must see it in terms of the necessities that permit it to work. Where the requisites are missing, the system has little chance, and it is rather beside the point to bemoan its passing where it never truly existed.

Even so, it is surely legitimate to ask whether its prospects are good or bad, whether it is on the rise, on the decline, or holding steady. And that, of course, is a major purpose of the present volume. But the answer not surprisingly is less clear than the question. Very few of these essayists reach a confident and unambiguous conclusion. Most are very properly concerned to assess the relevant influences and to consider contingencies. Most of them have confined their predictions to the country about which they are writing. And, it is fair to say, most of them are rather gloomy about the prospects.

Is there no basis then for a properly guarded optimism about liberal democracy? Of course there is, but it had better be very well guarded indeed. One problem is to avoid the numbers game of counting defaulters. The success of democracy in India and Japan must be accorded an importance far greater than its failure in a dozen small nations where it never had a chance anyway. In 1975 the Indian Emergency seemed to many observers to betoken the collapse of the world's largest democracy. The election of 1977—the fact that it was held and that its results were accepted—renewed the confidence of the supporters of democracy the world over. In the same era we have seen the recovery of democracy in Greece, in Spain, in Portugal. The nations of Germany, Italy, and Japan, which in the prewar period were its most bitter enemies, became in the postwar period its most enthusiastic practitioners. There is no question that liberal democracy is now again facing crises of magnitude, crises that deserve our real concern, but it has done so in the past and survived. It is not irrelevant that the nations least democratic in ideology and practice cloak their perversions in its nomenclature. Its vocabulary, its institutions, its traditions—all serve as shibboleths and facades for peoples who traduce its principles and renounce its substance. A guarded confidence is not irrational, though the rational optimist had better make sure he has read what Handlin, Honoré, and Sartori have to say on the subject.

If liberal democracy contains contradictions, so do other systems. That is no guarantee that it will soon self-destruct.[13] It is not only political systems but every human personality that is beset by contradictions. Men want *both* freedom and authority; that is what politics, and *a fortiori* political theory, is all about. It is not inevitable that a society any more than an individual will be destroyed by such contradictions. In the healthy society as in the healthy individual these dualisms are in balance—even if in tension.

Notes

1. The critics of liberal democracy are surveyed and analyzed in David Spitz, *Patterns of Anti-Democratic Thought* (New York: Macmillan, 1949).
2. No. 41 (Fall 1975).
3. Michel J. Crozier, Samuel P. Huntington, and Joji Watanuki, *The Crisis of Democracy: Report on the Governability of Democracies to the Trilateral Commission* (New York: New York University Press, 1975).
4. *The Crisis of Democracy*, Introduction (by Z. K. Brzezinski?), p. 9.
5. Robert Nisbet, *Twilight of Authority* (New York: Oxford University Press, 1975).
6. Theodore J. Lowi, *The End of Liberalism: Ideology, Policy, and the Crisis of Public Authority* (New York: Norton, 1969).
7. E.g., the article in *The Public Interest* cited above; *Time*, July 26, 1976, p. 31; *New York Times*, October 12, 1975, p. E13.
8. Daniel P. Moynihan, "The American Experiment," *The Public Interest*, no. 41 (Fall 1975), p. 6.
9. A contention masterfully expounded by George H. Sabine, "The Two Democratic Traditions," *The Philosophical Review* 61 (1952): 551–574.
10. J. A. Corry in *Prospects for Constitutional Democracy: Essays in Honor of R. Taylor Cole*, ed. John Hallowell (Durham, N.C.: Duke University Press, 1976), p. 67.
11. C. B. Macpherson, *The Life and Times of Liberal Democracy* (Oxford: Oxford University Press, 1977), p. 1.
12. Walter Lippmann, *The Public Philosophy* (Boston: Little, Brown & Co., 1955), ch. 3.
13. See the eloquent argument on this point in J. Roland Pennock, *Liberal Democracy: Its Merits and Prospects* (New York: Rinehart & Co., 1950), part 4. Note especially his list of "prerequisites," pp. 211–216, and his "Conclusion," p. 304.

WILLIAM H. GOETZMANN

2. Two Hundred Years of Liberal Democracy: A Beginning in Revolution and Independence

Though the concept of liberal democracy is not exclusively American, no other nation has been so consistently dedicated to that ideal. It forms the bedrock upon which rests "The American Dream" of freedom and unlimited opportunity for all—the acknowledged right of everyone in the society to pursue, as Jefferson put it, "life, liberty and happiness." In 1940, as the United States was faced with the demoralization of an ongoing Great Depression and the rising threat of world totalitarianism, Professor Ralph Henry Gabriel of Yale University boldly published his volume *The Course of American Democratic Thought*. That book presented in historical terms an American counter-ideology to the demoralization of depression and the threats of totalitarianism. He saw in the American democratic experience the forging of a set of ideals and principles that were inspiring, and yet tough and resilient enough to resist the awesome pressures and beguilingly easy solutions of the twentieth century. For him the essence of American democracy rested on three axioms: belief in a natural law that transcended temporal expediency, belief in the innate dignity of the individual, and belief in the mission of America to spread its enlightened principles wherever mankind was being oppressed or was in dire need. Since he was an historian, his book made clear that these principles had been derived from hard experience. They did not spring full-blown from the head of Zeus,

NOTE: Portions of this essay have previously been published in *Hemispheric Perspectives on the United States: Papers from the New World Conference*, ed. Joseph S. Tulchin (Westport, Conn.: Greenwood Press, 1978).

Jove, or any other god. They evolved, grew with time, and proved their value in many a perilous test. It is thus appropriate that we begin with history and concrete experience.

Before turning to that concrete experience, however—that "tale of the tribe"—I think it important to turn to the critical problem of definition. It is a problem that will recur several times throughout this essay since the concept of "liberal democracy," being live and dynamic, has continued to grow and evolve in our history. By way of preliminary definition, however, let us make use of an often-quoted chestnut, Lord Acton's pronouncement, "All power corrupts; absolute power corrupts absolutely." It seems clear that the concept or ideology of liberal democracy has always been, long before Lord Acton's time, directed toward the prevention of such absolute power and such absolute corruption. It is a philosophy rooted in the decentralization of power, in the democratic decision-making process, resting necessarily upon the broadest possible base of individual participation. It is the belief that individuals in society should control their own destinies. The great empty spaces and abundant resources of America, as Frederick Jackson Turner and David Potter have pointed out,[1] made it uniquely possible to test this philosophy in America.

Control over their own destinies by the individuals who make up society—the definition of democracy seems clear enough. But what does "liberal" democracy mean? For a long time "liberal" seemed to derive from "liberty," which in turn meant, in the context of monarchies and other forms of absolute government, that the people should be freed from governmental absolutism and left alone to pursue happiness in any way they chose. For much of the eighteenth and nearly all of the nineteenth century it meant laisser faire, the mainstay of the classical political economists from Adam Smith onwards. More recently it has taken on other meanings. It connotes an openness and a desire for change as opposed to the foot-dragging of conservatism rooted in tradition. Jefferson put it most succinctly when he said "The earth belongs to the living." It also connotes "liberality," open-handedness, a free-spending, everything-for-everybody mentality; the idea that one way or another the meek shall be either seduced or forced to inherit the earth. Put in its best terms, it connotes generosity, that virtue so eloquently symbolized by the Statue of Liberty. But, perhaps most importantly, it has come to stand for the protection of the people against concentrated power wherever it looms as a threat to liberty—in communities, in the economy, in government, in business, and in the arena of world politics. It is because the Americans believed they had perfected a philosophy and a technique for defending the people against concentrated power—that is to say, because the United States was and is a liberal-democratic nation—that they have been so eager to take up the cause of what Professor Gabriel called "The Mission of America."[2] Tom Paine, at the outset of the Revolution, provided the rallying cry, "Freedom hath been hunted round the globe. Asia and Africa have long expelled her—Europe regards her like a stranger, and England hath given her warning to depart. O! receive the fugitive and prepare in time an asylum for mankind!"[3]

Tom Paine takes us vividly back into history and the story of how the American liberal democratic experiment began—in revolution and the struggle for independence. These beginnings form a parable perhaps, or at least the basic text, upon which our subsequent experience with, and attitude toward, liberal democracy inevitably rest. In reciting this parable let us begin with the obvious.

Revolution and independence are not the same thing. The distinction has often been obscured in recent years and much more stress has been put upon *revolution*, admittedly a fashionable word these days, than upon *independence*. That is true for a number of reasons. Revolution is dramatic. It is story. It is epic. It is dynamic. It stirs the blood. Independence is a condition. Revolution connotes images and visions of struggle and heroism, of pamphleteers and ragged soldiers, of "times that try men's souls," of Tom Paine, George Washington, Simon Bolivar, and Louis Riel. Independence for the successful revolutionary is almost an anticlimax. It is abstract and it implies termination and stasis like the happy ending of a fairy tale or a motion picture, whereas revolution may be a permanent dynamic condition—an ongoing focus for the hopes and dreams of a people. Revolution is above all myth, the most powerful modern myth of our time, and certainly the most powerful myth, along with that of the frontier described by Frederick Jackson Turner, in American civilization. It behooves us then to be fully aware of the humanistic and spiritual quality of revolution as myth in the growth of American civilization. A tradition of revolution makes and has made the United States seem everlastingly the country of the future from the time that Tom Paine, somewhat over-optimistically, announced "the birthday of a new world" down to the present. The tradition of revolution also explains the North American's rage for novelty. Always in our history, it seems, "new" has been better. We have wished to be progressive, modernist, up-to-date. For a long time we were pathetically responsive to the latest European cultural fads, from phrenology and Walter Scott novels to Bauhaus architecture and existentialism. In recent decades we have seen the rage for the new virtually destroy our art as one school replaced another almost annually until we have gone from the "minimal" to the invisible. A similar rhythm prevailed in the nineteenth-century American preoccupation with the new in technology—a preoccupation that built a mighty industrial nation but forever altered the ecology of both land and people while at the same time generating a human mobility that has kept the nation in ferment. Steamboats with built-in obsolescence, railroads, bridges, superhighways, automobiles, motorcycles, strip culture, and the easy rider all have something to do with the North American myth of continuing revolution with its rage for the new. The United States in a bountiful continent for 200 years has been celebrating the "endless birthday party." The myth of revolution has supplied the dynamic. It has instilled the spirit in the revellers.

And yet most of our current scholars do not see the American Revolution as being very revolutionary at all. It is most frequently contrasted with the French and Soviet experiences and found wanting in revolutionary quality. The French Revolution, carried forward on the rising tide of Romantic folk-spirit, seemed once and for all to have overturned the established orders in favor of the masses. It has seemed a true social and class revolution. It produced an ideology—or at least a stirring rhetoric—of revolution that seemed addressed to the masses and promised, if not to abolish peasantry, at least to ameliorate its condition. Since the

United States has no explicitly acknowledged peasant class, its revolutionary leaders, alas, produced no such rhetoric. People like Jefferson and Franklin believed America to be a classless society, while leaders like Adams and Hamilton, if they believed otherwise, dared not admit it. American revolutionary leaders wished only to throw off the impediments of the British Empire so as to allow "the new man, the American" to realize the opportunities that nature's abundance offered to him. Crèvecoeur realized this, as did Tocqueville in the Age of Jackson.[4] But this meant that American revolutionary leaders, aside from Tom Paine, produced no rhetoric or ideology of cataclysmic class revolution.

Likewise in this respect they do not compare in their apocalyptic visions to the leaders of the Soviet Revolution. There was no powerful Hegelian dialectic to help them espouse clash and contradiction for its own sake. There was no Marxist teleology, no myth of the working class, to aid them in a country where everyone was of the working class and believed himself the better for it. And there was no brutal Tsarist repression, no downtrodden peasantry (except the Negro slave), no secret police, no Siberia.

By all current standards the American Revolution seems "prerevolutionary"—no peasants to liberate, no masses to disenchain, no classes to overthrow, no unsubtle appeal to a mass audience. From time to time, however, historians with a perverse, pragmatic bent have looked to the consequences of the two modern revolutions in France and Russia and have been mildly dismayed to find that as revolutions they have not accomplished so much after all.

Nonetheless the main scholarly battleground as it concerns the American Revolution today seems inevitably to invoke comparisons with the two "real" revolutions in France and Russia. One group of scholars has believed that the American Revolution was fought less over "home rule" than "who should rule at home" and has searched diligently for evidence indicating that a class struggle *was* somehow involved in *our* revolution too.[5] "New" historians have found startling evidence of such things as sailors' riots against their masters—to them certain evidence of a colony-wide class struggle.[6] Students of the Great Awakening often see that strange event less in religious terms than in socioeconomic terms.[7] The Awakeners all the way from Charleston to Boston were the true peasant masses pitted against the tie-wig elites and their pulpit puppets like Charles Chauncey and Jonathan Mayhew. It was these awakened peasant masses, inspired by Jonathan Edwards's millennial rhetoric of communitarianism—not to mention God's divine and supernatural light—who led the vanguard of revolution.[8] A recent "Courses by Newspaper" article even has George Washington numbered among this Awakeners' vanguard, absurd though that is to contemplate.[9] Still other interpreters point with pride to the period after the Revolution, to the democratizing provisions of the Northwest Ordinances, to the new state constitutions which carried republicanism to the extreme and enthroned the county legislator, to Shays's and other incipient rebellions, to the device of the constitutional convention, to the relative increase in the franchise (for men, not for women), and declare that the Revolution *was* after all class-motivated and class-propelled.[10] Another school points tellingly to the fact that the Federalists, in order to promote the Constitution and then stay in power, had to adopt the levelling rhetoric of republicanism, implying that no Federalist believed a word of it.[11] One of the abiding problems with this interpretation is, of course, the question whether republican yeomen in town or country considered themselves masses and classes, either in the revolutionary or even later in the Jacksonian period. This question should provide a field day for an emerging generation of cliometricians.

Certain interpreters of the Revolution remain old-fashioned. They still search for an ideological tradition among American leaders that not only provided the "cement" for revolutionary solidarity, but also bears comparison with the better-known rhetoric and ideology of France and Russia. The most notable work of this genre, Professor Bernard Bailyn's prize-winning *The Ideological Origins of the American Revolution*, sees the colonists being persuaded to revolt by appeals to classical models of Roman republican virtue, Puritan values, the English legal tradition, the works of British and continental philosophers, and most viscerally the English Whig tradition of "coffee house radicalism" best exemplified in *Cato's Letters* by Trenchard and Gordon.[12] Because the American colonies had a high degree of literacy, because the printing of pamphlets and penny papers was becoming the rage in America, because news travelled surprisingly fast in what was in the 1770s a seaboard nation, Professor Bailyn's thesis must be considered as something more than an old-fashioned elitist interpretation. But the ideological interpretation seems forced to concede that the Revolution itself was incidental, after the fact, that the real change had taken place some years before in "the minds of the people."[13] But then why the necessity for independence?

Perhaps this can be explained, and in explaining it we can possibly suggest still another characterization of the American Revolution.

The one notion that seems to have taken hold in "pre-revolutionary" North America is the belief in the natural right to liberty. First came the Pilgrims, then the Puritans, seeking religious liberty in their own peculiar fashion. To the south, on the Chesapeake, the one thing that the proprietors of the Virginia Company learned was the folly of attempting to attract plantation workers without giving them some chance to own their own land, and hence control their own destinies, in the vastness of America.[14] As the Middle Colonies developed, Pennsylvania prospered on its climate of tolerance—religious, economic, and even ethnic—which attracted thousands of settlers and not only made Philadelphia the most prosperous city in the colonies and the most tolerant, but also opened up the back country to rich and fruitful settlement. New Jersey was proprietary but in name only; the newly arrived settlers did pretty much as they pleased since the lordly owners were absentees, taking the waters somewhere in Britain. In New York, not only had the patroon system on the Hudson failed and Manhattan become a polyglot city of diverse peoples, religions, and occupations, but these developments were recognized by British authorities. When they conquered it from the Dutch they allowed most indigenous institutions to stand. Indeed, a main theme of British North American imperialism seems to have been the population of the colonies with whatever people seemed available and willing.

Religion at times became an issue because British rulers lived in an age when the spirit of the Reformation reinforced a natural imperial competition with Catholic France and Spain; consequently they endorsed, occasionally with enthusiasm, the holy aspects of the English mission to North America.[15] But when intense religious conflicts arose in the mid-seventeenth century, the reaction of Britain's rulers was always toward broadened toleration.[16] In the meantime, throughout the colonies, little by little, locally dominated political institutions began to develop, from the famous Virginia House of Burgesses to the New England town meetings built upon the bases of religious Congregationalism.

This whole broad imperial outlook on the part of Britain has been termed a policy of "salutary neglect," but it would be more accurate to say, on the contrary, that it was a policy of headlong, opportunistic, imperial development in which large numbers of grateful, loyal, functioning citizens were seen to be England's best resource in the competition with Spain, France, and Holland. To achieve this strength in the shortest possible time, within the broad outlines of a traditional mercantilist design, a middle-class, laisser-faire, or hands-off policy prevailed, one that even countenanced indentured servitude and slavery. This policy of opportunistic neglect Americans came to equate with liberty, and liberty they believed to be theirs by tradition, not only in their own long colonial experience, but also traditionally embodied in the rights of Englishmen under the British constitution. Eventually American philosophers, following John Locke, traced the natural right to liberty—or laisser faire—back through the best times in ancient history to the mythical origins of man in a state of nature.[17] Through a process of historicism they made these rights fundamental to the nature of man himself and the quest for them something holy.

The striking fact about all this is that for such a very long time, with minor exceptions, the interests of Britain and her North American colonies seemed to coincide. The bitterest struggles seemed to take place within the colonies themselves—partially owing to growing pains which continually jostled, threatened, or at times displaced the colonial leadership groups. The struggle of the Puritan orthodoxy to retain absolute control over its "visible saints" in the face of worldly alternatives was one such example.

The bitter war waged by the Awakeners against the so-called "Arminians" was another. These struggles were fought out on the plains of intellectualism with as much intensity as General Wolfe's fight with General Montcalm on the plains of Abraham. Moreover, by 1763, when the Peace of Paris ended the Seven Years' War, a new status revolution had taken place in North America, fully as profound as the ousting of the French from the backwoods heartlands of America. Religion per se had lost its monopoly on the definition of the "good life" in America. The Great Awakening had subsided for a time like a sudden storm blown out to sea, and with it had gone the minister's authority in the vanguard of continental leadership. New men ruled instead—merchants made rich on war profits, lawyers made rich on merchant's profits and squabbles, and, most important of all, a new intellectual class who gained great sway over the minds of Americans through the media of newspapers, almanacs, circulated letters, politically oriented sermons, manifestos, and pamphlets. Such figures as Samuel Adams, Benjamin Franklin, James Otis, Patrick Henry, John Dickinson, Thomas Jefferson, and Tom Paine immediately spring to mind. In place of the ministers' struggles over freedom of conscience and the merits or demerits of private revelation, these new men—the American philosophes—directed their energies to defining and arguing, using every basic strand of traditional western thought, the nature of human liberty in this world rather than the next.

But why had they arisen as contenders and leaders at all? Why did they feel compelled to precipitate a crisis within what seemed to be a harmonious British Empire, governed—by their own admission—under the most enlightened constitution and laws that western man had ever devised? It is quite clear that purely economic motives were not the most important. The Navigation Acts, with the exception of controls over sugar and molasses, were largely beneficial to the colonists. And as Oliver Dickerson has long since shown,[18] those acts were so loosely enforced as to make smuggling take on the character of legitimate business enterprise. The king seemed to wish nothing but goodwill for his colonies and even made an American, Benjamin West, his court painter. Both king and parliament were proud of their new-won North

American empire, and glory should probably have been enough. Parliament, as Namier and his followers have shown, was hardly a united body, but rather a collection of local representatives bound up with a limited set of constituents, parochial concerns, and the game or sport of jockeying for status and glory within the confines of the two Houses themselves.[19] Such a piece of witty one-upmanship as Horace Walpole's judgment of Charles Townshend—"He had almost every great talent . . . if he had had but common truth, common sincerity, common honesty, common modesty, common steadiness, common courage and common sense"—may have seemed at the time more important than a wise and far-sighted policy for the North American colonies.[20] In short, despite the great names of Parliament handed down to us by British historians, despite the striking personalities of Walpole, Pitt, Fox, Burke, Townshend, North, Grenville, et al., the British Parliament seems really to have differed little in its instincts from a Virginia House of Burgesses or a Massachusetts General Court. It was excessively local in character. At a time when worldwide intellectual currents were sweeping through western civilization and Britain itself had acquired a global empire, Parliament seemed almost testy at the inconveniences of interrupting its sport and attending to the responsibilities of its new empire.

The best way out was to delegate authority, and by 1763, in respect to foreign policy, Britain had developed the largest, most cumbersome bureaucracy of its time—a major triumph of spoilsmanship in the eyes of some. As Esmond Wright describes it, the following all had some control over the colonies: the Secretary of State for the Southern Department, the Board of Trade and Plantations (made up of merchants), the Treasury, the Surveyor and Auditor-General of the Colonies, the Commissioner of Customs, the Secretary-at-War, the Admiralty, the Admiralty Courts, the Surveyor-General of the King's Woods, the Postmaster General, and the Bishop of London. Wright observes, "The Admiralty alone had fifteen branches scattered in all parts of the town, from Whitehall to Cheapside; the Board sat in Whitehall, but the Navy Office was in Seething Lane, the Victualling Office in East Smithfield, the Ordnance in the Tower."[21] And, he might have added, the ships were docked along the Thames, and the Royal Observatory, which furnished the sailing charts, was administered by the Admiralty located in Greenwich. Clearly "foggy bottom" originated long ago in eighteenth-century London.

Beyond this, the experience of the Seven Years' War fastened a permanent, hostile bureaucracy on America. To a man, the British commanders who participated in that campaign, Loudon, Amherst, Bouquet, Sir William Johnson, and others, had nothing but contempt for the continentals. Most colonies had furnished supplies and men only with the greatest reluctance. And all of the successful campaigns in the vast war of forest and lakes were mounted by common British redcoats whose lobsterbacks alone had reflected imperial glory, from the wild Mohawk Valley to the unscalable heights of Quebec. Accordingly, General Thomas Gage was appointed commander-in-chief for North America to watch over the immense hinterland and to guard against the unruly Americans. In 1763 a new strategy was launched, which Gage enthusiastically carried out until 1774 when, too late, he was relieved. American settlers were to be kept out of the interior—the back country of Pennsylvania, Ohio, Kentucky, and Illinois. So, too, were British regulars, to avoid becoming enmeshed in another vast land war in the wilderness. Troops were to be stationed around the fringes of the frontier to keep the settlers out and to protect the Indians so that they might continue to furnish furs to British manufacturers. New York, because of its strategic location at the foot of the Hudson River Valley, was selected as the main headquarters of the British Army, and great numbers of troops were to be quartered there and sent out as reinforcements to frontier garrisons. Along with this, Britain sent its own agents among the Indians seeking trade and pacification so as to avoid another war. And finally in 1763 a Royal Proclamation was issued forbidding Americans to cross over and settle beyond the Alleghenies. This offended thousands of would-be American settlers and also groups of land speculators in the seaboard towns who hoped to profit by dealing in the greatly extended territories won by British arms.

Beyond all this, Parliament suddenly became aware—doubtless prompted by tax-paying clients from the landholding sections of the realm—that the war and the keeping of the peace had become very expensive. Revenue acts taxing the colonies for what, after all, could be construed as a war in their interests seemed essential. Unfortunately the primary act passed for securing revenue was the Stamp Act of 1765. That act fell most heavily on exactly the wrong group in America—the new elite of merchants, lawyers, publicists, and philosophes whose every document from newspapers and pamphlets to wills, cargo manifests, and land deeds had to bear the king's stamp. The Act directly threatened the most intelligent, aggressive, and recently triumphant elite in the colonies. That group, in addition, felt increasingly threatened not only by the rising military establishment and its pretentious if not contemptuous officer class, but also by still another British bureaucracy recently fastened upon America. This was the ever-growing number of customs agents, revenue collectors, English factors, insurance agents, bondsmen, inspectors, Vice-Admiralty Court officers, Royal governors and their growing staffs of agents and spies, to which now were to be added a legion of stamp sellers and an armada of revenue cutters and patrol boats. The colonial businessmen, farmers, shippers, and publicists decried the artificial status enjoyed by these new parliamentary favorites, and they bitterly resented the habitual extortion, over-zealousness, and racketeering that were common practice among those who swelled the king's bureaucracy in North America in pursuit of "the main chance." It was what today might be called "big government," with its real or imagined infringement on individual liberties, that seems most to have angered the colonists. It was not money alone or legalistic arguments over internal-versus-external taxation that aroused the colonists, but the psychological threat to their liberties and to the newly won leadership status of the vocal colonial elite. Moreover, the obvious venality, racketeering, and profligate behavior of the king's military officers and civilian agents helped build up, particularly in the minds of sober New Englanders and staid planters like George Washington, an image of rampant dissoluteness and immorality emanating from the mother country. The bad example of the low-principled, high-living king's agents in America began to change the colonials' image of Britain itself.[22]

Initially out of all this came the first Anglo-American confrontation, the Stamp Act crisis of 1765, which united the colonies for the first time in opposition to the crown. The mobs, the haranguing, the harassment of officials, which included hanging them in effigy, the sermons praying against episcopacy that somehow was linked with stamps, the writings of James Otis, the formation of the Stamp Act Congress, and the non-importation agreements—all these caused the Rockingham-Whig ministry to repeal the Stamp Act in 1766, but Parliament in an *obiter dictum*, the Declaratory Act of the same year, reasserted its power to tax and legislate for the colonies. In the decade that followed came the series of British Acts—pounded into the heads of every American school boy from that day to this—that seemed to lead inevitably to revolution. The creation of Vice-Admiralty Courts suspending trial by jury in one's own country; the Townshend Acts taxing the colonies on articles in such a way as to insure, as the *London Magazine* of 1766 put it, that, "The American is apparelled from head to foot in our manufactures ... he scarcely drinks, sits, moves, labours, or recreates himself without contributing to the emolument of the mother country";[23] the forcible quartering of troops in private homes; the hiring of Hessian mercenaries to hold down "freeborn Englishmen"; the Boston Massacre in 1770, in which five people were shot by soldiers; the granting of a tea monopoly to the East India Company; and finally the Coercive or Intolerable Acts—these events caused the colonists to take a more than casual interest in their liberties. Indeed in the critical decade between 1764 and 1774 liberty became an American obsession, a violent passion that led to revolution.

Behind all these imperial policies—indeed one of the chief causes for assuming the "hard line" that eventually lost America— was the continued advice of General Gage and the military-bureaucratic establishment in the colonies. In nearly every dispatch for a decade, Gage sounded the alarm, urged a "get tough" policy, and called for an ever-larger army and naval establishment.[24] Gage's dispatches and reports were echoed by other officers and by civil officials such as the Lieutenant Governor of Massachusetts, whose lavish house had been sacked by a mob. As the crucial decade moved along, and nearly every crown officer became a target of abuse, the advice flowing to Parliament and the king from those who were assumed to be the most expert—the men on the spot—counseled tighter restrictions, a greater bureaucracy in America, a larger show of military strength, and a policy of bringing America to heel. Neglecting to mention that such a policy would cement and perpetuate their own powers and potential wealth, the Crown's men on the spot glossed over their own countless peccadilloes, dishonesties, and bad judgments. They also failed to face up to the obvious. Such a policy meant civil war, an expensive conflict that Britain, should France be drawn into it, just might lose, along with her North American empire. So much dependence upon the "expert," the civil servant, the "man on the spot," the Tory colonial, seems almost an inescapable "pre-condition for takeoff" into a disastrous imperial war. More than any other factor, this proconsul strategy of offending the civil leaders while needlessly attempting harsh forms of military, economic, and bureaucratic coercion seems to have led to the American Revolution.

In any case, British strategy failed. Besides organizing the colonists as never before, it brought to the front the natural leaders in America. Further, it so mobilized the intellectual talents of those leaders as to generate a new kind of revolution—an ideological revolution. By 1776 the war, which had already begun in April of 1775 at Lexington and Concord, had turned into something quite different from a legal or military struggle. It had become the philosophe's war, an ideological battle that was made to represent the culmination of the Enlightenment struggle for the rights of man in a better environment shorn of the last vestiges of decadent feudalism. What better place than America—"Nature's Nation"—for the opening struggle in the great cause of liberty, a beginning which Tom Paine optimistically labelled "the birthday of a new world." The American Revolution as it developed through seven long years of war became a real adventure of the mind, a myth of creation, as well as a grim struggle of body against body. Thus the American Revolution did come to have its ideological dimension born out of the exigencies of an historical situation that involved "big government" and callous proconsulship in the service of imperialism. Liberty was nature's basic law and liberty was not now possible without independence.

Whatever interpretation one chooses to put on it, the American Revolution had one outcome that the French and Russian revolutions did not, but one of vital importance as a model for countries in this hemisphere and around the world—*independence* for a new nation. This all-important concept is largely taken for granted by North American cultural analysts who are mainly intent upon keeping alive the revolutionary myth. To others in the hemisphere and around the world, even those who have been born of revolution, independence cannot be taken for granted. The search for that elusive status or condition is an everyday—sometimes desperate—affair. Thus it is important to examine more closely just what independence consisted of for the North American.

I have already suggested that it meant openness, liberty—and to a very large extent laisser faire—in all things on the great and relatively empty continent. But that is too simple. Liberty meant a natural right to individual self-determination by man as a member of human society, which existed before government. The American's emotional belief in liberty as a given attests to the profound impact of liberal ideas on society at all levels. Without this emotional belief in the right to liberty the American would have found no cause for grievance against the king and his ministers, since the citizen had no profound rights to violate. But liberty and independence were largely perceived in Lockean terms, which meant that each individual had personal rights, that he also existed in society, that rights thus depended upon a certain mutuality among individuals, and that, recognizing this, men formed governments, delegating authority to them to secure these rights, both among themselves and with regard to outside social entities.[25] Independence thus meant that condition, both personal and in society, in which man had the ability to secure his true liberty.

Thus for the North American, independence in theory existed on all levels of life. It was personal, it was societal, and it was governmental, though it was always recognized that personal and societal independence took precedence over that of the state. In the United States from the beginning, owing largely to the philosophy of John Locke and a generation of Scottish Enlightenment thinkers, the individual and society were always more important than the state. That was true independence. The state existed to maintain that condition both internally and externally. But the state, i.e., the new United States of America, it was soon recognized, could not automatically guarantee liberty to every citizen under every condition; nor could it guarantee to either itself or its citizens true independence in the family of nations. Certain internal problems of liberty or independence were ignored or postponed by the founding fathers. A whole range of issues—states' rights versus national rights, the interpretation of the Bill of Rights and other clauses in the Constitution relating to liberties on every level, the question of slavery, and the status of the Indian—were all left either to the courts or to battlefields to decide, and some, such as the extent of women's liberties, have not been decided yet.

Likewise on the international level, independence—liberty and freedom of action as a nation—was not guaranteed for all times by the Revolution. Hamilton, perhaps more than any other founding father, worked assiduously to make independence a permanent condition. His financial plans for funding the war debt and creating a stable national bank were aimed at securing national credit abroad. His plan to encourage home manufactures looked towards continental economic self-sufficiency. His support for Jay's treaty with Britain was aimed at securing not only lasting peace with the mightiest power on earth through mutuality of interest, but also genuine recognition of America's existence by that power—a situation somewhat akin to that of Israel in the Middle East today. But these measures were not final. Throughout the early years of its existence, the United States struggled for independence, clearly through the War of 1812, and, I would maintain, throughout the first half of the nineteenth century. In those years the Balkanization of the country was an ever-possible threat, and economic growth was largely dependent upon foreign loans and on help from companies that were the equivalent of multinational corporations, such as world cotton brokers, the Baring Brothers Bank, and the foreign owners of our railroads, canals, mines, and cattle ranches. Americans soon learned that independence once achieved was not easy to maintain, that independence fully as much as revolution implies an ongoing, dramatic struggle. The citizens of the United States were never guaranteed "free security."[26]

Because of this, one is tempted to conclude that just as there was a myth of revolution that stirred America, there was also a myth of independence. The myth began with John Locke's fable of man in a state of nature endowed with his natural rights. Its story line—necessary for all myths—carries the weight of the American republican experiment: relative laisser faire, avoidance of extreme ideologies, faith in democratic self-government, notions of world security, and belief in a fundamental order that takes precedence over nations and states. Anyone who knows his American history can fill in his heroes and villains in this "tale of the tribe" in search of independence.

But it also seems clear that from the beginning, for the North American, independence was a relative thing. It was so in Locke's fable, which implied mutuality, and it worked out thus in the history of our people on all levels. Independence evolved in response to situations, and it was never perfect; indeed it involved a great contradiction: it was not possible without at the same time assuming a position of dependence, even deference, toward those from whom it was demanded. Independence depended upon mutuality among men, societies, and nations.

Since it did depend upon mutuality among men, society, and nations, independence was only a beginning. It meant that the Americans were free to create those institutional forms in society and in government that would most effectively guarantee and perpetuate liberty and independence on all levels. On a societal level republicanism seemed to offer the most promise. Even the Federalists, who favored a strong central government, were forced to embrace many of the tenets of republicanism.[27] This meant that a general consensus existed that saw virtue in yeomanry, private property, general equality, certainly equality of opportunity, the abolishing of rank and privilege, the separation of church and state, a guarantee of certain inalienable rights to the individual, and a representative form of government that was responsible to the people, that balanced powers and hence diffused them throughout the system. At the outset most people deplored the idea of monarchy while at the same time responsible leaders—the founding fathers—were fearful of excessive democracy. "Mobocracy" some of them called it.

The result was the Constitution of 1787 and the Bill of Rights, which crystallized the republican spirit, embodied the diffusion of power, and guaranteed not only inalienable rights but ultimate sovereignty to the people. Essentially the Constitution was a "compromise by combination" which, in true democratic fashion, encompassed the views of as many citizens as possible. It was a flexible charter that allowed for growth and change to such an extent that one historian has called it the first "romantic" or "organic" instrument of government.[28] It was also vague and it postponed, as has been suggested earlier, a number of basic decisions as to the role and powers of the states and the national government, the role of the courts, the sectional question, and the status of blacks, Indians, and women. Nonetheless the Constitution allowed for peaceful transfer of governmental power from the Federalists to the Democratic Republicans under Jefferson in 1800, thereby allowing the country to surmount one of the common perils of the newly independent nation lately born of revolution. In this case it offered convincing proof that republican democracy did work, that votes and voters counted.

For a long period after 1800, it was Congress not the presidency that was the focus of popular interest. The great heroes of the day were Henry Clay, Daniel Webster, and John C. Calhoun. John Quincy Adams gained much more acclaim as the people's tribune —"old man eloquent" in the House of Representatives—than he ever did in his one term as president. All of this meant that early American nationalism was fashioned out of confidence by the people in their representatives "met in Congress assembled." It also meant that for nearly a quarter of a century these representatives perceived a certain mutuality of interests among sections, classes, and individual citizens. Only differences over policy in the War of 1812 threatened to divide them.

During this same period the courts, acting as guarantors of individual liberties, gained the confidence of the people. Judges arose from grass-roots backgrounds, and trial by juries of one's peers was a visible sign that sovereignty—hence liberty—still rested with the democracy. With the electoral triumph of Andrew Jackson in 1828 the president himself dramatically appeared as the tribune of the people. Jackson's political philosophy, coupled with his "war" against the Bank of the United States, added a new dimension to the definition of liberal democracy. His party's slogan was "the world is too much governed" and Jackson was for small government; at the same time he saw it as his duty to use whatever powers he had to attack entrenched business monopolies like the Bank of the United States because they represented an undue concentration of power at the expense of the people. In the case of the Bank absolute power over the nation's money supply was bound to corrupt absolutely. So Jackson, as every schoolboy knows, destroyed the "monster bank." He also refused to let South Carolina take control over the fate of the Union in the nullification crisis of 1832, and he promoted the expansion of republican institutions across the country. Jackson became so powerful a public tribune that his party was eventually defeated. "King Andrew's" party was pulled down by the people who wished to return to the log cabin and hard cider of "Old Tip," William Henry Harrison. Liberal democracy had spoken again.

By 1845 liberal democracy had also expanded its horizons. It had spawned a sister republic in Texas whose constitution imitated that of the United States, and it soon reached out across the whole trans-Mississippi West in a contest with Mexico and Britain over the right to "republicanize" or bring liberal democracy to half a continent, while at the same time insuring independence against foreign interference with the great experiment. Even the crude mountain man saw himself as an apostle of what had become a state religion—liberal democracy. In the 1840s one of them wrote:

> Here lies the bones of old Black Harris
> Who often traveled beyond the far West
> And for the freedom of Equal rights
> He crossed the snowy mountain hights. . . .[29]

In 1861, however, liberal democracy confronted a problem it could not solve, and civil war resulted. Lincoln, the president-elect, could get no clear-cut majority, and in this case a liberal democracy that would include the Negro as man and as citizen clashed with a literal or Greek democracy that wished the world had stood still in 1787. Lincoln himself suspended basic and traditional liberties as an expediency of war, while at the same time proclaiming time after time a grand national vision of the future that lay before a "government of the people, by the people, and for the people." Liberal democracy, however, was never to be quite the same.

Constitutional amendments which freed the black and enfranchised him politically only raised further profound questions over the meaning of economic and social democracy. And after a brief experiment with the Freedmen's Bureau, for nearly seventy years the government on every level, perhaps reflecting the will of the majority, took no steps to protect the inalienable rights of its black citizens against the overwhelming power of the white majority.

In addition, the Civil War brought undreamed of economic concentration. Railroad monopolies, beef trusts, oil trusts, banking trusts, and grain trusts sprang up at every hand, protected by the courts under the 14th Amendment and wielding great private power at the expense of the people. Thus liberal democracy—individual independence—was threatened after the Civil War, paradoxically enough by both the tyranny of the majority in the case of Negro rights and the tyranny of the minority in the case of the trust-building moguls of high finance. Still, to a surprising degree, the people's representatives and spokesmen grappled with the problem. A whole series of native reformers came to the fore: Victoria Woodhull, first woman candidate for president in 1872; Edward Bellamy, a utopian socialist; Henry George, a California single-taxer; Samuel Gompers and Mother Jones, labor organizers; Eugene Debs, a perennial socialist candidate; Ignatius Donnelly, Mary Ellen Lease, Sockless Jerry Simpson, and the "Boy Orator of the Platte," William Jennings Bryan, all spoke for the farmers. Bully Theodore Roosevelt, the well-fed William Howard Taft, and the undernourished Woodrow Wilson all achieved heroic stature in the cause of reform. Congress passed law after law from the Interstate Commerce Act of 1887 and the Sherman Act of 1890 to the Clayton Anti-Trust Act of 1914 attempting to combat excesses of power at the expense of the people. Reform became an aspect of the revolutionary heritage and an American tradition in itself.

Reform depended upon a whole new conception of liberal democracy. The apparent rationalization or organization of American life after the Civil War, symbolized by cities, transportation lines, and factories with assembly lines—the emergence of a visible capitalist market place in Wall Street—made social life seem something of a game. That gaming quality was everywhere apparent in rags-to-riches success stories, and businessmen took to labeling their occupations "the oil game" or "the banking game" or the "real estate game" (the game of *Monopoly* was thus not an invention but an inevitability). In fact, as early as 1860 something called *The Game of Life* had appeared in American toy stores. But liberal democracy and the emergent reform tradition predisposed the American people to demand that whatever game life was, it must be played fairly and according to the rules. This meant that government took on a greatly enhanced role. Its function was to keep the game, however grim it was, honest. Government was the guardian of the old rules and values of individual opportunity, of meaningful democratic expression against undue concentrations of power by private individuals and combinations of individuals. "Liberal" came to mean that one felt it was the duty of government to protect the people against big business as it became more visibly anti-social.

A reversion to "normalcy" in the twenties, which meant that the "business of America was business," and that government, the treasury, oil speculators, and stockbrokers would all lie down together, not only distorted the all-American game of life; in 1929 it stopped the game altogether. Not only was there no fair play, there was no play at all. Bread lines, bonus marches, and apple selling were the only games in town, unless one went to Washington with a plan and a blueprint for society.

The New Deal ushered in a new era, in which social engineering has become by far America's largest industry and big government the nation's largest employer. In the meantime during the Second World War and the years thereafter, America fought continuously to save the world for liberal democracy. Business grew large, larger, multinational, imperial. Organized labor wielded an enhanced power—power to shut down industries, cities, towns, and the nation's entire transportation network, not to mention its major sports events and mass-media entertainments. Our most prominent economists could only speak lamely about the possibilities of "countervailing power" and a general all-around affluence due to increasing productivity. But in the postwar world liberal democracy faces overwhelming challenges, not the least of which is the obscuring of the individual in a computerized maze (the ultimate game) which has resulted in his increasing alienation from human society as he used to think it existed. Our most serious novelists have become prophets of paranoia, and they are losing even that role to the new journalists. Satire and black humor are the language of discourse even in the mass media. Liberal democracy is sometimes said to have produced, in the words of Ezra Pound, "a botched civilization" that bears striking resemblances to the selfish British Empire on the eve of the American Revolution.

And yet because of two hundred years of struggle for human independence—two hundred years of liberal democracy—we know more. We know for example that liberty and democracy are no good as principles if they apply to some and not to others anywhere on the globe. We know that however big or impressive the government, the far-flung corporation, the labor union, the media network, it is no good to man unless it is responsible to him, for it is not a *res publica*—a thing of the people. We know that life, liberty, and the pursuit of happiness are not possible without economic sufficiency, and that abundance not shared is not democratic or even humane. We know the enormous *costs* of achieving and sustaining life and liberty for each and every individual through war and peace. And we know that liberty depends upon mutuality and interdependence and unselfishness, which is why men formed societies and governments—and now world communities—in the first place. We have lived continuously with novelty and a revolutionary heritage; hence we know the value of flexibility. We are pragmatists in that we eschew absolutes and systems for their own sake; we adjust with zest to new situations; we make high culture out of turning incredible amounts of data into meaningful information; and we espouse an ethic of democracy—the greater the number of informed people who participate in the decision-making process the better. We are not a folk culture taking refuge in outmoded totems and taboos. We are inheritors of a revolution who at least have sense enough to struggle hard to bring unchecked power, wherever we see it, under the control of the people. In this sense liberal democracy is alive and well in this land. If one listens closely, the echoes of its sentiments can be heard everywhere, especially but not exclusively among the youth. These are the echoes, not of the Trumpets of Jubilee, but of the Battle Hymn of the Republic, that grim, determined song which is always with us, but which each generation must sing and celebrate anew.

Notes

1. Frederick Jackson Turner, *The Frontier in American History* (New York: Holt, 1920); David M. Potter, *People of Plenty: Economic Abundance and the American Character* (Chicago: University of Chicago Press, 1954).
2. Ralph H. Gabriel, *The Course of American Democratic Thought* (New York: Ronald Press, 1940), p. 22.
3. Thomas Paine, *Common Sense*, in *Basic Writings of Thomas Paine* (New York: Wiley, 1942), p. 56.
4. See J. Hector St. John de Crèvecoeur, *Letters from an American Farmer* (London, 1782); Alexis de Tocqueville, *Democracy in America*, 2 vols. (Paris, 1835).
5. This question was first raised by J. Franklin Jameson in *The American Revolution Considered as a Social Movement* (Princeton: Princeton University Press, 1926).
6. See Jessie Lemisch, "The Radicalism of the Inarticulate: Merchant Seamen in the Politics of Revolutionary America," in *Dissent: Explorations in the History of American Radicalism*, ed. Alfred F. Young (De Kalb: Northern Illinois University Press, 1968). Also see Lemisch, "The American Revolution Seen from the Bottom Up," in *Towards A New Past: Dissenting Essays in American History*, ed. Barton J. Bernstein (New York: Vintage Books, 1969), pp. 3–45, and Staughton Lynd, *Intellectual Origins of American Radicalism* (New York: Pantheon, 1968).
7. Edwin Scott Gaustad, *The Great Awakening in New England* (New York: Harper, 1957); Wesley M. Gewehr, *The Great Awakening in Virginia, 1740–1790* (Durham, N.C.: Duke University Press, 1930); Alan Heimert and Perry Miller, eds., *The Great Awakening* (Indianapolis and New York: Bobbs-Merrill, 1967).
8. Heimert and Miller, *The Great Awakening*, pp. 563–573. Also see Alan Heimert, *Religion and the American Mind: From the Great Awaken-*

ing to the Revolution (Cambridge, Mass.: Harvard University Press, 1966).
9. See John B. Jackson, Lecture VII, "The Landscape of Privacy," *American Issues Forum*, Courses by Newspaper, University of California, San Diego.
10. See notes 5 and 6 above. An extension of the same theme for the postwar period can be found in the works of Merrill Jensen, *The Articles of Confederation; An Interpretation of the Social-Constitutional History of the American Revolution, 1774–1781* (Madison: University of Wisconsin Press, 1948), and *The New Nation: A History of the United States during the Confederation, 1781–1789* (New York: Knopf, 1950).
11. The principal work in this school is Gordon S. Wood, *The Creation of The American Republic, 1776–1787* (Chapel Hill: University of North Carolina Press, 1969).
12. See Bernard Bailyn, *The Ideological Origins of the American Revolution* (Cambridge, Mass.: Harvard University Press, 1967).
13. The phrase belongs to John Adams. See Adams to Jefferson, August 24, 1815, in Lester J. Cappon, ed., *The Adams-Jefferson Papers* (Chapel Hill: University of North Carolina Press, 1959).
14. See Wesley F. Craven, *The Dissolution of the Virginia Company* (New York: Oxford University Press, 1932). See also William H. Goetzmann, ed., *The Colonial Horizon: America in the Sixteenth and Seventeenth Centuries* (Reading, Mass.: Addison Wesley, 1969), pp. 83–109.
15. Howard Mumford Jones, "The Colonial Impulse: An Analysis of the 'Promotion' Literature of Colonization," *Proceedings of the American Philosophical Society* 90 (May 1946): 131–161. See also Jones, *O Strange New World* (New York: Viking Press, 1964), pp. 194–226.
16. See Kai T. Erikson, *Wayward Puritans* (New York: Wiley, 1966), p. 135.
17. Jefferson especially developed a theory about this. See Gilbert Chinard, *Thomas Jefferson, the Apostle of Americanism* (Boston: Little, Brown, 1929), pp. 50–51. See also Thomas Jefferson, "Commonplace Book," ms. p. 135; and William H. Goetzmann, "'Savage Enough to Prefer the Woods,' the Cosmopolite and the West," in *Thomas Jefferson: the Man, His World, His Influence*, ed. Lally Weymouth (New York: Putnam, 1973), pp. 107–140.
18. Oliver M. Dickerson, *The Navigation Acts and the American Revolution* (Philadelphia: University of Pennsylvania Press, 1951).
19. The first of L. B. Namier's works on this subject was *The Structure of Politics at the Accession of George III* (London: Macmillan, 1929). Then followed *England in the Age of the American Revolution* (London: Macmillan, 1930). This has been expanded into a complete analysis of Parliament in biographical terms by Namier's many disciples.

20. Quoted in Esmond Wright, *Fabric of Freedom* (New York: Hill & Wang, 1961), p. 59.
21. Ibid., p. 30.
22. Bailyn, *Ideological Origins*, pp. 125–159.
23. Wright, *Fabric of Freedom*, pp. 34–35.
24. Ibid., pp. 73–76.
25. See the Declaration of Independence. Jefferson went to great pains to point out that the Declaration was not intended to be original but to express "the common sense" of the colonies.
26. I have reference here to statements by Ralph H. Gabriel and C. Vann Woodward twenty years later that seem to foster and perpetuate the myth of "free security." See Gabriel, *The Course of American Democratic Thought* (New York: Ronald Press, 1940), p. 11; and Woodward, "The Age of Reinterpretation," *The American Historical Review* 66 (October 1960): 1–19. For anyone who thinks America was secure diplomatically, see William H. Goetzmann, *When the Eagle Screamed: The Romantic Horizon in American Diplomacy, 1800–1860* (New York: Wiley, 1966). America's psychological insecurity is well discussed in Fred Somkin, *Unquiet Eagle* (Ithaca, N.Y.: Cornell University Press, 1967).
27. See Gordon Wood, *Creation of the American Republic*.
28. Ibid., p. 606.
29. Quoted in Charles L. Camp, ed., *James Clyman, Frontiersman* (Portland, Ore.: Champoeg Press, 1960), p. 64.

OSCAR HANDLIN

3. Liberal Democracy and the Image of America

From the perspective of the late 1970s, it is hard to credit the respect and hope the men and women of 1776 attached both to the United States and to liberal democracy. Standing at a moment when abuse, at home and abroad, of both the country and of the political system is commonplace, it takes an effort of the imagination to recall the time when both the country and the political system represented buoyant aspirations for all mankind. We shall not understand the present low estate in the world of the United States and of democracy without first reviewing the bases for high esteem in the past. Such a review will expose the continuing connection between the United States and liberal democracy, a connection responsible both for their high repute in 1776 and for their low repute today.

The idea of the New World existed in the imaginations of Europeans long before the discovery of America. For centuries, the discontented, the restless, and the ambitious conjured up visions of distant regions, alternative to their own, places which reversed whatever was inadequate or evil in their society. Stories about the holy land, about the destinations of pilgrimages, about the legendary empire of Prester John, about a hidden terrestrial paradise blended the descriptions of travellers with fiction in the wish-fulfilling dreams of readers and listeners. Thus, when the news of Columbus's landfall finally arrived, it was of an event long anticipated—hence the tremendous importance attached to it. And in the century that followed, as details of the wondrous features of the hitherto unknown continents reached the Old

World, speculation about their character continued to stir the emotions.

People who believed in a universe of tightly bound causes and effects could not but consider that there was some reason why this part of the earth's surface had so long been withheld from their knowledge. Like every occurrence in the universe, the sudden exposure after the long concealment was part of a divine plan, and, therefore, must have had some purpose. Speculation about that purpose inspired the holy zeal which moved not a few among the numerous types who came to the New World or thought about it. Their calculations ran as follows. Much was wrong with their own society. Inspiration, knowledge, or flashes of insight revealed the remedy. But the Old World, encrusted with habit and ancient institutions, resisted immediate correction. The New World, providentially, offered a field for experiment, a place in which to demonstrate the feasibility of the course the will desired.

A symbiotic relation thus developed in the thinking of generations of Europeans: the New World existed to right the evils of the Old. It was in that expectation, for instance, that the Puritans came to Massachusetts Bay, not as fugitives, not to abandon England to its corrupt rulers, but as experimenters who intended to build a city upon a hill which would demonstrate to men everywhere the lineaments of a righteous commonwealth. A hundred years later, Jonathan Edwards still wrote that God had designated America as "the glorious renovator of the world." And in the centuries that followed, other zealous men and women pursued the same star westward to plant in the wilderness models of secular or religious communities which would redeem the world.

I mention this continuing quest, not to describe its development within the New World but rather to indicate its continuing significance in the consciousness of Europe. To the people of that history-laden continent, America offered the opportunities of newness—an abundance of space unencumbered by tradition, habit, or rigid institutions.

The subtle alteration in the meaning of the very word America in the eighteenth century revealed the importance of the newly revealed hemisphere in the thinking of Europeans. Earlier, the term had applied to the whole of the two continents—to Peru and Mexico as well as to Virginia and Massachusetts. In the eighteenth century, for most Europeans, the meaning of the term gradually narrowed until it applied, first, to the English colonies on the mainland of North America and then, after independence, to the United States. So too, earlier, the word American referred to the aborigines, the indigenous inhabitants of the continent whom we would later call Indians; now, increasingly, it referred to the transplanted Europeans and their descendants who became citizens of the republic. America and Americans became synonymous with that part of the hemisphere that allowed Europeans to believe that a new type of society and a new type of man had appeared in the New World. And the idea of liberal democracy was born as much in these needs of Englishmen and Frenchmen as in the actual settlements of Pennsylvania or Massachusetts.

Enlightenment critics of the Old Regime easily projected onto the New World their vision of the political system intended to replace the troublesome vestiges of feudalism. Since man was naturally good and was made corrupt by the defects of the society about him, the American colonies offered a model of what man could be in his natural state—a cultivator of the soil, close to nature, an unaggressive neighbor tolerant of the beliefs of others although himself a follower of a rational faith, and a full participant competent to make his own decisions in the political and social life of the community of which he was a part.

Europeans possessed only a slight fund of actual information about the New World, culled from random travel accounts; but that did not in the least inhibit them. From Voltaire to Condorcet the French spokesmen of the Enlightenment stressed this image of America, not only as a model worth emulating, but also as a means of assailing their own society. Elsewhere on the continent also this same view of America obtained; near the end of his life, Goethe summed up the attitude of his generation in words which echoed and re-echoed through the decades that followed: *Amerika, du hast es besser—als unser kontinent, das alte.*

No group articulated the sensitivity of Europeans to America more clearly than the English Whigs, for whom the New World provided a fertile source of illustrative argument in their attacks upon the Tory system that dominated their country. James Burgh, not the ablest but the most representative, thus structured the whole of his *Political Disquisitions* about colonial materials; and Richard Price, in a widely read work of 1784, *Observations on the Importance of the American Revolution and the Means of Making It of Benefit to the World,* explained that independence was "one of the steps ordained by Providence to introduce these times." It would be true of the Americans as it had been of the ancient Jews "that in them all the families of the earth shall be blessed."

The Americans established a curious relation to this body of respected opinion which told them how wonderful they were. It was easy to believe these eulogistic writings; but, also, in a subtle fashion they shaped American opinion and American practice, creating an obligation to live up to these laudatory comments. Above all, they confirmed the older inherited view, not secularized, of a peculiar mission of universal significance in the American republic. John Adams put it thus in 1765: "I always consider the settlement of America with Reverence and Wonder—as the Opening of a grand scene and Design in Providence for the Illumination of the Ignorant and Emancipation of the slavish Part of Mankind all over the Earth."[1]

The faith in America's capacity to redeem the world erupted in the waves of rhetoric which accompanied the Revolution, a signal event not only in American, but also in European history and, many believed, in universal history. Independence, wrote a British Whig, was "a revolution made, not by chopping and changing of power in any of the existing states, but by the appearance of a new state, of a new species, in a new part of the globe." The events that led from the battlefield at Concord to the adoption of the federal constitution validated the ideas that emanated from a century of European political speculation—government by consent, operating through a system of representation and exercising powers limited by a written compact, that is, liberal democracy.

People on both sides of the Atlantic continued to express the belief in a future advance toward liberal democracy, with the

United States in the vanguard. That confidence drew support from the general faith in progress. Since the story of the future would be a record of steady, indeed inevitable, improvement as that of the past had been, what was most recent most clearly pointed the direction of developments yet to come; and, from that point of view, the very newness of the New World and the innovativeness of what had happened in the United States were reassuring.

In the nineteenth century, therefore, men and women on both sides of the ocean expected to follow the American way; revolutions in some places, peaceful evolution elsewhere, would take the rest of the world along the same path traced by the United States, the mother of republics. The severance of the other countries of the hemisphere from their European rulers was one indication of this tendency. Events in Ireland, France, Germany, Belgium, Scandinavia, Italy, and Austria, though not as decisive, nevertheless conformed to the general trend. Through the century, Americans were quite conscious of the model their new nation offered to liberals elsewhere. "A just and solid republican government maintained here," declared Jefferson in 1801, "will be a standing monument and example for the aim and imitation of the people of other countries." Later Herman Melville stated the case more explicitly in *White Jacket*: God had predestined and mankind expected great things from the Americans. "We are the pioneers of the world; we advance, the guard sent on through the wilderness of untried things, to break a new path in the New World. . . . Let us always remember that with ourselves almost for the first time in history of the earth the national selfishness is unbounded philanthropy; for we cannot do a good to America, but we give alms to the world."[2]

A great many politically aware Europeans agreed. Even radicals conceded a special place to the United States, as did the anarchist Bakunin; and the problems of American exceptionalism troubled many Marxists at the end of the century. Conservatives, of course, all along perceived the nature of the challenge to their authority in the American example. From Metternich to Napoleon III, they well understood that the republic was a source of subversion by virtue of the model it set for people everywhere. But the foes of America, though politically powerful, could not offset the influence on public opinion of intellectuals who almost unanimously (with a few exceptions to which I shall refer later) gave their allegiance to liberal democracy, as they saw it exemplified in the United States.

Moreover, in the nineteenth century the scope of American influence broadened. Among Europeans the New World idea penetrated beyond the relatively small groups of politically aware persons, whether statesmen or intellectuals. The great waves of immigration to the United States created a sense of its potential in much wider circles—artisans, yeomen, peasants, laborers. The mass of immigrants crossed the Atlantic for other compelling economic and social reasons. But the complex social, personal, and psychological preparations for migration generated a consciousness of unexpected possibilities. This intermingling of motives made democrats of peasants who never read a word of political philosophy. A poor boy like Michael Pupin, who fled from Idvor in Serbia where there was no place for him, cherished the image of another humble lad who had become president of the United States. Somehow the name of Lincoln had penetrated to that remote village; and the thought of it sustained the future scientist in the long migration, while he worked as farmhand and common laborer.

Equally important, the role of the United States as a model of political democracy spread to the non-European parts of the world. Until almost the end of the century, the republic was not an imperialist power; subject peoples therefore viewed it in a light different from that of countries that were. Moreover a network of missionary enterprises through the nineteenth century had dotted American institutions around the globe; and from them radiated lines of influence that spread through the Balkans to China and Japan and south into Africa and Latin America. We are far from being able adequately to appraise the work of these institutions but clearly they had an Americanizing, liberalizing democraticizing effect as well as one related to their primary religious objective.

Through the nineteenth century, also, American businessmen appeared to themselves and to others, not as exploiters, but a purveyors of modern democracy. Untainted by imperialism, abetted by a hands-off state policy, they exerted an economic influence by making goods cheap and commonplace, that is, by bringing to many ordinary persons the desired objects formerly so rare that only a few could enjoy them.

Much changed in the twentieth century; the process both altered the image of America and undermined the world's acceptance of the principles of liberal democracy. As the faith in one subsided, the attractiveness of the other faded.

To begin with there was an alteration in the United States itself. Industrialization and urbanization transformed the nation from a frontier wilderness with all its risks and opportunities into one vast mill town with all its constriction and its ugly social problems. Labor struggles from the 1890s through the Depression of the 1930s seemed to take a particularly cruel, heartless, violent form in the United States. The stories of Homestead, of Haymarket, of Sacco and Vanzetti, and of Scottsboro circulated widely among Europeans who interpreted them as demonstrations that oppression was as severe in the United States as elsewhere, indeed more so because of the absence of the restraints of tradition, aristocracy, and sense of social responsibility.

The republic suffered similar blows to its reputation by its venture into imperialism after 1898, by the racism behind its treatment of colored peoples, and also, after 1918, by the nativism and prejudice written into its new restrictive immigration policy. Then, too, the turn away from Wilsonian idealism and the retreat into isolationism in the 1920s and 1930s involved a rejection of the traditional conception of American responsibility for the fate of democracy everywhere in the world. All these trends were evidence that the United States had lost its exceptionalism, was a country like any other.

Corresponding to the changes within the country were changes in the way others regarded it. By 1920 America seemed no longer in the vanguard of human progress. The Russian Revolution had created a new model for reformers, and the attraction of that model in the decades immediately after the First World War detracted from the appeal of the New World republic. So, too, despite their slowness to cultivate international links, fascism and nazism also had admirers outside Italy and Germany. Thus, by the outbreak of the Second World War, writers who referred to the wave of the future no longer had in mind the experience of the United States but that of those other still newer societies.

The same assumption had taken hold within the United States. Mired down in isolationism, reluctant to assume responsibility for events outside their borders, many Americans also conceded that the country in which they lived was so exceptional that its experience could not apply elsewhere, that other societies would have to follow upon other models.

We must raise the question: Why? Why was there a turn in opinion against the United States, against liberal democracy? It was not merely disillusion with the outcome of the First World War that produced this result, though that factor was important enough in itself. Nor was it a response to the defects of America, which after 1930 passed through a far-reaching social revolution in the effort to perfect itself. Other more influential reasons were also involved.

The forces hostile to the United States, which were also the forces hostile to democracy, gained strength in those very decades of reform and amelioration. Even in the years just after 1945 when hopes were still being sounded that the defeat of the axis powers would permit the emergence of "One World," an undercurrent of anti-Americanism survived. It would not subside despite the liquidation of imperialism, despite massive domestic reform, and despite lavish foreign aid. And the identical elements hostile to the United States were everywhere the foes of liberal democracy.

Nowhere were these negative sentiments popular, in the sense that nowhere did they represent the opinion of large masses of the population. Of course, ordinary men and women did not have the freedom to register their preferences in every part of the world. But in the countries, like Japan, where people did have the opportunity to express themselves freely, polls regularly showed the United States to be the most admired foreign nation; and a quite distinctive culture there did not impede adoption of the forms of liberal democracy. Then again, ordinary men and women given a chance to vote with their feet, made the same choice; in the flow of world immigration the United States remained the leading destination among people in flight. Above all, wherever the least gleam of freedom flickered, popular culture revealed the attractiveness of American influences, in Moscow as in Paris.

Anti-Americanism was a sentiment of an elite, more widely diffused where powerful political organizations, whose interest it served, could give it currency.

The shift centered on the changed outlook of the intellectuals. In the eighteenth and nineteenth centuries intellectuals had been preponderantly committed both to the United States and to liberal democracy. In the twentieth century what was once a dissenting minority view became almost the consensus.

One can discern the growing distaste for the United States among intellectuals on both sides of the ocean from its origins 150 years ago. "The most odious and insupportable despotism that ever was heard of upon the face of the earth"—thus, Edgar Allan Poe on his native land in *Some Words with a Mummy*. Mark Twain, quintessentially American, articulated his bitterest emotions in criticism of his own country. "The red letter days of the calendar are April 1, which reminds us that we are fools and October 12, Columbus Day. It would have been wonderful to find America but it would have been more wonderful to miss it." So much for the American dream. No sooner did the ocean crossing become comfortable than the expatriates began their flight across the Atlantic to the more congenial cultural climate of the Old World. There is a direct line between these early statements eccentric within their own time and those now made trite by Gore Vidal and J.-P. Sartre.

Anti-Americanism has not displayed the random characteristics one would expect from highly individualistic, isolated people. The responses have been uniform, predictable, almost ritual in nature, the utterances not of free thinkers each wandering off in his own direction, but rather of people keeping time to the beat of a drummer, albeit a drummer different from the one who set the pace for their countrymen.

The importance of the intellectuals was a factor both of growing numbers and of control of the means of communication. The group had economic, social, and cultural interests of its own, although those were not often perceived, since its members generally denied those interests and presumed to speak for the society at large. Still those interests existed, as did the growing influence of the means of communication which expressed them.

In part, the hostility of the intellectuals sprang from dislike of what they referred to as the materialism of American society. One need not be surprised at the consciousness of the economic strength of the United States at a time when most of the world depended upon food exports from North America. Asia, Africa, Latin America, and Western and Eastern Europe, including the Soviet Union, became net importers of grain in the 1970s—surely a development worthy of comment. But the ability to feed a large part of the world was not the reference point of the criticism of American materialism, so much as the charge once associated with aristocrats, now voiced by intellectuals, of coca-colanization, that is, of a pervasive vulgarization of life. The United States was regarded as the source, or at least the prototype, of a culture built upon possession, upon the diffusion of an idolatry for material things; and it was on that account judged harshly.

The elitism of the intellectuals was thus related to a distaste for the culture of the common man. Intellectuals in all parts of the world disliked precisely that feature of American culture that represented the triumph of democratic ideals. If we revert to Poe we understand the nature of the enmity. The name of the tyrant in his story was *mob*. The intellectual's ever-present fear was of being swamped by the masses who threatened to crush cherished cultural values in the heedless pursuit of their own interest. As Mill had noted in *On Liberty*, the danger was greater in a democracy than in a stratified society where the location of power was clear and where appeals were possible to the enlightened sovereign. The popular will was a danger, not only in politics where it insisted upon wrong preferences, but in every aspect of life. The perils that Ibsen's *Enemy of the People* revealed in Europe were vastly magnified in the United States.

The truth was that intellectuals mourned the loss of America innocence. As long as the New World was an empty wilderness, they could inscribe upon it all the images critical of their own society. The latitude for doing so disappeared once an actual civilization, peopled by living men and women, preempted the formerly free space.

By the 1970s however something more had to be said: for by then other gods had also failed the intellectuals—in the Soviet Union and in China, for instance. Yet while few intellectuals would any longer defend the lands of Stalin and Mao as models to be emulated, few also made them such persistent targets for attack as they did the United States.

Some of this disparity in treatment arose from the habit of mind of Utopians who refused to discriminate among differences of degree in shortfalls from perfection, and who therefore opened themselves to an insidious moral relativism. When Jean-Paul Sartre returned in 1939 from studies in philosophy in Germany and announced that there was no genuine distinction between the Hitler Reich and the third French republic he spoke in a language that refused to make qualifications. So too did those who deplored the lack of civil liberties in South, but not North, Korea, in South, but not North, Vietnam, in Rhodesia but not Uganda. The flexibility of the standard of judgment always operated against the United States, of which more was demanded than of other countries. But it also bespoke the hidden unproven assumption that democracy, appropriate for the favored folk of favored climes, was not quite suitable for other, less developed breeds.

Moreover, by the 1970s, anti-Americanism had been firmly linked to hostility to liberal democracy. In most of Latin America, in almost all of Africa, in large parts of Asia and in Eastern Europe, it was not only the model of the United States which ceased to be attractive but also liberal democracy, with its insistence upon individuality and upon participation in the political process of large numbers of people undifferentiated by qualifications or party, class, or status. To the earlier array of enemies—radical socialists, aristocrats, and monarchists—who had once been democracy's severest critics were now added those who posed as its friends but fatally redefined its terms. We see the seeds early in the century among the critics of the bumbling inefficiency of parliamentary institutions. Few Englishmen were as influential in the opening decade of this century as H. G. Wells and G. B. Shaw, both progressives; and both sounded a persistent call for men of trained intelligence to cut through the shams of popular democracy to get things done. So, too, Max Weber in 1919 redefined the ideal democracy as one in which "the people choose a leader in whom they trust. Then the leader says, 'Now shut up, and obey me.' People and parties are then no longer free to interfere with his business. . . . Later the people can sit in judgment. If the leader has made mistakes—to the gallows with him."[3] Read sixty years later such calls for a superman cast an ominous light on the future. They deserve reflection now, when in other contexts, we hear the argument that "underdeveloped countries" cannot afford democracy, need an iron rule. Those calls also help explain why democrats of this sort continued to ridicule the illogicalities of American political behavior.

Despite the finicky distaste for popular culture and popular politics, intellectuals in the United States and elsewhere rarely chose to withdraw to protected enclaves. On the contrary they were ready to use and be used by the modern media of communications. Rationalizations were ready at hand. They owed it to the public to communicate through the *Today* show, or the book club, or the pages of *Playboy*. The temptations of opportunity drew them into competitions in which they were doomed. Those who succeeded despised themselves, as well as the suckers who made them rich and famous; and those who failed tasted the gall of frustration.

The lust for power compounded the dilemma. Every citizen was a participant in politics. The wisest and best-informed were obliged to make a special effort to shape policy. From Henry Adams to Ezra Pound to Norman Mailer, from Clemenceau to Malraux, the confident certainty of possessing a higher wisdom corrupted artists and writers who aspired directly or indirectly to govern and who came to hate the people who refused to follow, came to admire the man of power who used them.

The changes of recent decades have intensified the social consequences of the intellectuals and help explain their influence. The increase in the number of service and related occupations, the expansion of the bureaucracies of government and education, and the formalization of many sets of technical skills vastly expanded the ranks of the intellectuals and para-intellectuals. As a result, a crowd of uneducated college graduates led lives of quiet desperation at the little desks across which nothing of consequence ever moved. They formed a growing part of the intellectual audience; but they shared few experiences with persons not like themselves.

The intellectuals differed from the members of earlier middle classes in their relation to property. Some bit of knowledge was their primary capital. That they treasured. But knowledge as a whole had become complex, diffuse, and abundant—beyond the grasp of any one man. More often reading reviews than books, outside the narrow domain mastered, each individual acquired opinions at second or third hand, enjoying the critic rather than the performance. Hence gusts of fashion carried them all along and made them particularly susceptible to waves of self-hatred.

The captains and the kings.

The captains and the kings once held all governmental power. Now the kings are gone.

The captains remain. Year by year, the number of lands governed by force increases. Forget the optimism of the nineteenth century.

But those who now wield military power lack the support of tradition and of the institutional base that had sustained their predecessors of the Old Regime. A coup brings the colonel to power; a coup can displace him. He therefore seeks legitimacy; and in that quest the intellectuals are useful as formulators and purveyors of unifying ideologies and myths.

Hence if one looks away from the slogans and rhetoric, one finds in most parts of the world an unlikely alliance between the military and the intellectuals. The two groups are not the same; but each uses the other. And the United States still serves as a kind of mirror image reflecting the hatred of both the intellectuals and the dictators, for, however attenuated or qualified, government by consent and a culture that responds to the popular will freely expressed stand in opposition to the interests of both groups.

Notes

1. Oscar Handlin, *Truth in History* (Cambridge, Mass.: Harvard University Press, 1979), pp. 51 ff.
2. Ibid., p. 54.
3. Gerhard Masur, *Propheten von Gestern* (Frankfurt-am-Main: S. Fischer, 1965), p. 215.

ROBERT A. DAHL

4. Liberal Democracy in the United States

When I reflect on the future of democracy in the United States I often find myself wondering whether we Americans—or rather our predecessors on this soil—have not made a number of historic commitments that are fundamentally inconsistent with one another.

These historic commitments are not, of course, anything so simple as a clean-cut choice or decision but rather the usual messy, complex, and poorly understood process by which some more-or-less consistent set of values, beliefs, processes, and institutions gains ground over possible alternatives and then come to possess all the advantages of history, tradition, and things as they are.

First Commitment: The Constitutional Order

The first of these historic commitments was to a constitutional order intended to protect what were widely thought at the time to be the most important rights and liberties of individuals. One might reasonably locate the time of this commitment as the period from the Declaration of Independence (to be rather arbitrary about it) to, let us say, the end of Jefferson's first term.

Whatever the exact nature of that historic commitment, it was much less inclusive than the universalistic language of the Declaration or the Preamble to the Constitution might lead one to suppose. Interpreted in the simplest possible way, even among adults there was at least a three-tier system. At the bottom, where

NOTE: Portions of this essay have been published in substantially different form in "Removing Certain Impediments to Democracy in the United States," *Political Science Quarterly* 92 (Spring 1977): 1–20.

most nonwhites were found, were persons totally excluded from the system of rights. A second tier, which included white women and initially a substantial number of white men, consisted of persons who were denied the suffrage but enjoyed many, perhaps most, of the other constitutional rights. The top tier consisted of the white males who had the suffrage. By 1787, these were a majority of the white males in most states, and within a few years this tier encompassed all but a rather small minority of all adult white males.

What needs emphasizing, however, is not these exclusions or the struggles they led to but several other aspects of the first historic commitment. To begin with, it was not at the outset a commitment to democracy. The framers agreed on the desirability of a representative republic based directly or indirectly on the consent of the people secured through elections, but they were by no means agreed on who ought to be included among "the people." Thus they were able to agree on a republic but not on the desirability of a representative democracy based directly on universal suffrage, even among white males.

Second, the commitment was reflected in the very structure of the constitutional system itself, which in prescribing a separation of powers was intended to insure that no official of the government, least of all the president, could ever gain preponderant influence over the government, much less over the people.

Third, the particular rights that were thought to be of greatest importance were, as we all know, set out in the Bill of Rights, which was far more integral to the constitutional design than its form as a set of amendments might suggest.

Finally, more by implication and assumption than by explicit reference, the whole structure of rights and government took for granted the existence of a social and economic system based preponderantly on private property—which at the time was, of course, overwhelmingly in land owned by farmers.

Second Commitment: Democracy and Polyarchy

Sometime after the adoption of the Constitution and before Jackson left the presidency, this country made a second historic commitment, a commitment in favor of the democratic ideal as the very center of our philosophy. As an ideal it has since found fewer competitors over a longer period of time in the United States than quite possibly any other country in the world. Democracy is at the very heart, it is the very core and substance, of our political ideals. If our public agreement on that ideal, as a hope, an inspiration, an ambition, and a standard against which to evaluate our achievements as a people—if that agreement were to disintegrate, we would become an aimless people without either a meaningful past to shape our identity or a hopeful future to shape our aspirations.

Unfortunately, few words in political philosophy and popular discourse are more ambiguous than the word "democracy." To qualify it by the term "liberal" no doubt narrows the range a little, but not a lot. Some people would even argue that the qualifier is redundant, for although liberalism is not necessarily democratic, democracy must be liberal, that is to say, if it does not guarantee certain fundamental political and civil rights, then it is simply not democracy. In this way a democracy without free and fair elections, or one in which critics of the government are regularly thrown into jail, is a contradiction in terms; at the very least such a usage clashes with the practice of more than two thousand years of political discourse.

One must recognize, however, that the term has acquired a variety of meanings around the world, and that what I would unhesitatingly call a dictatorship, some people would call a democracy, and conversely. There is no need here to engage in a purely semantic exercise, though it might be interesting and worthwhile for, as George Orwell reminded us a good while ago, we are not likely to be truthful about the world if we are dishonest with the terms we use to describe it. Let me then specify as briefly and as clearly as I can what I mean by the term "democracy." Of its various usages, two are of particular appropriateness here.

First, democracy is an unachieved ideal summed up in its etymology as "rule by the people." Rule by the people is a formula intended to satisfy the principle of consent, according to which no adult should be compelled to live under a system of government and laws to which he or she refuses to give informed consent;

it is intended also to satisfy the principle that all adult human beings are fundamentally equal as moral beings, in the sense that the final judgment of each adult as to what constitutes the good for one's own self and for others is to be given equal respect and consideration. To state it negatively, the principle rejects the view that there exists a political priesthood whose members possess such superior knowledge of the good that they are entitled to rule over others.

The democratic ideal is given its particular content by the criteria it prescribes for determining how collective decisions ought to be made in any association of equal persons. As I see it, there are three such criteria. First, the criterion of *political equality:* that is, the rule for making final decisions must equally take into account the preferences of each member as to the outcome. The majority principle is usually thought to be one such rule, though it is not the only one consistent with the criterion of political equality. Second, the criterion of *effective participation:* that is, in order for the preferences of each member to be equally taken into account, every member must have equal opportunities for expressing his or her preferences, and the grounds for them, throughout the process of collective decision making. Third, the criterion of *adequate understanding:* that is, in order to express his or her preferences accurately, each member ought to have adequate and equal opportunities for discovering and validating, in the time available, what his or her preferences are on the matter to be decided.

Although I have formulated the three criteria a bit more abstractly than was common at the time, I think they catch much of the essence of the commitment to democracy that Americans made early in the nineteenth century. This second commitment was superimposed on, and often confused with, the preceding commitment to a specific constitutional order that was, like procedural democracy, also based on certain fundamental rights, some of which, like freedom of speech, were identical with those that would be required if the criteria of procedural democracy were to be met satisfactorily.

The government of a country—or for that matter the government of any kind of association—can be regarded as procedurally democratic, then, to the extent and only to the extent that it satisfies these criteria. The fact is, however, that no association—surely no large association and certainly no country—has ever met these criteria perfectly, or is likely to do so. Yet it is also true that in a number of countries, political institutions have been significantly shaped by claims based in the democratic ideal, and today the countries of the world vary significantly in the degree to which their political institutions approach these criteria.

Toward the end of the eighteenth century and on through the nineteenth century, in the United States, Britain, the English-speaking colonies and dominions, and Europe, advocates of the democratic ideal came to agree substantially that certain basic political guarantees were required if the ideal were to be approached in any association as large as even the smaller nation-states. To win the battle for democracy, that is, to democratize the existing regimes they saw about them, advocates of democracy pressed for and increasingly gained a set of minimal political guarantees protected by and embodied in political institutions.

By 1920, or thereabouts, such institutions were solidly, and at least up to now, irreversibly in place in more than a dozen English-speaking and European countries. In several of these countries women were still excluded from full citizenship, and in our own country, which had pioneered the development of democratic guarantees among adult white males, an overwhelming proportion of nonwhites continued to be excluded for more than 150 years after the rights were made available to most white men.

Despite these shortcomings, which in the American case have distorted the whole course of our political history, what in the late eighteenth century were mainly aspirations toward institutions still but dimly conceived have become in our own time so traditional that one hardly needs to be reminded what they are. They include, of course, the familiar guarantees of the first amendment, universal suffrage, free and fair elections, the right to run for public office, and thus to compete for votes and other support, the freedom to form political parties and other political organizations, the determination of basic laws and government policies by elected officials, and the like. Largely though not wholly in response to movements in ideas and actions over the past two centuries aimed at democratizing monarchies, oligarchies, dictatorships, and other nondemocratic regimes, institutions providing these guarantees at levels comparable to (and sometimes higher than) those in America exist today in something like two dozen countries. Because the term "democracy" is commonly used to refer both to the ideal and to the constellation of institutions just mentioned, it may help reduce the ambiguity if we reserve the term "democracy" for referring to the ideal, and use the term "polyarchy"—rule by the many—to refer to a governmental system distinguished by these kinds of institutional guarantees.

As regards the second historic commitment, it is fair to say that Americans committed themselves both to democracy as an ideal and to the institutions and guarantees of polyarchy. Now this commitment was not made in a political, social, or economic vacuum. It was facilitated by the previous commitment, which, by requiring elections and protecting a number of basic liberties, went a long way toward establishing the basic institution of polyarchy. The commitment to democracy and polyarchy was also strongly favored by an agrarian economic and social order unique in history up to that time, one that may not have been fully duplicated anywhere since that time. Tocqueville may have exaggerated, but surely he was basically right in stressing how much the American society, made up mainly of farmers, had created a condition of equality among white males that made democracy possible and likely (at least among white males). As he also rightly pointed out, our isolation made it unnecessary for Americans to support a large centralized military establishment, or to grant to the chief executive the kinds of powers that monarchs and their foreign ministers enjoyed in countries that depended for their survival more than the United States did on their military and diplomatic resources. In addition, with its norms of equality and individual liberty and autonomy, the agrarian society had no need, no place, no tolerance for a centralized regime, central bureaucracies, a sumptuous court, or a great capital city that would exert political, economic, social, and cultural dominance over the nation.

As we all know, however, the agrarian society was replaced and many of its institutions were dismantled or made over. Three later historic commitments have contributed to this profound change in the conditions that were so favorable to democracy and polyarchy. The agrarian order was displaced by a new social and economic order based on commercial and industrial capitalism and gigantic economic enterprises. Large central bureaucracies grew up that were aimed at overcoming some of the adverse consequences of unregulated capitalism. And the United States emerged as a world power. Each of the later commitments had some consequences that were adverse to the earlier commitment to democracy and polyarchy.

It is not at all clear whether the country would have rejected these later commitments even if it had foreseen the adverse consequences for democracy. Have the gains, after all, outweighed the costs? Might other alternatives have been adopted that were more consistent with the earlier commitment? To answer these questions responsibly would of course require an enormous undertaking that far exceeds the aims and possibilities of this brief discussion. Our purpose here is merely to call attention to some of the consequences of the later commitments that have been adverse to democracy and polyarchy, and to inquire—albeit all too briefly—whether there may not yet be ways of resolving, or at least reducing, the conflicts among our various historic commitments.

Third Commitment: A Private, Corporate Economy

Let us begin with the transformation of the socio-economic order. By the end of the nineteenth century, after much bitter contestation—more bitter, in fact, than the conflict over the democratic ideal and the institutions of polyarchy at the beginning of the century—the country committed itself to a new socio-economic order designed to encourage, foster, and guarantee the performance of economic functions mainly by privately owned corporations. The socio-economic order of commercial and industrial capitalism rapidly displaced the agrarian socio-economic order that had previously provided such a solid foundation for the democratic ideal. Despite some opposition, Americans in due course overwhelmingly and repeatedly ratified this new historical commitment. At the time, the emerging new order surely appeared to a great many Americans as if it were no more than a re-affirmation of the first historic commitment, which, after all, included an all but universal belief in private property. In time, however, despite continuing rear-guard actions by critics, the commitment came to mean de facto approval for the evolution of very large, even gigantic, privately owned corporate enterprises, the largest of which were one day to have gross incomes greater than those of most of the countries of the world. By the standards of all previous centuries, they are today themselves political systems of great opulence and power.

One of the consequences of the new order has been a high degree of inequality in the distribution of wealth and income—a far greater inequality than had ever been thought likely or desirable under an agrarian order by Democratic Republicans like Jefferson and Madison, or had ever been thought consistent with democratic or republican government in the historic writings on the subject from Aristotle to Locke, Montesquieu, and Rousseau. Previous theorists and advocates had, like many of the framers of our own Constitution, insisted that a republic could exist only if the citizen body contained neither rich nor poor. Citizens, it was argued, must enjoy a rough equality of condition. It was this equality of condition that Tocqueville reported he had found among American citizens, or at least among white males, in the 1830s.

Yet if Tocqueville were alive today, he would find a citizen body very different from the one he described. Recent studies have shown, for example, that:

- The poorest 20 percent of American families receive only about 2 percent of the family income. The poorest 40 percent receive only about 12 percent of the family income.
- At the other end of the scale, the top 20 percent receive about 50 percent of the income. The top 5 percent get about 24 percent of the income, and the top 1 percent about 11 percent.
- Differences in income among Americans are not declining; in fact, the best evidence indicates that they may be increasing.
- Despite a widely held belief to the contrary, taxes do not change

the distribution of income very much. One study shows that the sum total of all federal, state, and local taxes bears more heavily on the very poor than on any other income group.
- Some redistribution takes place as a result of the sum total of what economists call transfer payments, or governmental payments of benefits to individuals. Transfer payments comprise a substantial part of the income of the very poor and of people over the age of 65. Except for the very poor and the aged, however, the transfer payments are a small proportion of family incomes. Consequently, they do not have much effect on income inequality.
- Finally, wealth is highly concentrated. In 1969, the richest 4 percent of American adults owned 35 percent of the country's private wealth. The richest 1 percent owned 21 percent. Indeed, 8 percent of the private wealth of the United States is owned by only 70,000 persons, about one-tenth of 1 percent of the adult population.

It is true that polyarchies have survived in spite of great inequalities in wealth and income. After all, the American polyarchy has managed to exist in the midst of the inequalities just described. Yet the survival of polyarchy is one thing; attaining democracy is another. Inequalities in wealth and income generate a large gap between ideal democracy and the actual performance of political institutions. That is why Jefferson and Madison, like political theorists from Aristotle to Montesquieu, held that economic inequalities would seriously hamper democratic institutions and might finally undermine them.

The reasons are all but self-evident. Where wide differences exist in access to economic resources, there are bound to be great differences in resources for influencing the government—that is, in political resources. Economic resources are often directly convertible into political resources. This is plainly the case with campaign expenses, for example, or buying television time, or advertising, or bribing officials, or bringing economic pressures to bear on an official. But economic resources are also indirectly convertible into political resources. For example, economic advantages increase one's chances of getting an education, gaining higher status, having more time available for politics, and so on.

Economic advantages also help in providing psychological resources such as confidence and optimism, which strengthen both the incentives to participate in politics and the willingness to acquire political skills.

Solutions to the problem of inequalities are roughly of two kinds, and they are not mutually exclusive. One kind of solution looks toward reducing differences in wealth and income. Since this would almost certainly require redistributive policies by government, say by income and estate taxes, it would also appear to require still another historic commitment, this time to agreed-on principles of distributive justice.

If we do not make such a commitment, and the odds are that we cannot, then we must turn to the other alternative, which is to reduce the effects on political life of differences in wealth and income. For if we choose to permit such differences among our citizens, then it would seem that we must do everything possible to minimize their effects on politics. Surely it is flatly inconsistent with our public philosophy to hold that the mere possession of greater economic resources entitles the holder to more influence in government. Accordingly, we must do our best to confine variations in the individual use of money within strict floors and ceilings. In fact, I believe the time may come when we shall adopt the view that such basic rights of citizenship as in principle should be equally distributed among all adult citizens must include a standard bundle of political resources. These resources, like the vote, would assure a minimum level of participation for every citizen, and they might also impose a ceiling above which no citizen would be entitled to spend resources for political purposes.

Fourth and Fifth Commitments

Between the beginnings of the Great Depression and the end of the Second World War, this country entered into two more historic commitments that have had enormous consequences for the functioning of polyarchy and the prospects of democracy. In the 1930s, a substantial majority of the electorate committed themselves to the idea that the government—mainly but by no means exclusively the national government—should use its special capacities and powers to rectify some of the adverse consequences of the economic and social order. That commitment has not yet been, and is unlikely to be, reversed. Quite the contrary: it has been repeatedly ratified in one election after another, most notably perhaps when Republican presidents have taken office.

In the 1940s, the country added on still another commitment when it undertook to play a role as a major world power. Although it is often said nowadays that we have abandoned that commitment in the wake of our disillusion over the follies of Vietnam, that is far too facile an interpretation. Whatever judgment one may make about this country's performance as a world power—some of which seems to be abysmally bad—the United States unquestionably is, and for a long time surely will remain, one of the superpowers of the world, even if the old illusion of American benevolence, omnipotence, and omniscience has been pretty widely discredited in this country and throughout the world.

One of the results of these last two historic commitments has been the enormous expansion in government hierarchies (bureaucracies, if you prefer), both civil and military. Government hierarchies grew mightily—in both the absolute and the relative number of persons they employed, in their resources, in their expenditures, in their costs, and in their effects on the lives of Americans, and for that matter non-Americans as well.

Added to the earlier transformation of the socio-economic order, this development meant that most members of the American work force must now enter into a hierarchical system of authority, whether in the private firm, the government bureau, or the military. This was a radical, even a revolutionary, change away from the relative, even if highly imperfect, equality of status and authority sustained by the earlier agrarian order, as Tocqueville had reported it. It is hard to know which of the terms of classical political science best describes these modern hierarchies: some are monarchies, some are despotisms, some are oligarchies, and some are aristocracies of merit. Yet they most certainly are not democracies, no matter how generously one might stretch the term, nor are they polyarchies with the rights to oppose, to participate, and to displace rulers—rights that distinguish polyarchies from hegemonic regimes.

Thus, it is not going too far to say that taken together the three later historic commitments meant that the democratic ideal and the institutions of polyarchy were applied to one crucial set of authority relations, the control of elected officials, but not to another set that in its significance for daily life is perhaps even more crucial for most people: the government of the organization within which they work. In practice, then, the ideal of democracy became somewhat marginal to the concerns of daily life.

Proposals aimed at solving this problem confront serious difficulties of one kind or another. It is not at all clear that in the case of government bureaucracies and the military the problem can be solved at all without risking a loss of democratic controls over the bureaucracies and the military—a trade-off hardly to be recommended. Even in the case of economic enterprises, solutions are not easy. Yet surely we must confront the alternatives and examine their consequences, for a citizenry as highly educated as ours is becoming will sooner or later begin to wonder about contradictions between our commitment to the democratic ideal and the theory and practice of hierarchy in our daily lives.

The expansion of government hierarchies also facilitated another change that resulted from the commitments of the 1930s and 1940s, namely the transformation of the presidency into an office that has been variously called a plebiscitary executive, an elective monarchy, the American monarchy, the imperial presidency. Although some of the causes for the evolution of the imperial presidency may have been historically transitory, there were also enduring causes. These include the comparative advantages of the single executive in managing a large and enormously complex set of bureaucracies, providing leadership on innumerable questions of policy, conducting foreign and military affairs, often in an atmosphere of emergency (whether the sense of urgency is real or fictitious), and capturing the attention of the country and the world. Still other enduring causes would include the mystique of the presidential mandate, the position of the United States as a world power, the established constitutional doctrine, especially as to the "war powers" of the president, and the absence of alternative sources of leadership, particularly in the Congress.

The sort of unbalanced political system represented by the presidency of Richard Nixon did not develop by itself. It developed over many decades with the support—sometimes active, sometimes passive—of Congress, the Supreme Court, the political parties, the major political figures of the country, the newspapers and commentators, intellectuals, lawyers, political scientists, and the electorate. In this sense, the country gave its uninformed consent to a political system in which the government could frequently make crucial decisions without the consent of the people. Thus even though events have made the presidency the element most urgently in need of reform, the greater, more enduring challenge is to refashion a government that will rest upon the informed and active consent of the people.

It is hardly surprising that the foundations of the imperial presidency were laid by the very presidents and their supporters who sought to undo some of the adverse consequences of the socio-economic order the country had adopted earlier. If the commitment to an order based on the private ownership and management of large economic enterprises had, as I have argued, effects adverse to the earlier commitment to democracy, the commitment made in the 1930s was intended to overcome some of these adverse effects. Yet that commitment in turn helped to create the conditions for the imperial presidency which, as we now see, is itself inimical to democracy. Do we then confront a dilemma, to which there is no solution wholly favorable to democracy?

The Dilemma of Presidential Power

One horn of the dilemma is the political difficulty of bringing about changes that would diminish some of the consequences of those commitments that are unfavorable to democracy and polyarchy. I have in mind changes that would diminish great differences in income, wealth, and opportunities that are now created by the workings of our existing socio-economic order; or changes that would reduce the importance of these differentials in the political process; or changes that would alter the hierarchical structures that control the working lives of most Americans.

The difficulty of making changes like these is partly a result of certain special features of our political system, features not necessarily inherent in democracy and polyarchy. Indeed one prominent characteristic of the American constitutional and political system is that it makes great changes difficult. Any proposed change that arouses the opposition of an intense minority, as the proposals I have suggested inevitably will, is very likely to be blocked somewhere along the way. Moreover, it appears that those who stand to gain from existing inequalities of wealth and authority are rather more likely to participate in political life in this country, and more likely to participate effectively, than those who stand to lose by these inequalities.

Putting together a political coalition that can bring about changes intended to achieve greater equality is, therefore, a task of the utmost difficulty. Successful coalitions of this kind have been rare in American political life. I can think of only two in the last half century—that of Franklin Roosevelt, which endured as a successful reform coalition for about five years, and the much more narrowly focused civil-rights coalition that effectuated important changes during the presidency of Lyndon Johnson. The successes of both were the product of extraordinary circumstances. Ironically, both coalitions also contributed to the flourishing of the plebiscitary executive.

We may be reasonably sure, I think, that if there should be another period of reform aimed at reducing the major inequalities in American society, it will take place under the leadership of a president who will have regained at least some of the features of that lately fallen and largely unlamented structure of the imperial presidency. Although it now seems preposterous, from quarters still rejoicing that the late monarch has fallen we shall probably one day hear the cry: the king is dead, long live the king! Thus, do we find ourselves impaled on the other horn of our dilemma.

The usual solutions are, first, to elect better presidents, or second, to create better mechanisms to protect us from mediocre or bad presidents. The difficulty with solving the problem by electing better presidents is that the different roles of the president create conflicting demands that cannot be met except by a truly superhuman performance. Thus, the president's responsibilities as symbolic head of state and national model of morality are likely to conflict with his role as master politician, particularly with the things he must do if he is to be a successful leader of his party and initiator of policy. Any person who fights his way to the presidency by means of the brutal efforts required to win the nomination and the election, and who then successfully exploits the resources of his office to guide his policies through Congress and gain the support he needs in the country, is not altogether likely to have the character or qualities required to symbolize the country's highest traditions of morality.

To paper over the gap between high expectations and cruel reality, a great many Americans hold firmly to the belief that the White House transforms its occupant: it makes a silk purse out of a sow's ear. The transformation, alas, is largely in the eye of the beholder, who passionately wishes to see, and so manages to see, majesty and divinity where there are only the ordinary (or sometimes extraordinary) shortcomings of a mere mortal being. There is no evidence, as far as I know, to give any solid grounds for hoping that the highly imperfect person who reaches the presidency will, in the conventional and ever-hopeful phrase, "rise to the office." To be sure, the office may sometimes bring out the best in its holder. But it also may, and often does, bring out the worst. Indeed it probably does both.

What we need to confront then is an unpleasantness that the framers understood and that later Americans in their longing for a superhuman greatness in the presidency have too often forgotten. Because the worst that the office may bring out in the person who holds it may be very bad indeed, injurious to the life of the republic, and nowadays a danger to the world, the president's discretionary power must be carefully circumscribed. If we had assumed all along that the president was likely to use discretion badly if he were ever given half a chance, we would surely not have allowed the institution to evolve into the plebiscitary monarchy which a few years ago it seemed on the way to becoming.

Consequently, our perennial hope for better presidents is not likely to be realized except episodically—on the record, hardly more than once a generation, just enough to keep the hope alive. I do not doubt that we are all once again hoping—at this very moment—for just such a miracle.

Better mechanisms seem to me only a little more promising. Those that might be fairly easily adopted, such as the ever-recurring idea of a question hour in Congress for the president and his cabinet, would probably make very little difference in the end. Those that might really make a big difference, such as changing over to a parliamentary system, not only stand little chance of being adopted but are clouded with overwhelming uncertainty both as to their prerequisites and as to their consequences. Constitution-making hardly qualifies as an exact science.

I should be inclined to look elsewhere for a solution. I think we need to reformulate a few constitutional understandings which, if violated, would bring down upon a president the country's wrath; examples might include the reaction that followed Nixon's Saturday Night Massacre or FDR's proposal in 1937 to pack the Supreme Court. Now that we have finally learned how to operate the process of impeachment, we might keep the machinery oiled and ready for use.

One such crucial understanding should be that no president and no executive officer can ever expect to bind this country to a major policy unless that policy is based on the informed and active consent of the Congress and, ultimately, of a majority of the electorate. We should be better off, I think, if every president, every member of Congress, and every citizen understood that any president who violates this principle will be repudiated, his undertakings will be revoked, and if need be he will be impeached, convicted, and removed from office in public disgrace. No one ought ever again to forget that the president of the United States is only the chief executive officer of the republic.

After all, one of the nation's first great commitments, which it may yet renew, was that it would have a government derived from the consent of the people, and would neither honor nor knowingly consent to any other.

JO GRIMOND

5. Liberal Democracy in Britain

To believe that a human society can be run as a liberal democracy involves certain assumptions about the nature of man. The periods of civilization with which democracy has been associated were times when human personality was much discussed. I refer in particular to the late eighteenth century, the time of America's birth.

The intellectual attack on liberal democracy has come from those who feel that individual men are either somewhat unimportant—a view held by communists—or that men by themselves are incapable of leading good lives or running a good society—a view held by many religions.

It is apparently assumed by some people that there is no incompatibility between communism and democracy. The communist states call themselves democracies. If they do not allow free elections, they say that is because they are in a transitional stage. Once economic democracy and total indoctrination are achieved, then free elections may well be allowed, they tell us, though they will in any case be unnecessary. That is a doctrine for which there is no theoretical justification. Further, it runs contrary to all experience. In practice every communist state has subsisted and can only subsist on a tyranny of the most ruthless sort. Those who believe the promises of communism cannot do so on the evidence of history or psychology or science. They must indeed believe in miracles.

Between communism and liberalism there is a great and unbridgeable antagonism founded on different views about the nature of man. Communism is by no means the first dogmatic religion that has played down the individual. It is indeed not the first religion to preach predestination. Communism comes from the same stable as the more dogmatic form of medieval Catholicism or the Calvinism of Geneva. How is it then, one may ask, that communism, holding such untenable beliefs, has a grip on so much of the world? The answer is that "belief" is a word of many shades of meaning. The communist governors of their enslaved countries no more and no less believe in communism than medieval and Renaissance popes and ecclesiastics believed in Catholicism or John Knox in Calvinism. Belief is a useful justification for the pursuit of power. Communism panders to two deeply rooted instincts of mankind—the lust for power in some and the yearning for inescapable discipline in others. It is a discipline that many men find relieves them of the burdens of decision.

The other criticism of liberal democracy, which starts not from the perfectability of man and the claims of the elect but from the very opposite pole, has a great deal of empirical evidence to support it. Original sin is something of which there is all too much evidence in everyone. The human animal is aggressive. It is destructive. It is moved by lust, not least lust for prestige or power, to quite an extraordinary degree.

Liberals, while accepting the dangers of original sin, nevertheless believe that individuals by themselves are capable of running a good society. The history of human government might be read on the one hand as a recognition that some restraint on liberty, some force exerted on the individual, is essential in the light of original sin, while on the other hand it must be seen as containing a warning of the appalling effects of too much government. That is indeed the classic dilemma between freedom and order. But freedom should mean the freedom of a free community and order an impartial order under the law. Freedom sometimes used to be interpreted as freedom to exploit, and order sometimes still means the arbitrary tyranny of the dictator.

The view of society, of men in society, held by liberal democrats is the tradition that runs through Locke, Burke, Hume, Adam Smith, J. S. Mill, and the other Scottish political philosophers and economists down, say, to Lippmann in our time. Let us be clear that though this philosophy is individualist in that it believes that value resides in the individual and not in any abstraction—though it therefore believes in liberty for the individual to express himself—it does not believe that the individual can live on his own. It believes that what is interesting in human society is the interplay between individuals and the actions and reactions of the community. Government is the instrument by which the community meets certain needs—police, for instance. It draws its authority from the community. It comes, so to speak, "after" the community becomes self-conscious. Nor is it the only means which the community has of ordering its affairs. Once government assumes that it is the origin of political power, once it presumes in the name of religion, communism, superior knowledge, or the "right" of majorities or interest groups, trade unions, or bureaucracies to override the community, then tyranny is close at hand.

For most of history, government has been regarded as an evil, a necessary evil, but an evil from which springs oppression and war. Burke said that government was a contrivance of human wisdom to satisfy human want. There is nothing miraculous about it. If the human race was to live in peace and be able to improve its lot—to save, invest, and create wealth—it had to cooperate to discharge some functions. But the notion that bigger government is better government is contrary to all experience. In a way the astonishing thing is not that modern governments work badly but that anyone should think they would work at all. To entrust governments with more and more power—indeed to beseech them to take it—might seem in the light of history a sign of madness.

How has it come about? The founding fathers of America, true children of the eighteenth-century Enlightenment, were under no illusions about the corrupting effects of power. They devised a constitution which ensured that the executive was curbed and balanced. Their heirs in Europe and perhaps even in America are forgetting the age-old lessons of the history of politics.

The liberals of the first half of the nineteenth century perceived that in the good community there should be two systems at work, anterior, so to speak, to government: the rule of law and the market economy. Both were ways in which the community was kept together. Both enabled individuals in the community to use their talents, both were guarantees of freedom, and both were guarantees of equality.

The rule of law sprang from the morality of the community. I know there is a view that law has nothing to do with morality. I do not share it. Though the law has a different field from morality and should not attempt to control the whole moral field, yet it must rest upon some view of morality shared at least by the majority of the people concerned. Morality by its nature is the same for all. All therefore, in so far as they are moral beings, should be equal under the law. The growth of a secular morality strengthened the rule of law. From Kant onwards through the nineteenth century, the general interest and the general will were widely accepted with their moral imperatives such as the Golden Rule.

From the rule of law grew respect for constitutions. That Britain did not have a written constitution in the American style did not mean that her nineteenth-century statesmen were not deeply imbued with constitutional notions. What affronted Palmerston about European dictatorships was not the lack of a voting franchise: it was the lack of constitutional checks upon the autocracy. When Gladstone or Asquith wanted to make changes in the method of government, a bare majority was not enough. They were almost as conscious as was Burke of the need to respect the organic growth of the body politic and take into account the various branches of the state.

The free market enabled everyone in the community to exercise choice. That the choice of the poor was much smaller than that of the rich was all too true. But the choice of the poor was even smaller in the time of mercantilism. The free market allowed for the distribution of resources according to demand. Again, from some points of view that was unsatisfactory. But it contributed to a greatly increased output of cheap and sought-after goods. Further, not only has no other system allocated resources so well but socialist systems have often been compelled to fall back on it. Socialist planning with no free market will not work.

The founding fathers and those who thought along similar lines in North Europe had good reason for optimism. Nor did it turn out that their optimism was misplaced. America remains a miracle, a miracle only approached by Japan, which, if the efficient output of material goods is to be the criterion, should be a model for all underdeveloped countries. Nor let it be said that Americans, or for that matter Northwest Europeans, are disillusioned about the political and economic background of liberal democracy. In spite of all the professed admiration of communist countries, there is no rush to go there. The Russian record of creating human misery surpasses even that of the Nazis. If you want a memorial to the success of liberal democracy you have only to look at the Berlin Wall.

Nevertheless all is not well. Let me say at once that it never will be. In the democracies, it is true, there is a high level of material well-being, freedom, and education. But there are certain contradictions and difficulties in our situation. The rule of law and the market economy depend, as I have said, on a fairly general acceptance of morality. And morality, in turn, depends on an appreciation of the organic nature of human society and a respect for the individual in it. But today the importance of men and women is more and more attached to their role in society. In Britain people are regarded as members of a union, or a profession, civil servants, executives of a firm, or even as members of "the unemployed" or "the disabled." These organizations are run by their bureaucracies, whose main aim is to increase their empire and gain as much as they can in the way of pay and resources. The general interest—the interest of the community—goes to the wall. Society calls more and more upon government to intervene in particular situations instead of relying upon any impartial system. It is a reversion to the political situation before American independence. In the Middle Ages and the Renaissance powerful barons and later powerful moneyed interests disputed the authority of the crown or tried to use it for their own purposes. That is much more like the situation in Britain today than was the situation between, say, 1870 and 1914. It is a situation requiring political skills rather than rational argument. Mr. Heath suffered the classic fate of those who attack with inadequate forces uphill with the sun in their eyes. The miners defeated him. The age of Kennedy-Gaitskell, when it was taken for granted that the system would work and that everyone would obey the wisdom of those educated at Winchester, Oxford, or Harvard, is over.

I do not believe that the founding fathers or their counterparts in Britain could have foreseen the trend of events. I am sure that they would be as astonished by the popularity of communism as they would have been by a resurgence of the Inquisition. But with hindsight one can see that there were bound to be pressures on any liberal democratic constitution and contradictions between politics and economics.

We must not assume that democracy in its more extreme form was advocated in either Britain or America. In Britain, consonant with the fear of too much government, the job of Parliament was largely negative. It was to question, criticize, and thwart the executive. The government itself emerged either from the royal line, the Whig aristocracy, or the party system. Some of it came, and indeed comes, from the House of Lords. The prime minister is not elected as is the president. The British Parliament has never chosen the executive; it has never been a legislature in the sense that Congress is a legislature, the members of which actually initiate important legislation. The unwritten conventions of our constitution were abandoned, and as the party system became more rigid the potential power of the cabinet grew very great. The checks and balances have been eroded and there is no supreme court to act, so to speak, as long stop. But the British party system was essential both to give some democratic cohesion to the British electoral system and to give some shape and dialogue to our politics.

Contradictions between the political and economic systems have exposed the essential weaknesses of liberal democracy. For a period the presuppositions of a general interest, equality before the law, and the market economy were broadly accepted, and the system worked. But now the strike, or threat to strike, used not against the employer but against the public, has challenged the rule of law and the concept of an overriding general interest. Not only the weekly wage earner, but the civil servant and the white-collar worker look to what they believe (often quite mistakenly) is their own interest. And the market is much less effective. The planners, socialist or nonsocialist, claimed that the market was "unscientific," that rational human beings should not be at the mercy of "blind" economic forces or the whim of millionaires or large companies. In a curious phrase the market has been called the "rule of the jungle." That describes, however, not the market but much of socialist planning. For the rule of the jungle is the rule of the strongest—of the person who can use either industrial action or the machinery of the state. Today in Britain we are indeed in a jungle where the strongest unions and bureaucracies grab what they can get. The planners, i.e., those in control, are not free from the old vices that go with power. However repulsive may seem some of the habits of the old-style millionaires, yet there remains something in Dr. Johnson's dictum that men are seldom so innocently employed as when making money. At least power seeking is worse. And the combination of the two, which is clearly visible today, is worst of all. It was perfectly true that the completely free operation of the market with its booms and slumps led to great human misery. The social services and public works were an attempt to meet this problem by general provisions enacted by Parliament. The control of credit and the general acceptance of Keynesian economics were an effort to meet it by general policies affecting the whole economy. But paradoxically perhaps, as state activity has increased, Parliament in Britain has come to exert less power than the bureaucracy and the unions.

General essays in government are never sufficient to satisfy the bureaucratic urges in our society. So at every election political parties have to offer a program of government action. This program is seldom built upon a general view. It is rather a series of bribes offered to particular bureaucracies or groups of voters. It is usually in conflict with the economic and general needs of the community in two respects. The first is timing. The timing of politics is quite different from the timing of economics. Again and again governments take measures to deal with a current situation, but measures which will only take effect when the situation has changed.

Second, every program of every party in Britain in recent years has meant more state intervention, more interference with the market, more of the national income taken by the state, and more use of resources. Inasmuch as, even in the official statistics, production is hardly rising, and in terms of what the public wants is not rising at all, the inevitable result is inflation and a growing loss of efficiency, partly through the ever-increasing number of nonproducing bureaucrats and partly through lack of any adequate incentive to efficiency in the public sector. Resources are wasted and misapplied.

In fact, the democratic political system in Britain (and I suspect in most of the western world) is failing to cope with a situation for which its protagonists are not prepared. The origin and possible cure of the political problem is not understood. Let me take two examples: Lord Ashby, a distinguished scientist, has lately delivered a lecture entitled "A Second Look at Doom." Its themes are, first, that we are not only using up the world's resources at a dangerous rate but are becoming dependent for raw materials on the less wealthy part of the world, which will hold us for ransom; and, second, that our ecosystems are not self-adjusting and will therefore plunge us into chaos. He then goes on to say that we need international efforts "massive as those used to make the atomic bomb or put a man on the moon." But our wastage of raw materials, our position vis-à-vis the underdeveloped countries, and the difficulties of our cities—all these are caused by the very same type of thinking that has made the atom bomb or put a man on the moon. Both are the result of deliberate governmental planning. Both are a waste of resources. Neither has anything to do with the general good or the free market. The most successful development of underdeveloped countries in terms of material resources, as I have said, is found in the experience of the United States and Japan, the worst utilization of vast resources is in state-planned Russia. Lord Ashby's justifiable fears of the failure of our ecosystems brings me to my second example, the difficulties of the great cities—of which New York is perhaps the worst illustration. But the great cities are prime examples, not of the free market, but of constant public interference, constant increases in welfare of various types at the expense of production, constant subsidization of uneconomic activities. And by uneconomic I mean activities the public does not want to pay for.

What we need is to direct technological research by some system of values, insofar as—for humane reasons—we want to supplement the market. We should be encouraging intermediate technology; we should be developing tools suitable for the poor and the underdeveloped countries. But western governments are the slaves of technological determinism and prestige-hungry bureaucracies.

Until recently the market in Britain was strong enough to bear the disturbances and impositions put upon it by politicians and the bureaucratically minded. It is becoming doubtful how long that can continue. Taxes, subsidies, public bodies, all have proliferated to such an extent that the economic nexus which regulates society is in danger of snapping. And at the same time that the bonds of the community are in danger of breaking, a high proportion of our ablest people are in futile or at least unproductive and unessential occupations.

If liberal democracy is to develop its best in the next hundred years and shed its worst, certain ideas must be understood and accepted. The troubles are political or politico-economic. They stem from the growth of the bureaucratic attitude in all its forms, from the power of pressure groups and the resurgence of communist absolutism. We must reassert the primacy of the individual as a moral creature capable of developing his talents and making his choices within a community. A fault of the founding fathers and the subsequent generations was that they presumed the continuance of an aristocratic (largely landed) element in society which would stabilize it. They could not see the pulverizing effects of extreme economic or technological determinism treating human beings as monads to be manipulated either by a ruling bureaucracy or by inescapable laws. But in reasserting the individual we must also emphasize the community. And since the rule of law and the market have been so badly damaged we must ask ourselves whether they can be resuscitated or replaced.

As far as Britain is concerned, the rule of law could well be improved and extended. We probably need a bill of rights. Home Rule for Scotland and Wales will require a written constitution. The opportunity could be taken to write into such fundamental documents some protection for the generality of the community against vested interests.

As far as the market is concerned, we need to redefine its limits. It is perfectly true that many human economic relations and activities cannot be subject to the pure play of the market. It is also true that a system which gives interest groups vast political power to interfere with the market is inherently unstable. Most fundamental of all is the unequal start which boys and girls from different communities have in today's world.

There is a difficulty here between the need, for reasons of morality as it affects both the community and the individual, to allow some accumulation and inheritance of private property and the need for equality of opportunity. It seems to me that inheritance and gift taxes should be used as a means of transferring resources among the communities. A striking feature of our civilization is the great gulf—in spite, indeed perhaps because, of high taxation, subsidies, regional development, etc.—between the worst and the best areas. In his or her chances of education, health, jobs, housing, or indeed capacity to cope with life, the child of the poorer areas is still far worse off than the child of the richer. In Britain the social services are largely personal services acting upon the individual only after the individual is in trouble. Though very expensive, the sights of these services are set at reaching some minimum standard by centralized bureaucratic action. They fail to do enough either to improve the surroundings, and thereby prevent misfortune, or to involve the local community or the individuals concerned. Funds should be put at the disposal of the communities to develop their own way of life to its highest potential.

A free community is also a community that encourages life, play, art, expression. The recent history of art in Britain is instructive. Taken all round, the reputation of the British literary and visual arts and the design of clothes have seldom been higher than in the last thirty years. I attribute this partly to an informed, civilized, and communicating audience, a community so to speak, and to critics such as Leavis, and partly to the art schools. The art schools escaped the constrictions of formal education. They dwelt not in marble halls but in rather tatty old buildings repartitioned according to the needs of the artists. Women dressed as they liked. Regular hours were eschewed. They thought that art was central. They taught people to look again. They are now falling under the dead hand of bureaucracy.

As to the economy: here also there are two major questions to be tackled. Can a free economy run without much wider participation and ownership? To my mind it cannot. Is it not the inevitable result in a democracy that interest groups use political means to bend the economy to their liking? Yes. Therefore we should certainly copy the German policies of wider participation. But what if the great majority of workers do not want to participate actively? Are we not then faced with the possibility of companies being taken over by disruptive minority elements? Yes, we are. The solution lies in distinguishing between the workers' wish to be kept informed, to have a right to express their opinion when they find it necessary, and continual active participation in management, which is at best a long way off. By encouraging workers' participation we should at least be doing something to break down the gap between the political and economic systems.

We must clear our minds about the degree of government intervention and what is meant by "a mixed economy." In Britain the motives of the people who run nationalized industries are the same as those of the people who run private enterprise. But public industries are not subject to competition; they are inefficient, overmanned, and wasteful of capital. The motives of their unions or of those who advocate further nationalization is not public service but the assurance that taxpayers' money will keep them in their jobs forever. No doubt many in the so-called private sector behave very much like those in the public sector, but public monopolies are even more inefficient than private monopolies. Further, the public sector is not founded on any organic human situation. It grows for different reasons. It may soon be reaching a point of no return when freedom and efficiency, investment, and the incentive to work are so condemned that only a dictatorship will keep the country even at a painfully low standard of living.

What surely needs to be done is to try to disentangle once again the types of economic activity that are naturally services. They are probably few but they certainly exist, they are important, and they should be carried on for satisfactions other than monetary. One of the most serious incursions of the state in liberal democracies is into the field of voluntary work, though it often occurs from the best of motives. In our dislike of "charity" we are trying to run against some of the strongest of human instincts, the instinct to look after our families and neighbors.

When we move into the purely economic sphere it surely must be wrong to confine the market to the retail trades, betting, eating, drinking, and the production of luxury goods. The "public interest"—that vague phrase—is served by efficiency. It is perfectly true that efficiency is not a god to be worshipped but an instrument to be used. It needs to be regulated by a system of law and some of its products used for national and communal purposes. But people are all consumers. As consumers they want efficiency and cheapness.

In Britain, America, and the western world generally, the public interest is best served by such firms as Marks & Spencers, Macy's, and their equivalents, not by nationalized industries. The motor car has indeed brought problems, but the pleasure it has given is tremendous. If you compare the development of the British motor industry with that of the British aircraft industry—dominated by motives of prestige, bureaucratic constriction, and the inevitable tendency of public monopolies to hold up prices—you can be thankful that the motor car preceded modern socialist doctrines. Had socialism or state management existed 150 years ago we should not only still have had the stage coach but the coach drivers' union would have been demanding ever bigger subsidies. There are many activities (e.g., the Post Office and refuse collection) which fare so badly under public ownership that the possibility of farming them out should be considered.

The market system in Britain, and to some extent in Western Europe, has suffered from three tendencies—apart from government intervention—that have undermined its efficiency. First, the worship of size, served by the tax system. "The economies of scale," "bigger means better"—these were the cries of fifteen years ago. It suited the bureaucratic attitude in industry to create bigger empires and hope they would become monopolies. It suited the mood of technological determinism which presumed to tell the human race it must go wherever science and technology directed, regardless of morality or utility. It led in Britain to the collapse of several famous firms, particularly in the motor industry. In Italy and other countries it led to state control for no very clear reasons other than prestige. The taxation system, at least in Britain, favored amalgamations. Selling your business was at that time the one way of making money. Take-over bidders sold off assets. The big firm could feed itself from profits plowed back.

The next tendency involves the interrelated questions of restrictive practices and inadequate investment. It takes five British workers to equal one Japanese worker in the motor industry. Bethlehem Steel makes as much steel as the British Steel Corporation with half the number of employees. Such are the effects of our restrictive practices, which, incidentally, are just as bad in the professions (worse among lawyers) as they are in industry. In these conditions, and especially in view of the very high taxation on dividends, it is no wonder that investment in enterprise is low —especially when the gigantic British debt offers such yields on government stock. This lack of investment has led to demands that the government should invest. If this were to take place on a big scale it would lead first to inefficiency: governments invest according to bureaucratic pressures and organized groups. If indeed government intervention in the market destroyed the position of equity investment, then the government managers would have no stars to steer by and we should indeed be left in the jungle, at the mercy of whatever interest collared the Treasury. But second, and worse, government investment would fatally undermine liberty. The third tendency is the development of a fairly widespread cynicism about the conduct of the higher economic and financial management. The financial institutions have been too obsessed with making money for themselves, often by means that appear doubtfully honest. They seem to play too little part in supplying industry with the sinews it requires.

These tendencies must be reversed. Here we must consider the position of the social democrats. In Germany they appear to have accepted the principle that the market must dominate the economy. They have been largely concerned with foreign affairs, workers' participation (though the CDU and the FDP also have views on this), the social services, and the general regulation of the economy. In France and Italy it appears that their equivalents are being overtaken from the left. In Britain the Labour Party, though in government, commands only 28 percent of the electorate or 37 percent of those voting, and is in decline. Its social democrats are being driven to face certain questions. What proportion of the national income should go to the government? At present 63 percent passes through its hands. What is the mixture of the mixed economy? Has public control gone far enough? Some of their leaders are on the record as saying that if the government takes any more of the national income, freedom and democracy will be threatened. But they show little sign of calling a halt. Legislation to extend the government's demands is still passing through Parliament on Labour votes. The so-called cuts in public expenditure recently announced in fact add up to an increase. To my mind the British social democrats have been riding on the back of free enterprise, avoiding the ultimate dilemma. The idea that you can have total socialism, i.e., the public ownership of all the means of production, distribution, and exchange (as is written into the constitution of the Labour Party), in combination with democracy is absurd, and it is admitted by the majority of the Labour Party to be absurd. Indeed in the late 1970s many members of the Labour Party have been turning away from state ownership and embracing a form of codetermination, but state ownership is still enshrined in the Party Constitution, and that is the doctrine to which, as members of the Labour Party, they must subscribe.

As I have indicated, the main solution, I believe, lies in carrying democracy into the ownership and running of industry and in stressing the role of the community. But the elected Parliament too must take note of the need to husband the seed corn, use some of it for purposes not directly identifiable by the market, to protect the public against the corruption which is spreading in the West, and also to protect our surroundings and resources.

How are these objectives to be achieved so long as liberal parliamentary democrats constantly feel the need to advocate more immediate expenditure? There are certain procedural improvements that might help. In the British Parliament at least, the purpose of taxation is inadequately understood. Today governments control the supply of money. If they want more money they can print it. They do not have to "buy" it from a third party. Taxation more than ever, therefore, is concerned with restraining demand by individuals or firms so that resources may be available for government purposes without rampant inflation. But taxation on the very rich has a negligible effect on demand. Taxation on the poor, apart from being unjust, is often offset by increases in wages. Taxation is effective, therefore, on a narrow but deserving band of taxpayers. As an instrument of demand management, it is becoming increasingly ineffective for its main purpose and damaging to the economy.

It is a fault of British parliamentary procedure, too, that taxation and expenditure are never discussed together. Nor are alternative expenditures discussed together, nor is there any budget of resources. If Members of Parliament were forced to consider how they paid for things at the moment they voted for these things to be done it would at least alert the public to what was happening.

Parliaments, too, will have to equip themselves better for such managerial roles as are properly theirs. We must accept the idea that the democratic representative today is expected to play a more positive role than his predecessor. But the negative, critical —obstructive if you like—role must not be abolished. Apart from a more logical handling of the business before it, the British system demands some form of counter-civil service. The ombudsman is an embryonic and somewhat mistaken attempt to set up such a service. The counter-civil service must not be in addition to our already overinflated public service. Its successes must be judged by quite different criteria. It must be lodged not in the bureaucratic but in the democratic side of government. It must be associated with that community development that I have mentioned. It must be a counterpoise to the power of bureaucratic government and vested organizations.

It is true that human ecosystems are not as obviously self-righting as those of nature. Man is endlessly and pointlessly destructive. We have eroded many of the natural forces making for equilibrium. We suffer from a greatly weakened code of morality. There is little attempt to keep to standards of behavior. At the same time there are elements at work that are positively disruptive. Our means of communication, for instance, the press and television, excite violence and triviality. The thuggery in Northern Ireland, and some of the kidnappings and bomb throwings, are stimulated by the publicity they receive. Our education does far too little to inculcate the general interest or teach boys and girls to view society as a whole. Communism and a certain defeatism in the West have been fostered partly by the appetite of the press and television to magnify the blots on our society and ignore the appalling dishonesty, inefficiency, and oppression behind the iron curtain, and fostered also in Britain by the failure of our educational system to teach any general morality or indeed the understanding of the rules essential to the conduct of a free society. Bad planning and bad architecture have broken or distorted natural communities. Contrast the success of much of the anti-pollution legislation in our cities with the troubles of urban housing and urban traffic. The first has been achieved by general legislation and admittedly of a largely negative kind—the control of smoke, effluents, etc. It has aroused no sectional interest. It has been associated with no search for prestige. The latter is bedeviled by competing interests. The personal cars which ministers, senior civil servants, and company executives demand have been free from economic forces and are used in disregard of the public interest. The public will not accept one morality for the bureaucrat and another for everyone else. The same tendency is creeping into housing and offices. Meanwhile the conventional fashion is to praise public transport, which is kept in unnecessary profusion and expense by vested interests, and to demand subsidies not only for transport but for housing, special services, etc. The general ecosystem of the city is not studied, nor is its natural development encouraged.

Parliaments have to look again at their functions. They now have a duty to find some consensus in accord with the possibilities of the situation. The communities they are supposed to serve must not be pulled apart by insulated demands from interest groups for more resources. They must spend more time in monitoring trends, capital expenditure, and the success or failure of legislation, and less time in trying to appease pressure groups by new legislation.

British governments have a variety of weapons already at hand or ready to be forged—but they have neglected them.

To the overseas observer American politics seems, on the one hand, more sophisticated than British. Our Public Accounts Committee is not nearly as effective as the oversight committees of the Congress. And there is, I believe, a very welcome disposition in America to examine government to see if it is really beneficial. There seems a healthy readiness to question whether more government expenditure is always desirable. But at the same time the emergence of general policies seems somewhat bewildering. The system of direct primaries has been advocated in Britain as a means of preventing small caucuses from throwing out M.P.s who may well be acceptable to the majority of their party. But the 1976 struggles between President Ford and Governor Reagan or among the several Democratic candidates appear to have been more about personalities than policy. The apparent power of personally recruited staff owing allegiance more to the individual candidate than to the public interest seems to have been an unwelcome element in Watergate. And the genesis and execution of the Vietnam policy appears to have been a story of good intentions undermined and finally lost to sight. Democracies in fact are not very good about having those "great debates" which are constantly called for. But again this seems to be because on the one hand we expect too much of rational debate, which, alas, commands limited interest, and on the other hand the democratic system only occasionally focuses effectively on main issues. It took a long time for Britain to decide about, say, the Common Market, and no democracy has really put either inflation or the situation vis-à-vis the communist dictatorships into a perspective which ordinary people can appreciate.

These latter faults are to a great extent the result of the atrophy of political skills. One hopes those skills may some day return.

To sum up: liberal democracy demands continual respect and attention. It demands recognition of the organic, changing, but continuous growth of the community. It requires recognition of the ultimate value attaching to individuals in the community apart from the roles they play. It demands the rejection of economic or technical determinism, in favor of a system which studies human relations and seeks by political skill to promote a satisfactory but varied series of such relations. It demands activity. It demands thought. If it is taken for granted, the devils of dictatorship, apathy, and bureaucratic attitudes will take over our society.

Liberal democracy must learn the age-old lessons—that human beings are power hungry; that too much government becomes tyranny; that centers of power outside government should exist but need to be kept within bounds and must accept responsibilities wider than the furtherance of their particular empires.

Liberal democracy must foster industrial and social democracy. It must re-examine our economic developments and seek to ameliorate the contradictions between our political and economic needs and capacities.

It must encourage a mixed economy which is not simply a muddle. It must reject the notion that the public sector in the mixed economy should be that ground which sectional interests, anxious to free themselves from economic change, have succeeded in winning. The mixed economy should mean effective and fairly widespread general control. It should mean that some operations are removed from the market, subjected to different tests and motives, and treated as services. But it should mean also that most operations that could benefit from competition are submitted to competition.

Liberal democracy has to reform its political institutions. The hand of the governed must be strengthened against the establishment. Political parties no longer do this. Many important issues fall outside or across the lines of party policy. Fewer people now have faith in the parties, feel that they can be trusted to represent them, or agree with their position on all issues. At the same time the government must present the issues in an intelligible form, setting out the resources available against possible public tasks. The government may have to take an historically large share of gross domestic product, but it should use it not to bolster up particular industries in trouble but to undertake general improvements, for instance in the environment.

The timing of democratic action must be improved. Modern communications must be used for the dissemination of information and not merely sensationalism. Planning must not be viewed as merely taking a "snapshot" of the present position and then from that static photograph projecting trends by a computer.

Planning requires a careful monitoring of the changes in society and nudging it this way and that towards creating conditions in which the good society can flourish.

I sometimes speculate what would have happened had the history of America gone differently. Had you remained a British colony you would still be a country of some ten million people living along the east coast. You would observe the Queen's Birthday. Visitors such as myself would be courteously advised by immaculate bureaucrats with first-class degrees that expansion west of the Alleghenies was not in the plan and was impossible.

Had you gained your independence lately you would have been told that all capital must be borrowed from international sources. (Where, in the assumed absence of America from the world scene, it would have come from, I do not know.) All development must be undertaken by the state, you would have been told, and in consequence there would have been very little development except in white-elephant prestige projects of gigantic size.

We must learn from history and remember that communities are living, changing, and unpredictable. We should not despise the arts of politics or disdain the present. Certainly let us have some vision before us, but in the meanwhile we have an all too short life to enjoy. So far, with all its faults, with all the troubles which beset it, life, liberty, and the pursuit of happiness have never flourished except in a free democracy. Let us extend the legacy of the founding fathers.

B. K. NEHRU

6. Liberal Democracy in India

There are so many kinds of democracies afloat in the world today that it is desirable to be reasonably clear about our terms of reference.[1] I understand "liberal democracy" to mean a system of government in which the executive and the legislature are both chosen by the free exercise of the will of all the people, where the judiciary is independent of the executive, where the rule of law prevails, and where the individual is assured of certain rights—akin to those contained in the United Nations Declaration of Human Rights—which the state cannot, at least in normal times, take away.

This kind of democracy is of comparatively recent growth in the world. Until the American and French revolutions, the normal organization of government all over the globe historically involved the concentration of all power in a monarch who governed, in the western countries, by divine right. In India, too, the sovereignty of the king was absolute except for an indeterminate and ill-defined obligation to act in accordance with the canon and customary laws; he was expected to preserve tradition which did, to a certain extent, protect the rights of the individual.

No matter how the British were governed at home, the British in India carried on the tradition of absolutism. All power was concentrated in the Viceroy and Governor-General and though toward the end some of it was delegated to elected or appointed Indians, the Governor-General's overriding authority always remained. Right up to Indian independence the citizen of India had no rights against the state which it could not take away if it so wished. Meanwhile, the Indian intellectual, for a hundred years

—ever since the beginning of English education in India—had been absorbing the ideas of the American and French revolutions and of the liberal thinkers of Europe and the western world. The ideas of liberty and democracy and freedom of the individual gained popularity in proportion to their absence in practice. Those freedoms that were particularly missed were the ones involved in the struggle for independence—the freedom of speech and expression, the right of assembly and organization, the freedom from arbitrary arrest and detention without trial, and equality before the law.

The Indian national movement—till Mahatma Gandhi took command of it in 1920—was essentially an upper-class movement. The changes that Gandhi wrought in the Indian National Congress are of great importance for our purpose, for they explain not only how it was that liberal democracy flourished in India when it died out in much of the rest of the decolonized British Empire, but also how Indian democracy subsequently developed in practice. Gandhi changed the constitution of the Congress so as to convert it from a class movement to a mass movement and from an elitist organization to a popular one. Membership in the Congress was opened to everybody who accepted its creed, without regard to race, religion, sex, wealth, or education, and who paid dues of four annas (roughly ten cents) annually. Congress sought to establish committees in each village and town of the country. Above them were, in ever-increasing circles, the "tahsil" or "taluka" committees, the District Committees, the Provincial Committees, and finally, over them all, the All-India Congress Committee, which could be likened to a Parliament with a small "Working Committee" that corresponded to a Cabinet. Almost all offices in all these organizations were elective, and the term of office was short so that elections were frequent.

The British had introduced some constitutional forms into the government of India in the nineteenth century. Constitutional reforms were made at intervals till, under the Government of India Act of 1935, Indian-elected legislatures and ministers in the Provinces were given an appreciable measure of responsibility. But in contrast to the Congress franchise, the franchise for the governmental legislative assemblies remained very restricted.

Even at the time of independence, property and educational qualifications limited the franchise to 14 percent of the population.

The constitutional forms and representative institutions of government were common to the whole of the Indian Empire. One of the purposes claimed for them was to give to the Indians experience of the democratic process and get them used to the manner in which representative institutions worked. The old Indian Empire now consists of four independent countries—Pakistan, India, Bangladesh, and Burma. Among these India alone remains a democracy; the democratic process did not long survive in the others, where Gandhi's Congress had not been as strong. This long official tuition in democracy did not work; it was Gandhi's shorter but much more intensive and broad-based lessons that have endured.

The other basic change that Gandhi made in the nationalist movement was to teach us that national independence could not be achieved through petitions; sanctions had to be developed and used to wrest power from foreign hands. Gandhi was against violence in principle; armed insurrection was, in any case, in the Indian conditions of the time, impractical. The weapons he invented have been translated into English as "non-violent non-cooperation," "passive resistance," and "civil disobedience." In essence they consisted of withdrawing all cooperation from the agencies of the government, refusing to submit to the orders of authority, disobeying the laws of the land, and doing all this without violence. A general movement of this kind could, and sometimes did, bring all governmental activity to an end. What is important for our purpose is that for a whole quarter of a century, and throughout the country, defiance of authority and disobedience of the laws was synonymous with nationalism, patriotism, and the fight for independence Also, inevitably, the members of the administration, in particular the magistracy and the police, whose function it was to enforce the laws, became identified in the people's minds as enemies and opponents of freedom.

The Constitution of independent India was framed by a Constituent Assembly which was elected indirectly on the very restricted franchise that prevailed under the Act of 1935. It had, naturally, a predominance of the property-owning classes; there were large and very influential contingents of lawyers and of graduates of Indian or British universities, all of whom tended to follow British modes of thought and practice—political, legal, and constitutional. The atmosphere in which the Assembly met was one in which the minds of its members were dominated by the denial of individual freedoms and the exercise of arbitrary powers by the executive, from which they had so long suffered. Being reasonably affluent themselves, they were perhaps not as acutely aware of economic questions as the country was later to become. They also tended to give less importance than was warranted to the difficulties of maintaining order in a vast and poor country and to the problems of running a complex administration.

The Constitution that emerged was a long and very libertarian document. It gave us a federal structure of the parliamentary type, with a division of powers, particularly financial powers, weighted in favor of the center. It was universally accepted that this was desirable because of the danger that the diversity of the constituents of the Indian Union—states as large and as different from each other as the countries of Europe—might lead to the development of local nationalisms and movements for secession. This part of the Constitution has worked well; though there are occasional demands for increased autonomy for the states, the general consensus continues to be that the center should remain strong.

The concern of the Constituent Assembly to guarantee the freedoms of the individual against encroachment by the executive led to the adoption of a set of provisions in the Constitution which have caused great difficulty in practice. Part III of the Constitution enshrines an elaborate set of fundamental rights and declares that any law in violation of them shall be invalid. These rights can be subdivided into the right to equality (which includes the prohibition of discrimination on the grounds of race, religion, caste, sex, etc.), the right to freedom (of speech and expression, of assembly and association, of religion, of languages, and of the person), the right of minorities (to protect their separate culture and education), and the right to property of which the individual may not be deprived except on payment of compensation. Not satisfied with a wide definition of fundamental rights, the makers of the

Constitution gave special powers to the courts "to issue directions or orders or writs, including writs of habeas corpus, mandamus, prohibition, quo warranto, and certiorari, whichever may be appropriate for the enforcement of" these rights. It is interesting that many people who had had experience of running the government pointed out that defining fundamental rights so broadly, making all of them justiciable, and giving the courts wide and enhanced powers for their enforcement would make government impossible. But so great was the euphoria of freedom and the zeal for liberty that this advice was brushed aside.

Considering the stresses and strains which democratic constitutions must necessarily suffer in poor countries, and having regard to the additional stresses and strains to which any central government of India must be put because of India's size and diversity, the Indian Constitution has, on the whole, worked reasonably well. The regional pressures were largely contained by the predominance of the Congress Party as a national party throughout the country; its predominance owed not a little to the towering personality of Jawaharlal Nehru, whose tenure of the prime ministry lasted seventeen years.

The political pressures generated by economic difficulties, however, were not so well contained. The overriding need of the people in a poor country is to increase their standard of consumption; their insistent demand is that this should be done here and now. Increased consumption can come only from increased production. The capital necessary to increase production can be raised from within the country only by further decreasing immediate consumption, for capital is only the difference between current production and current consumption. Such an attempt is hardly likely to be popular with the electorate. The dilemma of a democratic government in a poor country is that if it acts in the best long-term interests of the people it ensures its own demise. Democratic governments are therefore not likely so to act; on the contrary, they normally tend to please the electorate by increasing the share of consumption in the national product through measures such as an increase in wages and salaries and other public expenditures. The acuteness of this dilemma is reduced to the extent that capital is available from sources outside the country for then productive capacity can be built up without reducing the standard of living of the people.

The government of India was certainly not free from this dilemma. Its difficulties were compounded by many factors. First, the per capita income of India being among the lowest in the world, the economic needs that were not satisfied were so basic that the discontents generated by the lack of their fulfillment were intense. Second, the population explosion coincided with the independence of India. Between 1891 and 1921 the population of India increased at an average rate of 0.01 percent per annum; between 1951 and 1971 the comparable rate was 2.3 percent, a result of the health measures taken by the government under the combined pressure of morality and public demand. Third, the Congress Party was wedded, for historical and other reasons, to an economic policy of which the overall effect, though unintended, was to give primacy not to an increase in production but to greater equality in distribution.

On the credit side was the fact that India started its independence with substantial foreign-exchange balances. When these balances were exhausted the World Bank organized a substantial aid program for India, the success of which was due in no small part to the leadership and the generous contributions of the United States. Further, the tradition of sacrifice in the national interest which had been established during the struggle for independence was still alive, as were the many leaders of gigantic stature and utter selflessness who had led the country to independence and whose influence was great. This enabled a rate of internal saving to be achieved which for so poor and free a society as India was remarkable; it also kept very much in check the discontents which lack of adequate economic progress would otherwise have generated.

As time went on these advantages disappeared; more normal conditions took over. Revolutionary enthusiasm gave way to more typical human motivations; political leadership reverted to what is usual in other democracies. The internal rate of saving could not be maintained; the inflow of foreign aid, in real terms, was substantially reduced—with America unfortunately leading the retreat as it had led the advance. Foreign investment which, theoretically, could be a valuable external source of capital never achieved much importance in India; the terms of trade which should, in justice, be the major provider of capital for the underdeveloped world continued to move to India's disadvantage. The combined result of a quarter of a century's effort at economic growth, though very considerable, has not, when translated into per capita terms, been sufficient to satisfy the demands of the people.

In the meantime population continued to increase—and, because of inadequate economic growth, so did unemployment. As the result of an increased emphasis on education, the proportion of the educated among the unemployed continued to grow. Whether or not the troubles of the educated are, in theory, entitled to priority, the fact is that great numbers of educated unemployed youth often cause social and political instability. Though employment of both the educated and uneducated has increased and is increasing fairly fast, the number of unemployed of both categories is also increasing and will continue to do so for a fairly long time. The body politic will therefore be under considerable strain on this account.

The economic policy of the government of India since independence has been considerably influenced by the left wing of the Labour Party in England as well as by the Soviet Union, both of whom have historically been supporters of the cause of Indian independence. India has attempted to put into practice a centrally planned economy, relying to a substantial extent on physical controls which, as is the nature of all controls, have gone on increasing in coverage and complexity, and some would add—impotence. Like most underdeveloped countries India has also enlarged the sphere of the ownership by the state of the means of production. This close regulation of the Indian economy and the increase in public ownership have also naturally placed great economic power in the hands of those who already wielded political power. Simultaneously with this increase in the power of the politician and the functionary has been a very substantial reduction, in real terms, of the emoluments of civil servants and ministers. The consequence has been the introduction of an element of corruption into an administration earlier noted for its honesty

This concentration of economic and political power has also made the post of minister (or even that of a legislator who can influence ministerial action) much more desirable in India than it is in other democracies. By the same token, what a candidate is prepared to do to get elected is more extreme than elsewhere.

The strains produced by our inability to solve our economic problems would have been easier to contain if there had not been operative a combination of psychological factors which made it difficult to enforce the laws of the country. As I have pointed out earlier, one of the targets of attack for the nationalists during the independence struggle was the members of the administration who were then, naturally, under British control. The fact that these administrators were now under the control of Indian elected ministers and obeyed their orders did not for quite some time penetrate the minds of the people and the politicians—and perhaps has not yet fully done so. One of the consequences has been a distrust and a denigration of administrators, and a second is that administrators have, therefore, often tended to play safe and to enforce the law only sparingly if they felt that enforcement would be unpopular. Still another result has been the interference in local administration by elected representatives and local politicians, such interference being almost always designed to prevent the law's being applied to the detriment of the lawbreaker if he happened to be a supporter of the politician concerned. The strong influence of family and caste loyalties in India adds to this tendency to interfere. Such interference is not unknown in other democracies; but the social harm it causes is much less in a rich and developed society than in a poor and underdeveloped one.

Another holdover from pre-independence days has been the idea that resistance to authority is good in itself. The difference in disobeying the dictates of a group of foreigners, whose sole claim to power was the physical force they could command, and the orders given by the duly elected representatives of the people, who could be changed at the next election, tended to be disregarded. The definition of democratic freedom that came to prevail was that a man was free only if he could disobey with impunity any law, rule, regulation, or convention requiring disciplined behavior, if he so desired. Often enough this attitude was strengthened by yet another holdover belief from the pre-independence era, namely that the law was really meant to hold down the underdog. And in encouraging this general atmosphere of lawlessness, a large section of the totally free press was not altogether without blame.

The prime example of lawbreaking was set by the politicians themselves—often from the opposition parties. In the first five general elections held in India after independence, the opposition parties—divided among themselves—were never able to defeat the Congress. That party therefore began to have for them, in their frustration, the irremovable characteristics of the British government, and they began to use against it the same unconstitutional and undemocratic methods that they had used against the British. Within the legislative assemblies of the country, rules of parliamentary procedure were disobeyed with impunity. Reasoned debate was replaced by shouting matches, exchange of abuses, physical obstruction, and various other antics—all of which made a mockery of parliamentary government. There was no lack of rules of procedure to check this behavior; there was no lack of majorities to support the Speaker. What was lacking was the political will to enforce the law.

It is no wonder that this example of high-level lawbreaking found a ready following. At first the disobedience of authority and the breach of laws were infrequent and tentative; when it was discovered that there was not only no attempt to enforce the law but, on the contrary, much support from many quarters, disorder rapidly became general. The disorder was not confined to any party or region, and no party or region can be held blameless. Government clerks did not come to the office on time or pay much attention to their work when they came; industrial labor struck work as and when it pleased without regard to its own union rules and contracts. Bank clerks went one better by spending their working day in drinking tea and abusing their managements while insisting on doing their work after office hours and claiming overtime; the railways worked as and when their staff ordained; the airlines became irregular; rudeness, sullenness, unhelpfulness in all the public services became general. Students at the universities seemed to be perpetually on strike; they insisted that they must be given their degrees and diplomas without study or examination; those who refused their demands were subjected to humiliation and violence. *Dharnas*[2] and *gheraos*[3]—both criminal offenses under western as well as Indian law—became our contributions to the democratic process! The frequency of the breaches of the law accelerated as it became increasingly clear that all laws could be broken with impunity. It was evident that a continuation of this trend would only result in anarchy.

This rapid advance toward chaos was brought to an abrupt and successful standstill by the Proclamation of Emergency in June of 1975. The founding fathers of the Constitution had been well aware that a country like India could be subject to enormous strains and that the very libertarian Constitution that they were adopting might not be able to keep these strains in check. They had, therefore, provided constitutional means to give to the executive virtually unlimited power for a limited period through a device called a "Proclamation of Emergency." The effect of such a proclamation is that no law passed by Parliament shall be invalid on the ground that it is in contravention of the Fundamental Rights and freedoms guaranteed in Part III of the Constitution. In short, it converts the Indian Parliament, for the duration of the Emergency, into a sovereign body (like the Parliament of the United Kingdom, for example), but it does not abolish the rule of law. If, for example, the executive wishes to detain a person without trial, Parliament must pass a law authorizing such detention. The courts can inquire whether such detention is in consonance with the provisions of the law under which action is purported to have been taken, but the courts cannot question, for the duration of the Emergency, whether that law violates the Fundamental Rights.

The effect of the Emergency, under which a number of people were placed under detention without trial and under which the press was subject to censorship, became evident in every aspect of Indian life. First, as if by a miracle, without the enactment of any new laws and without the necessity of actually using any force, it restored respect for the law, including such things as acceptance of normal rules of orderly behavior. That would indicate that the disease of lawbreaking and indiscipline had as yet taken so little root in the body politic that it could be cured by a simple threat that the law would be enforced. Second, the return of discipline had an immediate effect on production. If people work instead of agitating or marching in processions or practicing sit-ins or going on strike, production in the country is naturally increased. And the very remarkable and immediate effect of increased production was palpable to the people at large. Third, although the increased corruption described above did not disappear, it was appreciably reduced, seemingly for fear that the law was now being enforced. Smuggling, hoarding, black marketing, and the evasion of taxes were also much reduced. The combined consequence of all this was an enhanced availability of consumer goods which had for years been in short supply, a fall in prices—as against continuous inflation—and a great surge of revenue to the central exchequer.

Perhaps more important than all this was the psychological shock that the nation received. People had been complaining for years about the rapidity with which the country was going downward; there had been for years much shaking of heads at the indiscipline, the lawlessness, and the corruption that was increasing. The downward drift was now checked abruptly; it is certain that it had gone so far that there was no other means of checking it except through the shock treatment that was now applied.

What is important, however, is where we go from here. Is India destined to be a dictatorship, as some foreigners think, or is it going to revert back to its soft, permissive, and chaotic ways as many Indians fear? My own opinion—now as then—is that neither will happen. The truth is that the Emergency was generally popular and well received, though it is certainly true that many measures taken under it were widely disliked and condemned. All in all, however, it showed that the Indian is prepared to risk some loss of individual freedom for the sake of order and economic progress. A great deal of thought is now being given to the changes in the Constitution and in our institutions that may be necessary to ensure that the good produced by the Emergency—the respect for the law and for discipline generally—should become permanent, while the evils of arbitrary action that accompanied it should not endure. It is agreed and proclaimed by almost all political parties and political leaders—including, repeatedly

Mrs. Gandhi—that India must continue to be a democracy. The only exceptions are some small and ineffective groups on the extreme left and the extreme right.

There are several valid reasons why there is such unanimous agreement that India cannot be governed except democratically. Foremost among them is the strong individualism of the Indian and his allergy to regimentation. In both respects he resembles greatly the citizen of the United States. Second, the democratic process, even though imported, has by now taken strong root—thanks to a quarter of a century of a Gandhian Congress followed by another quarter century of constitutional democracy in government. Third, the educated classes are still by and large dominated by the political theories of the West. It is true that there is an increasing number of intellectuals who hold that the liberal democratic process is a particularly inefficient way of ensuring economic growth with justice in an underdeveloped country—which is, after all, the crying need of India—but their influence is still limited; perhaps in another generation, if economic conditions do not improve, they may begin to dominate.

In addition to these general arguments is the very practical consideration of the size and diversity of India. India is a country of minorities, which is not surprising, for it is in reality a union of diverse social units with an overall cultural, historical, and emotional unity which makes it into a nation. In European terms India corresponds to what may some day be a United States of Europe. In Soviet terms it is a union of republics of different nationalities. It is not possible, all are agreed, to govern one-seventh of the human race without the establishment of a consensus. But though all are agreed that the selection of the executive and the legislature must take place through the classical liberal democratic process of periodical elections on the basis of a universal adult franchise, there are many, many differences beyond this point.

First, there is the question of the relation between the executive and the legislature. The Constituent Assembly opted for the parliamentary form of government rather than the presidential principally because, it argued, India had had no experience of the latter. There was general agreement then that India needed a strong executive and that view has since found even wider support. Many voices have been raised in favor of a system such as the presidential that will obviate the executive's being weakened by being put continuously at risk, as it is in a parliamentary system. But it would appear that the tradition of a parliamentary system is by now so strong that this kind of fundamental change in the Constitution is not likely to be effected.

The second major area in which amendments to the Constitution are necessary is in the treatment of the Fundamental Rights. There is considerable feeling that for Indian conditions they have been too broadly drawn, and that the ease with which they can be used to override the expressed will of the legislature is far too great. There are many undoubtedly democratic countries—Britain and Canada to take two examples—where the citizen has no rights which cannot be overridden by the ordinary law of the land. There are suggestions that all these rights be made nonjusticiable, in other words that while they should remain in the Constitution as directing the lawmakers not to infringe them, they should not be used as authority to upset the decision of the lawmakers if they do in fact choose to disregard the Constitution's directive. There are other less drastic suggestions that, while the more basic of the Fundamental Rights, such as those guaranteeing the inviolability of the person, or freedom of religion or speech or equality before the law, should remain as they are, those that have caused the most administrative troubles, such as the right to property, should be made nonjusticiable. Article 31, which guarantees the right to property, has already been amended four times; even so, litigation based on it is still delaying in much of the country the basic land reforms that are vital to economic progress. There is little doubt that many of the measures now being taken to control India's population, a matter vital to its very existence, would be held up by the courts in normal times, as being violative of one or the other of the Fundamental Rights.

The power of the courts and their procedures is another matter to which thought is being given. There is general agreement that the power "to issue directives or orders or writs for the enforcement" of the Fundamental Rights has proved to be far too wide and has been grossly misused to obstruct even the most routine administrative processes.[4] There are suggestions that this power should be reduced, or, alternatively, that it should be restricted to the Supreme Court, which would exercise it more responsibly. There is also a proposal for a more fundamental change according to which the power to interpret the Constitution should be taken away from the Supreme Court, to whom it was given following the American Constitution, and given to a Special Constitutional Court which would have on it representatives of other branches of the government, as in France, Germany, or Italy.

Another and more controversial area in which changes will be made—some have been made already—is the press. That freedom of speech or expression is a cardinal principle of the democratic polity is not questioned in India. But that freedom is not absolute in any country; it is always subject to restrictions in the interest of such things as public order, decency, morality, protection of reputations, and the like. Differences of view arise as to the content of these restrictions, which must necessarily correspond to the mores, the needs, and the ethos of individual societies. In India it was felt, as early as the second year of the Republic, that the wider national interest required much greater restrictions on the press than are customary in the western world. The Press Act of 1951 was accordingly passed and seems to have worked without causing any damage to the democratic process. In 1954, as the result of pressure from the journalistic lobby, which was then very strong, it was discontinued. A similar measure has recently been reintroduced in a somewhat strengthened form and will probably soon become part of the law of the land.

It would be foolhardy in the extreme to attempt to forecast the development of liberal democracy in India in the years to come. Democracy in India, ever since its establishment after independence, has had a content of freedom for the individual second to no country in the world. It is doubtful, however, in light of the paramount Indian need—which is for economic growth—whether the absoluteness of this freedom has been to the benefit of the country. The Proclamation of Emergency brought us up with an unpleasant start against the reality that this degree of freedom— and the libertarian and permissive attitudes that went with it— was taking us in a direction the reverse of where we wanted to go. The unexpected and widespread support accorded to the

Emergency suggests that the country would welcome certain restraints on individual liberty if they are necessary for social order.

The Emergency and the loss of individual liberties it involves—though most of this loss is theoretical—is temporary. While India will continue to be governed by representatives elected by the free choice of all its people, the shape and content of Indian democracy will depend in the long term almost entirely on the rapidity (or slowness) with which the Indian economy can grow. The more rapid this growth, the larger the area of individual freedom the society will be able to afford. The only discontents in India strong enough to tear the fabric of society apart are economic discontents, though they manifest themselves in diverse forms. The pace of India's economic growth, where lack of capital is the major constraint, does not depend on India alone; it depends on a wide variety of external factors, and principally on what kind of new international economic order, if any, the world is going to have. The future of liberal democracy in India is tied, as nowhere else, to the seriousness with which the developed countries take their responsibilities as members of the world community.

Postscript

A number of developments have taken place in India since this essay was written, the principal among them being that a general election has been held in which the Congress Party was defeated and the opposition parties, which merged into a single Janata Party, were returned in absolute majority and now form the government.

The basic thrust of the argument in my essay was that (i) India would not become a dictatorship, for it could not be governed except democratically, but that (ii) on the restoration of the democratic freedoms, it would not return to its soft, permissive, and chaotic ways, for (iii) the Indian is prepared to risk some loss of individual freedom for the sake of order and economic progress.

The mere holding of the elections (which were free and fair—as the results showed) proved that the democratic process could not for long be suspended. As to just what the election results meant, there are two views. One is the straightforward view that they showed that the Indian electorate was not prepared to accept the loss of individual liberties which the Emergency had entailed. The other view is that it was not the loss of those liberties that the electorate resented, but the rapid deterioration, particularly during the last year of the Emergency, of the manner in which the executive exercised its untrammelled authority. In support of this latter view may be cited the fact that whereas the Congress was wiped out in the north of India (which was its principal stronghold) it came back in substantially increased strength in the southern states. The explanation given is that while the laws, rules, regulations, and directives issued under the Emergency were the same for the whole of India, executive actions were kept within the rule of law in the southern states and were, therefore, welcomed by the people. By contrast in the north the Emergency degenerated into the exercise of arbitrary and coercive powers, often at the behest of extraconstitutional authority and without legal sanction, for objectives which frequently had nothing to do with the common weal. It was this, rather than the Emergency itself, which angered the people. Where the truth lies time alone will show.

The restoration of full individual liberty by the new government has resulted, however, in the immediate recrudescence of the strikes, demonstrations, student unrest, and other manifestations of disorder which, over the years, were making India ungovernable. The new government has not yet had time to handle this situation, which is undoubtedly, to a certain extent, a reaction against the suppression of the previous nineteen months. But whether or not these manifestations can be controlled within the framework of our libertarian attitudes and the parliamentary system remains a most critical question for the future of democracy in India.

Notes

1. This essay in no way reflects the views, the thinking, or the policy of the government of India. I have given expression in it to my own personal

views as a student of Indian affairs who has had very favorable opportunities for observing them over a long period of time.
2. *Dharnas*: A "sit-in" or "squatting"—the occupation of premises to prevent the occupant from using them.
3. *Gheraos*: surrounding a person to prevent all movement.
4. An actual case will illustrate what happens: the superannuation (retirement) age for senior public servants in India is generally 58. There is a provision under which they may be retired on full pension at 55 if the appointing authority is satisfied on the basis of the record that the man's competence or integrity are not of the required standard. In my last appointment (as Governor of Assam) I had occasion to retire one administrator in this fashion: his incompetence was patent, his integrity doubtful. All he did was to go straight to the court next door, file a petition claiming that a whole series of his Fundamental Rights had been violated, and praying that the court should stay the execution of my order until such time as the case was decided. He got his stay order, and the courts were so congested that the case did not come up for trial for three years. The gentleman in question sat in his office all that time drawing his full salary; when he reached the age of 58 he withdrew his petition.

TONY HONORÉ

7. Liberal Democracy in Southern Africa

In October 1976 Mr. Ian Smith, the Rhodesian prime minister, presented to his Rhodesia Front caucus the proposals for a settlement of the Rhodesia crisis brought to Southern Africa by Dr. Henry Kissinger. The caucus accepted the proposals, which included a transition to majority rule within two years, but the "agreement" came to nothing and the supposed parties to it soon resorted to mutual accusations of misunderstanding and bad faith. From a psychological point of view, however, that abortive agreement was a turning point in Rhodesian affairs. It was the first public acknowledgement by the white minority that white rule could not continue indefinitely in the circumstances of that country.

To understand such events as these and appraise their significance, one must avoid being caught up in the tumble of the events themselves and see them instead in their historical setting, in which social divisions, ideology, and political institutions interact with one another. Indeed that may be taken as the theme of this essay—the relation and interaction between racial divisions, democratic theory, and democratic institutions in Southern Africa. That theme does not, of course, depend on particular events —even important recent events—so I shall try to maintain a broader and more distant perspective. Indeed, too much concern with recent events often tempts professors into prophecy, at which they have a poor record.

Of no part of the world is this truer than of Southern Africa, that graveyard of prophecy. In *Modernizing Racial Domination* (1971) Heribert Adam demonstrated the falsity of several theses advanced by Pierre van den Berghe in 1965. Van den Berghe, like many others, looked forward to revolutionary developments and was rash enough to foresee conditions favorable for them within five years.[1] Yet nothing revolutionary occurred in the quinquennium 1965–70. In 1971 Adam in his turn looked forward to an evolution by which more and more African countries would settle for peaceful coexistence with the South African republic.[2] Yet the trend in 1976–77 was rather toward confrontation. In 1975 Leonard Thompson surmised that South Africa had entered a period of internal instability pointing toward fundamental change.[3] Was he a better prophet? The township riots which began in Soweto in June 1976 may point (though the South African government denies it) to an unstable situation. But were they a prelude to a shift in political power?

Before embarking on so uncertain a voyage I believe it may be a help to begin with a declaration of interest. I grew up in Cape Town, at an all-white (or nearly all-white) school. There in the thirties my hero was the liberal imperialist Jan H. Hofmeyr (1894–1948), whose perceptive biography by Alan Paton is one of that fine writer's finest achievements.[4] In those days the preservation of a common roll for Cape African voters (abrogated in 1936)[5] and later of African representation in the senate by white senators evoked the passion of a small group of white liberals to whom Hofmeyr (who resigned in 1938 on the latter issue, trivial as it may now seem) was the leader and guide. Frustrating and indeed counterproductive as was Hofmeyr's political career, the tradition in which he stood, derived from the Cape liberalism of the late nineteenth century, has never quite died. The Progressive Reform Party,[6] which won eleven seats in the 1976 Republican Parliament, is the latest embodiment of that tradition. But in the twentieth century liberalism has never stood in the mainstream of subcontinental politics. I mention it not to endorse it as a politically viable movement but because, whatever our opinions, we view the world from the ineradicable perspectives of our youth.

Southern Africa: Liberal Democracy

It is probably wise to begin by setting out the basic demography of Southern Africa and defining liberal democracy, for the first is easily forgotten and the second is a controversial concept. Estimates for the population of the Republic of South Africa in mid-1974 gave 71 percent Africans (17.7 million); 16½ percent whites (4.1 million), of whom over 60 percent were Afrikaners; 9 percent mixed-race colored people (2.3 million); and 3 percent Asians (700,000), mainly Indians. These proportions are not very different from the guesses that James Bryce, writing in 1897, gave for what were then the four colonies and republics of the Cape, Natal, Orange Free State, and the South African Republic or Transvaal. The Africans were then about 69 percent of the people, whites 20½, colored 9, Indians 1½. In eighty years the proportions of the races have remained remarkably steady, though whites are now a sixth instead of a fifth of the whole. But the total has increased sixfold, so that 4.1 million has turned into 24.9 million. Estimates for the five peripheral states give 1.1 million for Lesotho (independent 1966), 630,000 for Botswana (independent 1966), 380,000 for Swaziland (independent 1968), 750,000 for Namibia, for which independence is projected in 1978 or 1979 and 6.1 million for Rhodesia, of which the whites comprise some 4½ percent (273,000), Africans 95 percent (5.8 million), and Asians/colored ½ percent (29,000). In 1911 Southern Rhodesia (as it then was) had 96 percent Africans, 3 percent whites, and ½ percent colored and Asians, so that the white element has grown in proportion to the rest, but not enough to sustain a long-term military crisis.

Something must also be said of the internal structure of the Republic of South Africa, since maps tend to give a seriously misleading picture, omitting both African homelands and townships. Apart from the four white provinces which are the successors to the colonies and republics of Bryce's time, we have since the 1960s African homelands[7] which range from KwaZulu with a population of 2.2 million to small enclaves like Qwaqwa on the Lesotho border. But more than this, under the apartheid policy the urban areas, though in principle predominantly white, have been divided into white towns and the African, colored, or Indian townships around them. These urban areas contain just over 3.2 million whites and (officially) 4.9 million Africans (1970),[8] and it is these Africans, needed for their work but threatening by their numbers the viability of any white homeland, that constitute the main impetus of and also the main obstacle to the policy of apartheid or separate development. The African townships—such as Soweto, the scene of the 1976 riots—are administered not by the white municipalities but by special boards responsible to the central government.[9] There is no municipal self-government to parallel the partial self-government of the homelands or Bantustans, though urban Africans are represented by Urban Bantu Councils which have a consultative role. There are two other important differences between townships and homelands. The homelands are, unlike the Reserves which preceded them, no longer expected to be self-supporting. Their development is a concern of the central government, in competition, of course, with other claims. But the townships, which have but slender sources of revenue, since there is no home ownership in them, and hence no property on which a rate or tax can be levied, are expected to be self-supporting. Consequently the public utilities are rudimentary. The second difference, implied in what has been said, is that Africans have not so far been allowed to own land in the townships but only in the homelands. They are supposed to be temporary residents in the white areas, welcome only for their labor. Yet this is simply a fiction, as the law itself admits, for under the influx-control legislation an urban African who satisfies certain requirements as to descent, residence, and employment has the right to remain in his township.[10]

In the upshot, then, the Africans of South Africa are divided two ways. First, ethnically, into the various homelands to one of which everyone is supposed to be affiliated, even if he has never seen it.[11] Second, according to his relation to the white areas, in which he is either a settled resident with a right to remain, or a migrant worker on a short-term contract, or an illegal resident concerned to dodge the law, unless indeed he is a genuine homelander living in his ethnic area. It is not easy to put figures on these groups, but one may guess at 19 percent (3.6 million) Africans in white rural areas, 27 percent (4.9 million) officially living in white urban areas, of whom about half are migrants and half settled residents, perhaps 4 percent (0.7 million) illegally resident in the towns, and 50 percent (9.2 million) who at any given moment are present in the ethnic homelands.[12] The fact that, twenty-eight years after the inception of apartheid, only about half the

African people are at any given moment in the ethnic homelands[13] is an indication that the policy of separate development will have to be either abandoned or reinterpreted.

Next, liberal democracy. We must come to some understanding about the meaning of that term and the sense, if any, in which liberal democracy has existed or now exists in Southern Africa. It would be easy to make a case for the proposition that there is nothing either democratic or liberal about the South African Republic or indeed about the régimes in Namibia, Rhodesia, Lesotho, and Swaziland, which all fall in the area with which this paper is concerned. I shall concentrate on the Republic, however, for the moment, since it sets the pace for the periphery.

Over four-fifths of the people of South Africa are excluded from political power, or at least from central political power. Can such a state be called a democracy? In considering that question we must remember that in most of the societies which are or have been generally termed democratic, most or at least many people have been excluded from voting, let alone from the direct exercise of power. This was true of classical Athens, with its helots; of republican Rome, with its slaves; of women in nineteenth-century England; and even of twentieth-century western states that disfranchise children, felons, idiots, or peers of the realm. The arguments against extending political power to these various classes have at all times been rather similar: lack of experience, capacity, education, stability, maturity, or social responsibility. Much the same is said in Southern Africa about the extension of political power to black or brown people. It is difficult to describe a society as undemocratic because black people are excluded but acknowledge it to be democratic when women or children are kept from the vote. The difference between democracy and autocracy or oligarchy is largely a matter of degree. A democracy is a society in which political power is shared by a wide class of people, not merely a small group of the wealthy or well-born. In the Republic the white group, according to mid-1974 figures, constitute 16½ percent of the population (4.1 million) and though not all these are voters, the dispersion of power among them seems great enough to justify the term "democracy." It would, perhaps, be more precise to speak of a "white democracy" (or, according to the case, a "male democracy," an "adult democracy," etc.).

The adjective "liberal" I take to connote a distinction between societies in which the voters who endorse or elect the government are relatively free and equal and have a choice of government, and those (for example people's democracies) in which the voters, lacking that free and equal status, also lack the effective power of choice, though they may be called on to express an opinion for or against a particular government. It is a delicate matter to say whether these conditions of liberal democracy are fulfilled in a given society. They seem to require a certain degree of social and economic equality among the participants in power, a reasonably wide diffusion of property and education, and the liberty to organize political groups or parties, at least within certain limits; and so we may say that these requisites, too, are among the conditions of liberal democracy. Clearly these conditions exist among white South Africans, who enjoy compulsory school education, a high standard of living, and a choice of political parties. But, no less clearly, according to this definition, democracy and dictatorship are not incompatible. The white democracy exercises a dictatorship over the nonwhite population.

Liberal democracy in white South Africa has in fact a continuous history of over a hundred years. It may be said to begin with the grant of representative government to the Cape Colony in 1853 and to ripen into the fully fledged form which is familiar in Britain with the grant of responsible government (by which the executive is responsible to the legislature) in 1872. The same process took place in Natal also, in two stages, in 1856 and 1893. The British model was thereby introduced into South Africa: democracy with a flexible and unitary constitution, the executive responsible to the legislature, single-member constituencies and majority voting on the first-past-the-post system, not to mention the conventions of parliamentary behavior and privilege which grew up in England. All later manifestations or imitations of democracy in Southern Africa have retained these features, or most of them. In the National Convention of 1908–9 which led to the formation of the Union of South Africa, the British features were in every case preferred to the suggested alternatives: federalism, multi-member constituencies, proportional representation, rigid procedures of amendment.[14] Analogies with the United States, Canada, and Australia were weighed and consciously rejected.

Perhaps more surprisingly, so were those derived from the Boer Republics, in particular President Kruger's Transvaal, where the head of state had executive power, and where, in a populist society, meetings and grass roots counted for almost as much as formal debates and legislation.[15] Though populism is a permanent feature of Afrikanerdom it has never since received formal recognition. The only constitutional innovation in 1910 was the entrenchment by section 152 of the South Africa Act of the Cape nonwhite franchise, which could thenceforth only be altered by a two-thirds majority in Parliament.[16] This was a compromise between Cape politicians who wanted to extend the nonracial franchise to the other provinces and those of the North and East who wanted to abolish the nonwhite vote in the Cape. It must be recalled that most of the Cape nonwhite voters were colored, not African, and that the gap between colored and white seemed in the Cape, after centuries of coexistence, by no means the unbridgeable chasm that it seemed in the other provinces. But the device of a semirigid constitution had no permanent place in South African democratic practice. After a long legal and constitutional wrangle the nonwhite voters were removed to a separate electoral roll—Africans in 1936[17] and colored voters in 1951–56[18]—and then simply disfranchised in 1960[19] and 1968.[20] It would be difficult to find a parallel to this process of direct disfranchisement,[21] though of course subterranean ouster, via property or educational requirements, has been common enough. If to be candid is a merit, Afrikaner racialism has a long lead over its British counterpart.

Thus the white South African democracy is modelled on the British, and the change to a republic in 1961 made no difference; the president replaced the queen but acquired no extra power.

In Rhodesia responsible government was introduced in 1923 following the referendum of 1922 which rejected union with South Africa.[22] The Rhodesian constitution like the South African followed the standard British model. In the 1961[23] constitution, which was enacted in the period of the abortive Central African Federation, a bill of rights and a rigid procedure for constitutional amendment were introduced. In modified form these have survived the Unilateral Declaration of Independence of 1965 and the change to a republic in 1970[24] so that the resulting Rhodesian constitution is of the new-model British commonwealth type, unitary but rigid. The same is true, since these are all products of the British colonial administrators, of the independence constitutions of Botswana (1966),[25] Lesotho (1966, suspended in 1970),[26] and Swaziland (1968, abrogated by King Sobhuza II in 1973).[27] The constitutions of the South African homelands or Bantustans, which have mixed legislatures of elected and appointed members, are rather like restricted versions of the responsible-government systems with which the Cape and Natal were endowed in 1852 and 1856. The elected members are chosen by adult male suffrage and in nearly all the Bantustans the chief minister has in fact, though he is not constitutionally required to have, the support of the majority of elected members. To this Vendaland is a (relatively unimportant) exception.

One can summarize the democratic typology by saying that all the structures in Southern Africa are of the unitary parliamentary type derived from Britain, but that they appear in variants which range from the responsible government species, popular with the colonial office in the mid-nineteenth century, to the post–Second-World-War model, with its entrenched rights and rigid procedures of constitutional amendment. Constitutions of the second type were influenced of course by the experience of the United States, but they seldom remained in force for more than a few years.

The long existence of white dominance, or, as we may say, of white democracies in South Africa and Rhodesia has two important political effects. One is to enhance the determination of the white group to retain political power. The other is to obstruct the efforts of white governments, who are more sensitive than their voters to international opinion, to reach an accommodation with their black citizens and neighbors.

Two Perspectives

The prospects for liberal democracy in Southern Africa depend on the answer to an awkward conundrum: is liberal democracy in the subcontinent dependent on white supremacy? Is a democratic form of government viable among relatively poor, ill-educated people who have a history of inferiority to shake off? In trying to answer this in a South African context I shall concentrate on two historical periods, the 1890s and the 1960s. In the first of these it was treated as self-evident that colored people were, exceptions apart, incapable of self-government. British colonies fell into two classes, Crown Colonies governed from London and self-governing colonies. The former were situated mainly within the tropics. "The self-governing colonies, on the other hand, are all situated in the temperate zone, and are all, with one exception, peopled chiefly by Europeans. It is because they have a European population that they have been deemed fit to govern themselves, just as it is because the tropical colonies have a predominantly coloured population that the supremacy of the Colonial Office and its local representatives is acquiesced in as fit and proper."[28] These are the words not of a reactionary settler but of the urbane and liberal James Bryce, who visited South Africa in 1895 and wrote an absorbing account of the country in 1897. He is, from my point of view, a cosy observer through whose eyes to view the scene, for he held the Regius Chair of Civil Law at Oxford from 1870 to 1893.[29] He was also a close student of the American scene, which he described in two volumes on *The American Commonwealth*, published in 1910, in which he was able to compare America with Southern Africa.[30]

Bryce visited South Africa at a critical moment. The colonization of Rhodesia had begun in 1888, the Jameson raid of December 1895 was soon to discredit Cecil Rhodes, and the intransigence of Sir Alfred Milner, sent from Britain to be High Commissioner and Governor of the Cape in 1897, forced the Boer Republics into war in October 1899.[31] In these events the colored and African people played almost no part. White men insisted, and they accepted the notion, that the white man's quarrel was none of their concern, though the alert among them were perfectly aware that the nonwhite élite had political rights in the British colonies and none in the Boer Republics.

What was this white man's quarrel? In nineteenth-century South Africa Britain wavered between a policy of retrenchment and one of advance. The first, dominant in the 1850s, left the

Boer Republics of the North and East to their own devices and declined to extend British protection to African tribes who felt threatened by white expansion. This policy was meant to save money and avoid foreign entanglement. The second, which sporadically gained the upper hand from 1869 onwards, sought to extend British influence and territory. It was variously rationalized. There was the missionary motive, to extend good government to the underprivileged. There was a strategic argument that British colonies were not safe unless bordered by areas loyal or allied to the British crown. There was a desire to annex sources of mineral wealth. There was a quasi-religious fervor which saw value in the sheer multiplication of subjects owing allegiance to the British sovereign, like the worshipers of a tribal god. But behind these motives, often based on false premises and beliefs, lay something, I believe, far more primitive. In the late nineteenth century some British statesmen and adventurers thought of themselves as engaged in an international competition to be pursued for its own sake, a form of challenge and emulation, which drove them in practice to a game of continental tic-tac-toe. Unless British symbols occupied the vacant spaces on the map, those of Germany, Portugal, Belgium, or the South African Dutch, as they were then called, would preempt them. What harm this would do was never properly explained, and indeed could not have been. Britain itself, apart from the brief Danish empire, has at all times lived in the midst of neighbors of foreign allegiance. Her colonies could quite well have done the same. This is a point which Bryce, speaking after the outbreak of war about the supposed menace presented by the Boer Republic of the Transvaal, makes with a cogency not disguised by his restraint.[32]

But to Rhodes, Chamberlain, Milner, and later Smuts,[33] in their various temperaments, the game of imperial tic-tac-toe had an irresistible fascination, the more so since they conceived themselves entitled to cheat when it was not working out as they liked. In the war of 1894–96 the Chartered Company, under the inspiration of Rhodes, conquered Lobengula and the Matabele and in 1896 Rhodesia became British, though under the company's administration.[34] Rhodesia may be called a Crusader state.[35] The immediate object of its seizure was to hem in the Boer Republics, but the adventurers and settlers who went north were also fired by a strange mixture of idealism and greed, like that which sustained the Latin kingdom of Jerusalem for eighty-eight years until shortage of manpower undid it.[36]

The Jameson raid of December 1895[37] was more obviously a breach of the rules since the company's men under Jameson invaded a white state, the South African Republic. This invasion, quickly suppressed, gave a decisive impetus to Afrikaner nationalism, and instilled in many Afrikaners a permanent suspicion of the English. In sponsoring the invasion Rhodes abused the confidence of his Afrikaner political ally Onze Jan Hofmeyr, and the deceit, which Rhodes dismissed with the cynical and untrue remark that Hofmeyr would have done the same to him if he could,[38] left a permanent wound. It was the war of 1899–1902, however, that set the seal on the nationhood of the Afrikaner and gave it an enduring mythology. To the Boers of an earlier age Bryce attributes dissociative instincts. He remarks that "they were resolved to make their government absolutely popular, and little disposed to brook the control even of the authorities they had themselves created. They had, in fact, a genius for disobedience; their ideal, if one can attribute any ideals to them, was that of Israel in the days when every man did what was right in his own eyes."[39] How different was the disciplined nation, conscious of its destiny and institutions, which emerged from the war and, in 1907, regained political power in the conquered Transvaal.[40]

Although nonwhites were only observers in 1899–1902, the course of the war was crucial for the future of race relations. In principle most British statesmen and English-speaking South African politicians were in favor of an élitist, not a racially demarcated, constitution. They accepted a franchise based on property or educational criteria, not race. To the Boer Republics this was anathema. The constitution of the South African Republic expressly laid down that the people did not admit any equality of black and white in church or state.[41] Had the British gained a decisive military victory they might have insisted on writing élitism into future South African constitutions. In the event, the struggle dragged on inconclusively for over two years, in part because paradoxically the British declined to use the dark-skinned

Indian Army against whites. Article VIII of the so-called treaty of Vereeniging in 1902 provided that the question of granting natives the franchise should be postponed until after the grant of responsible government to the old Boer Republics.[42] This ensured that no native franchise would be granted. Would speedy victory really have made a difference? Rhodes and Milner believed theoretically in "equal rights for every civilised man," but only said so when they had lost political power.[43]

At the peace of Vereeniging Britain lost its last chance of coercing South Africa into multiracial élitism, since, as all appreciated, the Transvaal was the political heart of South Africa, by virtue of its gold if for no other reason. Thereafter Britain, committed to restoring self-government to the former republics, could do nothing positive for her nonwhite subjects.

Bryce was not blind to the coming storm between black and white and he perceived the problem of black-white relations as more serious though less urgent than that of adjustment between the Dutch, as he called them, and the English. He was taken aback by the force of white feeling.

"The traveller in South Africa is astonished at the strong feelings of dislike and contempt—one might almost say of hostility—which the bulk of the whites show to their black neighbours."[44] He surmised that the cause was not, as in southern states of America, political resentment, for which there was no reason, but a feeling derived from the old contempt for slaves, together with physical aversion and incompatibility of character and temperament. That blacks should be excluded from political power was sensible. "It is easy for people in Europe, who have had no experience of the presence among them of a semi-civilised race, destitute of the ideas and habits which lie at the basis of free government, to condemn the actions of these Colonies [the Cape and Natal] in seeking to preserve a decisive electoral majority for the whites. But anyone who has studied the question on the spot, and especially anyone who has seen the evils which in America have followed the grant of suffrage to persons unfit for it, will form a more charitable judgment."[45] He favored a restricted nonracial franchise. Looking to the future of race relations, he foresaw that while in 1897 "the black man accepts the superiority of the white as part of the order of nature," once Africans had received education and (characteristic touch) "developed a much higher intelligence" there would "if the feeling and behaviour of the whites continue to be what they are now" be serious trouble. "And if trouble comes, the preponderance of numbers on the black side may make it more serious than it could be in the United States, where the Southern whites are the outmost fringe of an enormous white nation."[46] What was the remedy? "Could [the white] be got to feel more kindly toward the native, and then treat him if not as an equal, which he is not, yet as a child, the social aspect of the problem—and it is not the least serious aspect—would be completely altered."[47]

In 1897, then, the most humane and liberal white observer, though deploring the manners of white South Africans, did not consider blacks the equal of whites or support the extension of the franchise to persons without property or education. How different, at least verbally, when we move to the 1960s.

On the surface the 1960s was a period of immobility. In contrast with the fevered excitement and violence of the 1890s, the decade following Sharpeville (March 20, 1960) saw the repression of the African National Congress, the arrest or dispersion of the main revolutionary leaders, and the inauguration of a period of political quiescence. But ideologically and economically it was a period of gestation. For it was the time when the Bantustan policy began to acquire momentum. In 1959 Prime Minister Hendrik Verwoerd revealed to a startled National Party congress that the consolidation of African areas, or Bantustans as they are often called, was to be the blueprint for the future. "The Bantu will be able to develop into separate states. That is not what we would have liked to see. It is a form of fragmentation that we would not have liked, if we were able to avoid it. In the light of the pressure being exerted on South Africa, there is however no doubt that eventually this will have to be done, thereby buying for the white man his freedom and the right to retain his domination in what is his country."[48] There could be no clearer statement of the motives for and objects of the policy. "I can see only one road ahead," he was to tell the Republic's House of Assembly two years later, "however difficult it may be and whatever further consideration it may require as one progresses from step to step, and that is the policy of separate areas. Then the leaders of the various groups can meet, as is done at a Prime Ministers' conference or when different nations meet, on a basis of absolute equality in a consultative body to discuss matters of common interest. I foresee that the eventual outcome of this policy will be no discrimination and no domination."[49]

The ultimate strategy of white South Africa is, therefore, to consolidate and defend a white homeland, successively sloughing off the surrounds until the periphery becomes a girdle. Or a noose? This policy was admittedly a late resort. Even in 1954, when the Tomlinson commission (1950–54) reported, Verwoerd rejected both self-rule and economic subsidies for the Bantu areas. By 1959 he had swung around. Why? He had become prime minister and had learned something of the international scene.

Verwoerd had been, among other things, a professor of psychology. Professors like to find theories to guide and justify their conduct. He was no exception. Indifferent to African aspirations, he was sensitive to international reproach. By the late 1950s a number of governments, though not their peoples, were jettisoning the embarrassing cargo of white supremacy. It was the international society, in which governments have to live, that set the pace. After the admission of China to great-power status during the 1939–45 war, the military achievements of Japan during the war, the grant of independence in 1948 to four Asian countries including India (according to Smuts, as "an awful mistake"),[50] the Suez crisis of 1956 demonstrated in Africa itself that, to the surprise of many white people, Egyptians could master the art of navigation. Above all the multiplication of international agencies, negotiations, and contacts of every sort brought home the impossibility of racial discrimination at the international level. There can be no international apartheid.

Nevertheless formal equality is compatible with great disparity in influence. The permanent membership of the Security Council of the United Nations formalizes that very disparity. Verwoerd saw the future of South Africa in similar terms. It would consist of formally equal states of different ethnic affiliation, but the economically dominant white state would exercise a hegemony proportionate to its resources. Of the effectiveness of the policy of divide and influence, de Gaulle—returned to power in 1958—had given a brilliant demonstration.

During the 1960s the policy of separate development began to take shape, first only in the Transkei, which became a self-governing territory by the Transkei Constitution Act of 1963.[51] Its constitution, somewhat like that of Northern Ireland before suspension, may be called a system of partial responsible government. Some members of the legislature are elected, on universal adult suffrage, but most of it is nominated (or appointed), largely from among chiefs or other persons who by custom have official duties. The legislature elects the executive, and is empowered to make laws on a range of matters wider than that open to a white province (and added to from time to time), but excluding military and foreign affairs, communications, and currency.[52] The budget is largely subsidized from central funds and the homelands, especially from 1965, are to be developed by the Homelands Development Corporations, i.e., with outside capital. In the current stage of development, incorporated in the Bantu Homelands Constitution Act of 1971, there are seven self-governing homelands with this modified form of responsible government, while the Transkei on October 26, 1976, passed to the ultimate state of constitutional development, independence, but too late to secure the international recognition which would have come to it had the separate development program been put into effect without regard for white electoral opinion. In 1959 then, Verwoerd committed white South Africa to a policy of which we subsequently saw the consequences in Prime Minister Vorster's attempt to secure the passage of power to well-disposed African successor states in Namibia and Rhodesia.

Subject to one qualification, the process of fragmentation is irreversible. Knowing how the Cape nonwhite franchise was whittled down and then abrogated between 1936 and 1968, one might suspect that the self-governing territories would be liable to instant obliteration if they should prove awkward. But as the intransigent Michiel C. Botha, Minister of Bantu Administration and Development, said in 1970, though the Parliament (of the Republic) has the legal capacity to replace the homeland constitutions it will not do so. The Bantu nations will continue their political evolution on their courses toward their independent destination.[53] The thin end of a racially separate wedge is no different from the thin end of a multiracial wedge.

The qualification is that the homelands and their leaders should want to move toward independence. An independent homeland, even if subsidized by the Republican government, has in principle lost its claim to share in the economic resources of the white state, and in any event subsidies can be used to manipulate policy, as the French have demonstrated in independent Saharan Africa. Yet Africans, not to mention colored people and Indians, have helped create an industrial state; indeed, from a Marxist or even a Lockean point of view they have made overwhelmingly the greatest contribution to its present prosperity. It would be folly to renounce an inheritance and especially a share of the land to which they have in their own eyes the major claim.[54] Even Bophuthatswana, bordering on independent Botswana with which it has an ethnic kinship, indicated in the first half of 1977 that its rulers were not willing to accept independence unless there were radical changes in the racial policies of the Republican government. The other Bantustan territories, moreover, have no intention of opting for independence, and since they would not now be accorded international recognition, there is little incentive for them to do so, even if the Republic were to offer them more and better land.

After this brief delineation of the policy that has evolved from apartheid to separate and now parallel development (or "plural democracy"), I should like to return to the contrast between James Bryce in 1897 and Hendrik Verwoerd in 1959. Whatever he may have thought privately, the hard-nosed conservative of this later age would not for a moment have endorsed in public the reactionary opinions of his liberal predecessor: "Destitute of the ideas and habits which lie at the basis of free government";[55] "Treat him not as an equal, which he is not."[56] In the world of today the self-governing homelands have universal adult suffrage at eighteen and are supposed to be moving toward an age in which there will be neither discrimination nor domination.

We are all the prisoners of axioms which stand beyond falsification. The axioms of our day postulate majority rule, but subject to certain limits and modes. Majority rule does not apply to the international community, in which the tiny population of Barbados counts as the equal of India's millions. It applies only within geographically defined units, but even there the criteria for defining the units are unclear. Hence in Ireland the principle of majority rule is not in dispute, but the area in which it should be applied divides Protestant from Catholic. Nor does majority rule apply to foreigners. Berlin is said to be the second Turkish city in the world, but the Berlin Turks do not vote in Berlin. Verwoerd understood how to exploit these limits and modes. Since the disruptive task of carving up the world's surface anew so as to allot a fair share to each individual human being can hardly be contemplated, so long as territorial sovereignty remains an unchallenged though deeply undemocratic dogma, the new geopolitics, of which "parallel development" is one example, aims at persuading people to identify themselves with this or that parcel of soil, the narrower the better. These geopolitical salmon must swim upstream, for South Africa is a psychological unit with a long history. What could show better the attachment of its inhabitants to the whole area than the words "Afrikaner" and "African," which mean the same but designate two entirely different claimant peoples, each jealous of its right to the land.[57]

A Possible Scenario

The time has come to peer into the future. In doing so I believe we shall see at least three fixed points. The first is that the white population of Southern Africa will not in any circumstances voluntarily agree to live under African majority rule, present or future. The second is that the nonwhite peoples of the subcontinent are increasingly conscious of their dignity and common interests. The third is that the political equilibrium of Southern Africa depends in the last resort on the balance of power between the United States and the Soviet Union.

The first assumption, that whites will not concede majority rule, though they may make lesser concessions, rests on the experience of dominant minorities throughout history. Such minorities, even though they thought it just to extend political rights, have yielded power to a majority conceived as distinct from themselves in four cases only: (i) after defeat in war, (ii) through internal revolution, (iii) in deference to external threat or coercion, and (iv) when the extension was thought to offer no threat to their own continued power. As to war-borne democracy, Napoleon's armies brought the bourgeoisie a share of power in the lands his armies conquered. Defeat in war followed by revolution helped the Bolsheviks seize control of Russia. In Africa majority rule has come about through outside coercion: the metropolitan power in Kenya, Algeria, Mozambique, and Angola made the white settlers of those countries surrender power by a combined exercise of military and constitutional authority.[58] Of course that is a very brief synopsis of a complicated story. The metropolitan power forced that concession only when it was no longer prepared to face the national and international cost of a colonial war. But even in these cases, the white settlers, far less numerous than the four million whites of Southern Africa, did not freely concede majority rule. In Southern Africa the conditions for constitutional coercion of the white minority do not exist. There is no metropolitan power with authority over the Republic of South Africa, and in Rhodesia the authority of Britain has not been recognized by the white Rhodesian government since November 1965. Britain, as the metropolitan ruler, surrendered its power to insist on a nonracial franchise for South Africa as long ago as the peace of Vereeniging in 1902.[59] In Rhodesia on the other hand Britain tried from 1965 onward to reassert its constitutional authority but failed. The reason for the failure is clear. Rhodesia had never been administered as a colony. It passed in 1923 straight from the rule of Rhodes's British South Africa Company to responsible government by white settlers under a nominally nonracial franchise.[60] There was no administrative structure on which constitutional pressure could be brought at any level below the governor and the judiciary.

One must not, however, underestimate the possibility of economic coercion. White Rhodesia is economically at the mercy of South Africa, and South Africa itself, as an industrial country, would be embarrassed by a united, but only by a united, boycott by other industrial nations.

The fourth method by which a minority has come to extend power to a majority is by the sort of enlargement of the electoral body of which 1832 and 1867 are examples in Britain. The competing political parties may think that the extension of the franchise is harmless, in the sense that it will not threaten their power, and wise in that it will dampen the clamor of the disfranchised. Again, one party may think that it stands to obtain an electoral advantage from the extension, as did Disraeli when he attempted to "dish the Whigs" in 1867. This sort of extension is not possible in modern South Africa because it is seen as the thin end of a wedge ending in majority black rule. It is true that there was a nonracial franchise in the Cape Colony and Natal which survived the grant of responsible government to those colonies in 1854 and 1892, though in Natal it was in effect rendered nugatory by a high property qualification which reduced the African voters to just six.[61] This franchise was tolerated because of the insistence of the metropolitan power, whose wishes could not then be disregarded. From the point of view even of liberal Cape politicians the nonracial franchise was not something desirable in itself but rather a safety valve, harmless so long as the nonwhite voter had no real political influence.[62] In Rhodesia there has always been a nonracial franchise,[63] which the metropolitan power was able to require while it possessed constitutional authority and which has been retained since in the hope of satisfying international opinion. But from the beginnings of responsible government the efforts of white Rhodesians have been directed toward ensuring that the nonracial franchise could not be converted into an avenue leading to African majority rule.[64] The factors that brought about universal suffrage in nineteenth- and twentieth-century Britain do not therefore exist in Southern Africa, where the imprint of racial consciousness overrides any electoral advantage that a political party might hope to secure through an extension of the franchise to nonwhites. Political suicide is not an option.

If for white South Africans majority rule is not in the cards,[65] whites must find other ways of coping with a rapid though so far mainly psychological transformation of the black scene in the

1970s. A number of reasons account for this transformation. The high rate of economic growth in South Africa has led to an upward shift in the grading of the various races on the scale of skilled employment. If the number of skilled and semiskilled jobs grows proportionately faster than the population, then—even under a system of industrial apartheid—there is a consequent shift in the skill required of the average member of each race even if his race does not move up relative to the other races. In the last ten years this trend has been most noticeable in South Africa, and to a lesser extent the economic progress of Rhodesia since UDI in 1967 has had the same effect. In practice, of course, industrial apartheid has not been rigorously enforced, except where white unions are able to detect infringements quickly and to press against them, as in the South African mines.

Such an upward economic shift, which leaves relative positions largely untouched, can have two effects. The satisfaction derived from economic advance may dampen political ardor. In the sixties that seems to have happened in South Africa, and the dampening, or at least the slowing, of political demands was helped by the fact that the political organization of the underground movements was destroyed in the aftermath of Sharpeville. In the seventies a resumption of those demands has occurred. It seems that with a slowly rising standard of living, African, colored, and even Indian South Africans have become conscious to an extent unprecedented in recent history that their political and above all their human status has not advanced to a commensurate degree, that the government and many white officials lack *ubuntu* or humanity.

The National Party government has notably failed to take account of the class differentiation which improved economic status brings with it. So the group-areas legislation has been ruthlessly applied to the Cape colored community, many of whom are economically middle class, and is depriving them of their historic home in Cape Town in favor of a sandy, outlying area. This crime against history, which (if we are to speak the language of homelands) is an expropriation of the colored homeland, may be heavy with political consequences. Apartheid did not require it. It did arguably require the government to refuse home ownership in the

African townships, such as Soweto, which surround the white cities. This policy is conformable to the theory that urban Africans are citizens of Bantu homelands, and, even if born or long established in the town, are visitors to a fundamentally foreign country, or as the Minister of Bantu Administration, Michiel C. Botha, recently put it, "the basis on which the Bantu is in the white area is to sell their [sic] labor and nothing else. The same principle is applicable to the white in the Bantu homelands."[66] But since these established urban Africans have security of residence under the law (for they cannot be returned to their homelands if they comply with the conditions of the influx-control legislation), the pass has in effect been sold. If apartheid means racial separation into geographically coherent blocks of land, it cannot be put into practice consistently with the needs of an economically sophisticated industry. Home ownership and municipal self-government in the African townships could have been accommodated by a shift in theory from geographically coherent to geographically fragmented apartheid, for which the existing Bantu homelands provide ample precedent.[67]

From the Afrikaner point of view, then, some mistakes have been made, but even without them, a growth of black consciousness was to be expected. Although the Bantustan policy presupposes that Africans can be divided into a number of tribes or nations such as Zulus, Venda, and the like, the urban-influx legislation belies this, since it treats all Africans whatever their ethnic affiliation on the same basis, that is to say, apart from their right to reside in the towns under section 10 of the Bantu (Urban Areas) Consolidation Act, they are all a work force which must somehow manage to be simultaneously present and unseen. In a township like Soweto,[68] which has at least 800,000 African inhabitants of all tribes (perhaps over a million since illegal migrants avoid the census), a common African consciousness has inevitably grown up, the more so as tribal customs, even if they survive the move to town, take on a cultural rather than a moral significance in the new environment. The African townships therefore hold a quasi-permanent population among whom tribal influences are waning plus a migrant group whose homeland connection is much stronger. But since the tendency of the Bantustan policy is toward treating the three segments of the African people—the settled urban African, the migrant worker, and the settled homeland inhabitant—alike, the government itself fosters, though without meaning to, a common African consciousness. Even the Bantustan leaders, who can be regarded as a conservative force, recognize common bonds, and meet to concert policy.[69] A leader such as Gatsha Buthelezi, who is in a sense committed to Zulu ethnicity, of which Inkatha Zulu is the organized expression, does not—indeed cannot—reject, at least in principle, a wider African or black consciousness.[70]

Black consciousness, or "Black Power," which is its radical expression, is not confined to Africans. Indeed one of its main aims is linguistic: to bring about a situation in which the term "black" is applied without strain to coloreds and Asians, to the "brown" people, as well as to Africans. From about 1973 the movement has made headway not just among Africans but among colored leaders such as the Labour Party chairman Alan Hendrikse (recently arrested)[71] and Professor R. E. Van der Ross, rector of the colored University of Western Cape, one of the centers of rioting in August 1976. Van der Ross has said of black consciousness that "it can and will lead to Black Power when the people have developed a consciousness and find that they are being frustrated." After asserting that "there are no movements in South Africa anywhere near the extreme manifestations of Black Power seen in America" since "the violence among the blacks in South Africa is a violence of passion," he concludes, "Black consciousness is a wholesome philosophy. . . . As I understand it, black consciousness makes people who are not white aware that they have a dignity of their own."[72]

I quote the words of Professor Van der Ross since he, like the Bantustan leaders, is an appointee of the National Party government, not, like Hendrikse, a radical. His views, and those of the colored youths who have shown their consciousness in white Cape Town with their feet and fists, point in different ways to a growing interracial solidarity.

Yet a number of warnings and qualifications are called for in case anyone should see in the growth of black consciousness a harbinger of imminent revolution. First, all the weapons, all the instruments of coercion, apart from the strike, are in the hands of government.[73] The state now has power under section 10 of the Internal Security Act, 1976, to detain any person without trial—until he dies. Its object is of course to behead the opposition from time to time. A legalistic state has resorted to the ultimate denial of the rule of law, life imprisonment without trial. Second, the differences between nonwhite peoples cannot be thought away. They have persisted in independent African Africa and have been deliberately fostered in South Africa. Even without artificial sponsorship, the pride of a nation like the Zulu would certainly not die. For them at least a great common history is a source of strength not to be foregone. Certain racial conflicts, especially between African and Indian, are not easily obliterated, as the recent history of East Africa demonstrates. It is by no means clear (nor could it be expected) that the Indian community, with its relatively high standard of living and its bitter memories of its 1949 massacre at the hands of Durban Africans,[74] has, despite some tentative acknowledgements, accepted the notion of an all-encompassing black consciousness, to the same extent as the colored. Third, it should be remembered that intermediate between ethnic consciousness on the one hand and black consciousness on the other lies African nationalism, which in most of the continent has proved a potent political force.

The final warning in connection with the growth of black consciousness must be that it need not necessarily be interpreted as a revolutionary consciousness. The proper interpretation is still a matter for debate. No doubt the events of 1974 and 1975—the Lisbon military coup; the independence of Mozambique and Angola; the triumph, with Cuban assistance, of the MPLA in independent Angola—have had their effect in South Africa and even more in Rhodesia. They have set up hopes of radical change. They have infused a sense of black capacity and dignity which encouraged the youngsters of Soweto to rebel against the plan to teach them history, geography, and mathematics in Afrikaans. But this teenage rebellion, insofar as it is not just the effervescence and vandalism of youth, which in June 1976 set off a chain of demonstration and riot that has not yet subsided, might be interpreted in a reformist sense. Perhaps the protests were motivated by the youngsters' concern to secure for themselves a better education, a more secure future in the township society to which they have been born rather than a desire to destroy it. The truth is that revolutionary leadership, like reformist leadership, is generally middle class, and its motives waver between personal frustration and vicarious anger. I should not like to guess the direction in which the middle-class leadership which we now see emerging in the townships and the colored community will turn. What seems certain is that the hope of radical change is not likely to die as it nearly died in the 1960s. The independence of Namibia, which now has been made certain, and the struggle for African rule in Rhodesia, to which Botswana, Zambia, Mozambique, Angola, and Tanzania are committed, and to which South Africa is not resolutely opposed, cannot but fire the imagination of black South Africans. Nor is it easy for the National Party in South Africa to retreat from its advanced positions without demoralizing its own troops. Rational as is the policy of defending interior lines, consistent indeed with the theory of apartheid, it is difficult, when it comes to the point, for white and black alike not to allow their imagination to be gripped by the domino theory of black takeover.

The third fixed point as we gaze at the future is that the outcome of the power struggle in Southern Africa depends on the relations between the United States and the Soviet Union. To neither of these powers, I believe, is Southern Africa, despite its chrome, a crucial area. Their interest is rather indirect. The United States would not wish the Soviet Union to secure a predominant influence even in an area of marginal strategic interest because of the destabilizing effect of shifts in spheres of influence. The Soviet Union and the Marxist powers would like to figure as the liberators of Southern Africa if it could be done without too great risk and expense. Here a distinction must be drawn between military intervention in South Africa and in Rhodesia. For the overthrow of white South Africa the Soviet Union must intervene with a naval and air force capable of establishing air superiority. In Rhodesia military intervention of the Angolan type could, on the other hand, be relatively quick and effective. But it would still be an international adventure not lightly to be embarked on send troops into a country of which Britain is technically the recognized sovereign. At least it would be necessary, as a preliminary, for the Marxist powers to recognize an alternative government of Rhodesia, which at the moment would be a very implausible act. Nor could it be undertaken without an assurance of South African neutrality. The likelihood is therefore that the Marxist powers will limit themselves to supplying aid and arms for the neighboring states which are seeking by guerrilla activity to infiltrate the white bastions and undermine the self-confidence and devotion of a part, at least, of the white population by subjecting them to long periods of military service and high taxation. In these circumstances it seems likely that, while the white Rhodesian government, with its deficient manpower, is as surely doomed as the Crusader states of the twelfth century (those prototypes of imperial adventure), it can and will prolong its resistance. For those who defend their way of life, which means their standard of living, the natural right of self-defense adds conviction to desperation. Nevertheless, the force of numbers,[75] and the consensus outside Rhodesia in favor of majority rule, will in time bring Africans to power there.

South Africa is another matter. It is not a Crusader state, but a country of permanent mixed settlement. It is relatively secure against military threats from outside its borders. If we assess the chances of internal revolution we must take account of the fact that no such revolution has ever occurred in an industrial country. The nearest parallel is perhaps Northern Ireland, where the Catholic group, though a minority in the North, is a majority in Ireland as a whole. The racial and economic divisions of South Africa are not likely to prove easier to bridge than the religious and economic divisions of Northern Ireland, and the dismal failure of power sharing there is no good omen for the prospects of consociation of any sort in industrial South Africa.

One must predict, then, that in South Africa revolutionary consciousness will develop steadily, and a black leadership capable of seizing its opportunity will be waiting for a sign. The elements of a revolutionary situation are slowly assembling, and in a revolutionary situation it is immaterial that the majority is satisfied with things as they are. For what matters then is not one's private thoughts but one's public professions. What responsible African could confess, with African sovereignty stretching to the north and east, that he is content to play a subordinate role in a white-ruled state? Are we not witnessing the overture to a tragedy in which Afrikaner and African, for reasons inescapably compelling to themselves, are set on a collision course, leaving the English, the colored, and the Indians to scramble from ship to ship as they see the chance?

I believe that the clash is not inevitable. But avoiding it will call for political skill on the part of both Afrikaner and African, a quality which, if history is a guide, both tribes possess.

Notes

1. Pierre van den Berghe, *South Africa: A Study in Conflict* (Middletown, Conn.: Wesleyan University Press, 1965), p. 263.
2. Heribert Adam, *Modernizing Racial Domination: The Dynamics of South African Politics* (Berkeley: University of California Press, 1971), p. 121.
3. Leonard M. Thompson, "White over Black in South Africa: What of the Future?" in *Change in Contemporary South Africa*, ed. Leonard Thompson and Jeffrey Butler (Berkeley: University of California Press, 1975), pp. 400, 413.
4. Alan Paton, *Hofmeyr* (New York: Scribner, 1965).
5. Representation of Natives Act, no. 12 of 1936.
6. Formed on July 25, 1975.
7. The expression "homelands" (tendentious of course) is found in the Bantu Homelands Development Corporations Act, no. 86, of 1965 and especially the Bantu Homelands Constitution Act, no. 21, of 1971
8. P. Mayer, "Class, Status and Ethnicity as Perceived by Johannesburg Africans," in *Change in Contemporary South Africa*, pp. 138, 140 n. 8
9. The Bantu Affairs Administration Act, no. 45 of 1971, sets up the administrative structure.
10. Bantu (Urban Areas) Consolidation Act, no. 25 of 1945, s. 10.
11. Ethnic distribution in 1970 about 3.9 million Zulu and Xhosa, 1. Tswana, 1.5 Sepedi, 1.4 Seshoeshoe, 0.7 Shangaan, 0.4 Swazi, 0. Venda, 0.2 southern Ndebele, 0.1 northern Ndebele.
12. Note 8 above and also F. Wilson, "Political Implications for Blacks of Economic Changes," in *Change in Contemporary South Africa*, pp 168, 175.
13. Though the proportion has arguably increased from about a third to

half between 1960 and 1970: E. Kahn, *1970 Annual Survey of South African Law,* pp. 49–50.
14. Leonard M. Thompson, "The Compromise of Union," in *Oxford History of South Africa,* ed. Monica Wilson and L. Thompson, vol. 2 (New York: Oxford University Press, 1971), pp. 350–363.
15. The main provisions of the constitution (Grondwet) of the South African Republic gave expression to the will of the people, e.g., article 9 of the 1858 constitution: "The people do not accept that colored and white inhabitants be placed on an equal footing in church or state."
16. South Africa Act 1909, ss. 35, 152. The entrenchment of the Dutch (later Afrikaans) and English languages by s. 137 remains even under the Republican constitution: Republic of South Africa Constitution Act, no. 32 of 1961, s. 108.
17. Native Representation Act, no. 12 of 1936.
18. Separate Representation of Voters Act, no. 46 of 1951; High Court Act; Appellate Division Quorum Act, no. 27 of 1955; Senate Act, no. 53 of 1955; South Africa Amendment Act, no. 9 of 1956. See W. S. Livingston, "Court and Parliament in South Africa," *Parliamentary Affairs* 10 (1957): 434–453.
19. Promotion of Bantu Self-Government Act, no. 46 of 1959, s. 15.
20. Separate Representation of Voters Act, no. 50 of 1968.
21. Hence some members of the 1908–9 National Convention thought, against all the local evidence, that it would not happen. *Oxford History of South Africa,* vol. 2, p. 498 n. 1.
22. Ronald Hyam, *The Failure of South African Expansion, 1908–1948* (London: Macmillan, 1972), pp. 47–71.
23. Southern Rhodesia (Constitution) Order in Council 1961.
24. Act 49 of 1969, ss. 78, 80, 91 and Second Schedule.
25. Botswana Independence Act 1966; Botswana Independence Order 1966, S.I. 1966, no. 1771, schedule 2.
26. Lesotho Independence Act 1966; Lesotho Independence Order 1966, S.I. 1966, no. 1172, s. 3 schedule; Lesotho Order no. 1 of 1970 suspended the constitution from January 30, 1970.
27. Swaziland Independence Act 1968; Swaziland Independence Order 1968, S.I. 1968, no. 1377, ss. 2(1), 4, schedule; and Swaziland Government Gazette Extraordinary, XI, no. 878 (April 17, 1973).
28. J. Bryce, *Impressions of South Africa,* 3rd ed. (London: Macmillan, 1899), pp. 346–347.
29. See his inaugural lecture, *The Academical Study of the Civil Law,* of 25 February 1871 (London, 1871) and his valedictory lecture, *Legal Studies in the University of Oxford,* of June 10, 1893 (London, 1893).
30. *The American Commonwealth,* rev. ed., 2 vols. (New York: Macmillan, 1910).

31. See, e.g., Godfrey H. L. le May, *British Supremacy in South Africa 1899–1907* (Oxford: Clarendon Press, 1965), pp. 1–37.
32. *Impressions*, introduction, p. xliv: "an unfriendly neighbor is less dangerous than a disaffected colony."
33. On Smuts's geopolitical fantasies, see Ronald Hyam, *The Failure of South African Expansion, 1908–1948* (London: Macmillan, 1972), pp. 23, 28, 32, 36.
34. Matabeleland Order in Council 1894; Southern Rhodesia Order in Council 1898.
35. On which see Joshua Prawer, *The Latin Kingdom of Jerusalem: European Colonialism in the Middle Ages* (London: Weidenfeld & Nicolson, 1972).
36. Battle of Hittin (July 1187).
37. Jean van der Poel, *The Jameson Raid* (Capetown and New York: Oxford University Press, 1951); E. Pakenham, *Jameson's Raid* (London: Weidenfeld & Nicolson, 1960); Monica Wilson and Leonard Thompson, *The Oxford History of South Africa*, vol. 2 (1971), pp. 313–320.
38. Gerald Shaw, *Some Beginnings: The Cape Times 1876–1910* (London and New York: Oxford University Press, 1975), pp. 80–81.
39. *Impressions*, pp. 126–127.
40. Le May, *British Supremacy*, pp. 209 f.: "We are in forever," said Smuts of the results of the Transvaal election of February 22, 1907 (ibid., p. 211).
41. Note 15 above. In the 1889 revision the reference to church and state was omitted.
42. Le May, *British Supremacy*, p. 149.
43. Ibid., p. 177.
44. *Impressions*, p. 351.
45. Ibid., p. 360.
46. Ibid., pp. 367–368.
47. Ibid., p. 369.
48. A. du Toit, cited in *Change in Contemporary South Africa*, p. 41.
49. *House of Assembly Debates*, vol. 107, col. 4552 (April 14, 1961).
50. J. C. Smuts, Jr., *Jan Christian Smuts* (London: Cassell, 1952), p. 507.
51. Act 48 of 1963, the preamble of which stated that "the policy of separate development envisages the gradual development of self-governing Bantu national units in the traditional Bantu homelands."
52. Its legal status is described by E. Kahn, *1963 Annual Survey of South African Law*, pp. 56–70.
53. *House of Assembly Debates*, vol. 30, cols. 3495–3497 (September 7, 1970).
54. Chief Minister Ntsanwisi of Gazankulu (November 15, 1974): "We would lose our claims to South Africa's wealth and be abandoning our claims to an economy we have helped to build up."
55. Note 46 above.

56. Note 48 above.
57. The Afrikaans neologism "Afrikaan" (= Bantu African) is self-consciously awkward. The "Afrikaner Bond," founded in 1879, was originally open to English and colored people, but as the latter took little interest, "Afrikaner" soon acquired the narrower primary meaning; *Oxford History of South Africa*, vol. 2, p. 303 n. 3.
58. Jeffrey Butler, "Changes within the White Ruling Caste," in *Change in Contemporary South Africa*, pp. 79, 84.
59. Note 43 above.
60. Claire Palley, *The Constitutional History and Law of Southern Rhodesia, 1888–1965* (Oxford: Clarendon Press, 1966), part 1.
61. Leonard M. Thompson, *Politics in the Republic of South Africa* (Boston: Little, Brown, 1966), p. 27; Leo Kuper, "African Nationalism in South Africa 1910–64," in *The Oxford History of South Africa*, vol. II, pp. 424, 430.
62. John X. Merriman (1906), "To me personally the idea of a Native franchise is repellant but I am convinced that it is a safety-valve and the best safety-valve," cited by A. du Toit, "Ideological Change, Afrikaner Nationalism, Racial Domination," in *Change in Contemporary South Africa*, pp. 19, 23.
63. Palley, *Constitutional History*, pp. 135–136, 169–171, 243–246, 309–312, 416–424.
64. Prime Minister Ian Smith to CBS (March 16, 1976): "We may in the end lose. But I think it is better to lose while you are standing up and fighting rather than crawling out on your knees."
65. E.g., Prime Minister John Vorster (November 16, 1975): "If there are people who are raising your hopes that there will one day be one man one vote in the white Parliament for you, then they are misleading you, for that will never happen."
66. Speech in Maritzberg, reported in the *Cape Times*, August 30, 1976.
67. Thus, KwaZulu consists of 48 major areas and over 100 "black spots," L. Schlemmer and T. J. Muil, "Social and Political Change in the African Areas: A Case Study of Kwa Zulu," in *Change in Contemporary South Africa*, p. 111 n. 7.
68. On Soweto, see P. Mayer, note 8 above, with ethnic distribution, p. 142 n. 13.
69. E.g., Declaration of seven homeland leaders reported in the *Cape Times* August 23, 1976: "The black leaders meeting here regard themselves and are considered by millions of their people as part and parcel of the liberation movement." In January 1975 they jointly demanded home ownership in white areas, the abolition of influx control, the right of blacks to control their own local authorities in white areas, trade-union rights for black workers, and the release of political prisoners.
70. On Buthelezi, see L. Schlemmer and T. J. Muil, "Social and Political

Change in the African Areas: A Case Study of Kwa Zulu," in *Change in Contemporary South Africa*, p. 107.
71. On August 26, 1976, the (colored) Labour Party rejected the government's proposals for (separate) colored constitutional advance on the ground that it rejected racial power though it supported black consciousness.
72. *Cape Argus*, August 28, 1976.
73. Albert L. Sachs, "The Instruments of Domination in South Africa," in *Change in Contemporary South Africa*, p. 223.
74. *The Oxford History of South Africa*, vol. 2, pp. 461–462.
75. The mobilizable Rhodesian forces (10,000 to 12,000 men) plus 8,000 police are of the same order of magnitude as the army of the Latin kingdom (1,200 knights, 15,000 foot soldiers) destroyed by Saladin at Hittin in July 1187.

STANLEY R. ROSS

8. Liberal Democracy in Mexico

When these essays were planned, it seemed logical that a representative of our neighbors to the south should be included in this broad-ranging appraisal of the state of liberal democracy in the world. After all, the American Revolution, which broke the imperial ties with England, did serve as an example to others in the hemisphere and in the newly founded nations there was considerable copying of the federalist form, the tripartite division of government, and the listing of individual rights. And Mexico loomed large as the likely candidate because of its long struggle for both modernity and a more democratic society, including the first of the twentieth-century nationalist social revolutions. Finally, there is an inevitable curiosity about the evolution, functioning, and democratic potential of the dominant official party in Mexico.

Once it was decided that an essay on Mexico should be included, there was no question that the most appropriate person to undertake such an assignment was Daniel Cosío Villegas—distinguished Mexican historian, economist, political scientist, publisher, teacher, diplomat, essayist, and founder of cultural institutions. After all, Don Daniel had penned hundreds of analytical essays about his nation's political system, not to mention his monumental historical works. Cosío Villegas was invited and had accepted an invitation to participate, but on March 10, 1976, death intervened and brought to an end the multifaceted career of this remarkable man. So we are denied the opportunity to know what Don Daniel would have had to say on this fundamentally important topic. We do know that it would have interested him greatly and that he would have brought to it those distinctive and noteworthy characteristics which economist Victor Urquidi defined as "his lucidity, his extraordinary intelligence, his analytical capacity, and his love for historical truth."[1]

Obviously, I am being called upon to fill some oversized shoes. It will be my purpose to try to provide some sense of what Don Daniel might have said as well as some views of my own on the present state and future prospects of liberal democracy in Mexico.

At a symposium on the United States and Mexican independence movements held in Mexico City in January 1976,[2] I was struck by the insistence of several Mexicans that their country's liberalism was rooted almost anywhere other than in the United States. While such assertions are perhaps better understood in terms of the current world, it is true that the Enlightenment and the French Revolution were other sources of inspiration for Mexicans seeking to free themselves and establish a nation. It is also true, nevertheless, that intellectuals of New Spain looked to the United States for inspiration since that neighbor's success in achieving independence, together with the French Revolution, was decisive in both the development and the timing of the Mexican struggle for independence. With the tie severed and the short-lived empire of Iturbide having run its course, the Mexicans turned to the establishment of a republic mainly on the United States model. The basic state papers of the northern neighbor were readily available and extensively discussed as the Constitution of 1824 came into being. A federal system was established, as was a division of powers. If the fundamental law owes much to the Spanish Constitution of 1812, it also owes a great deal to the United States model of 1787.

Independence from Spain was achieved, but little else changed. The preeminent *peninsulares* or *gachupines* were displaced, but the rest of the pyramidal colonial structure, divided along economic and racial lines, persisted. No longer a part of the Spanish Empire, Mexico remained colonial in the economic sense. Worst of all was the absence of a tradition of self-government and of meaningful political experience for those now called upon to direct a nation which lacked cohesiveness in any sense. Small wonder that Mexico alternated between periods of anarchy and despotism, frequently with a wide gap between constitutional form and actual practice. Tragically, the years were marked not only by coups, civil wars, ineffective control, and separatist movements, but also by external conflict, both diplomatic and military, with Spain, France, and the United States, the last resulting in substantial loss of national territory.

During the second quarter of the nineteenth century, Mexican liberalism started with the premise that man has the capacity to govern himself and improve his lot. Liberals theoretically supported political freedom and social equality of all peoples. It was in the mid-nineteenth century that Mexico experienced the second of her three genuine revolutions—the War of the Reform. The movement represented an effort to complete the work of independence, to bring Mexico into the nineteenth century. It sought to encourage the small landowner as the backbone of a more democratic society. It endeavored to curb institutions inherited from colonial times, such as the church, the hacienda, and the army—institutions that had alternately challenged or ignored the Mexican polity, or sought to convert it to their own interests. The Reform also represented the substitution of mestizos—particularly middle-class mestizo professionals—for the creoles who had tried unsuccessfully to govern Mexico since independence.[3] The Constitution of 1857 incorporated these objectives as well as a full panoply of traditional liberal rights and freedoms, including various measures intended to secure separation of church and state and the superiority of the latter.

A decade later, the conservatives having been defeated and discredited through the French invasion and the Maximilian episode, liberalism was triumphant with the restored republic. The liberal movement in general and the Constitution of 1857 in particular were identified by many Mexicans not only with the quest for social justice, but with nationalism and patriotism. Despite the "we are all liberals" syndrome, there were factional as well as personal differences, and these facilitated the emergence and rise to power of Porfirio Díaz—the long-term dictator who contributed significantly and in more than one way to the modernization of Mexico.

Porfirio Díaz brought political peace and economic progress to

Mexico. The price paid was high in terms of the loss of political liberty and experience in self-government, the resurgence of the church, the expansion of the hacienda system, the devastating destruction of the Indian landholding communities, the suppression of labor, and the introduction of a favored and exploitative foreign capitalism. Those who were ignored and left out of the Porfirian way of life—those on whose backs the facade of order and material progress was erected—ultimately would rebel and destroy the dictatorship.

Later observers and analysts were to note that despite constitutional guarantees of freedoms, liberalism could come to be interpreted by the state as favoring the powerful, both national and foreign, and liberal regimes too often were unable or unwilling to deal with social issues. It is customary for official historians of the Mexican Revolution to view the Porfirian era as the old regime, as a discontinuity in the course of Mexican liberalism,[4] and as an aberration in the Mexican struggle for a modern society and a democratic way of life. However, it was Cosío Villegas who, in his *Historia Moderna de México*, without in any way being an apologist for the Porfirian era, demonstrated the continuity between the Restored Republic and the Porfiriato. It was during the latter period that the "scientific politics" of Comtean positivism emerged and attained striking influence. Its advocates attacked doctrinaire liberalism or "metaphysical politics" with its emphasis on individual liberty, legislative democracy, and the weakening of executive power. Scientific politics would be applied to the practical ends of economic development, social resuscitation, and political unity. They favored more administration and less politics, since from their point of view society should be administered rather than governed.

Despite the almost universal adherence to the ideology—or, as one leading scholar has called it, the myth—of the Reform,[5] there was constitutional debate and contention. And despite their theoretical antagonism, liberalism and positivism became thoroughly intermingled, with both remaining as potential ideological sources for the continuity of ideas during and after the Revolution. Cosío has shown the persistence of a liberal political opposition, particularly in the press, during the Porfirian era. And it was from liberal clubs shortly after the turn of the century that criticism of the failure to enforce the Laws of the Reform and the resultant resurgence of the church emerged. The precursory Mexican Liberal Party of Ricardo Flores Magón broadened its goals and used a liberal appeal as well as a liberal name beginning in 1906 and continuing through three armed assaults on the regime. This was despite the fact that its leadership was moving toward an anarcho-syndicalism, openly proclaimed in 1911. While contributing to the awakening of the population, the movement's ideology made it a fringe group outside of the mainstream of the Mexican Revolution. Most industrial workers were not ideologically radical. They sought justice, including a place of dignity within the new industrial national society. They identified with liberalism as a search for social justice within the framework of national independence from foreign penetration and domination. First politically and then with arms in hand, they followed Madero.[6]

Francisco I. Madero, who initiated the first phase of the Mexican Revolution, was devoted to French egalitarianism and to Anglo-Saxon democracy. It was with reluctance that he turned to force to oust the aging dictator, and he quickly compromised in the late spring of 1911 to avoid further bloodshed and to restore constitutional government. In his campaigning as well as in his revolutionary statements, Madero advocated effective suffrage and no re-election as the means by which the people would establish a democratic polity under which the people's representatives would undertake to solve their socioeconomic problems. While there is a serious question as to whether Mexico was ready for democracy and whether that would have been the best way of achieving the urgently needed socioeconomic changes, there can be no doubt that the circumstances were hardly propitious. Madero did proclaim the goal of a democratic polity, which became part of the revolutionary tradition, and in the process he gave the Mexican Revolution a symbol and a martyr.

The overthrow and death of Madero—the apostle of Mexican democracy—unified the revolutionary forces against Huerta the usurper. The unity before the common foe disintegrated once Huerta was defeated, and division developed among various revolutionary leaders and factions. Partly from conviction and partly from the need for popular support, revolutionary decrees were promulgated. Thus did a political upheaval become a social revolution.

Frank Tannenbaum, late dean of Mexicanists in this country, called the Constitution of 1917 "the most important single event in the history of the Revolution. It definitely marked off the past from the present and future in Mexico. . . . it once and for all set a definitive legal program for the Mexican Revolution and laid the legal foundation for all of the [subsequent] conflicting currents. . . ."[7]

The constituent assembly of Querétaro was convened in December 1916 to give a legal basis for Carranza's power and to reform the fundamental law of 1857. Instead, by early February, the delegates had produced a document which provided the legal framework for a far-reaching social and economic revolution. The Constitution of 1917, although much more of a twentieth-century social code, would prove to be as remarkably flexible a document as had the United States Constitution of 1789.

That flexible character is principally due to the fact that the Mexican charter embodies two contradictory conceptions of the role of the state and of the relation of the individual to the government. The Constitution of 1917 reiterates all of the concepts of democratic government contained in the Constitution of 1857.[8] Freedom of association, worship, and speech, representative government, universal suffrage, periodic elections, the separation of powers, the independence of state and municipal governments, the right of trial by jury, and the right to property are all retained. Indeed, the political ideas of the American and French revolutions find their restatement in the Constitution of 1917.

However, there were those who recognized that historically the enunciation of such principles had not protected Mexico from either political chaos or tyranny. If the Revolution was not to prove a useless or incomplete effort, something would have to be done to redress the balance in Mexican society so that the state could contend with such entrenched institutions as the church, the hacienda, and foreign interests. Accordingly, the delegates attacked and sought to bridle or destroy the rival institutions while strengthening the state. The hopes for social betterment and for redeeming man from injustice were written into the Constitution in the form of Article 27 dealing with land and the subsoil, Article 123 dealing with labor, and Article 130 dealing with the church.

The delegates recognized that these articles conflicted with the principles of personal freedom such as the right to property, the right to work, and the right to religious freedom. Those principles were consciously compromised, however, on the ground that social interest was more basic and took precedence over the interest of the individual. Much of the obviously divergent policy of subsequent Mexican governments has stemmed from this contradiction, with presidents choosing to emphasize one or the other of these commitments. Under the Constitution, it would be possible to have the strongly revolutionary regime of Lázaro Cárdenas (1934–40) expropriating foreign petroleum holdings and carrying out large-scale agrarian reform, and the more conservative administration of Miguel Alemán (1946–52) with its emphasis on industrialization and foreign investment and on agricultural productivity rather than land distribution.

The fact of fundamental importance is that the Mexican government was given very extensive powers to define and implement the program outlined. New pillars of support were created in the form of two moral, social, and political agencies: the semi-collective *ejido* and the trade union. These institutions with collective interest stood between the individual and the state and took precedence over the former. The extended powers also are to be found in the nation's reassertion of its rights to the subsoil, the power to control monopolies, the sharp reduction of the institutional power of the church, and the limitation of foreign rights. As Tannenbaum wrote, "The Constitution of 1917 provided the Revolution with a program that could be called into action to justify public policy and political expediency."[9]

Following the overthrow of Carranza in 1920, the constructive phase of the Revolution was initiated as the program detailed in the Constitution began to be translated into legislation and action. It was a decade of cultural renaissance, agrarian reform, subsoil legislation, anti-clericalism, educational reform, and attention to the place and future of the Indian. These were years of excitement and innovation. These were years when the revolutionary regimes were threatened from within and without. Internally there was conflict with the church and externally the danger of one with the United States. Further, each change of administration was accompanied by armed rebellion or at least abortive coups. There were major armed conflicts in 1923–24 and 1929 and abortive challenges to the dominant Sonoran group in 1927.

A political crisis of imposing dimensions occurred in 1928 when Obregón's candidacy to return to the presidency after an intervening term provoked an anti–re-electionist movement. Obregón triumphed in the election, but was assassinated by a religious fanatic before assuming office.

The resulting political vacuum threatened political stability and revolutionary rule and could only be filled by Plutarco Elías Calles. For the next six years, Calles remained as the *jefe máximo* while three others nominally ruled. To avoid a recurrence of military rivalries and regional politics provoking armed conflict with each political succession, the National Revolutionary Party was created to provide a mechanism whereby individual ambitions and regional aspirations could be recognized and reconciled without recourse to military might.

These were years of transition and years of depression. There was cynicism and corruption. Revolutionary vows were forgotten, with the exception of a conscience-salving anti-clericalism. There was need for a reaffirmation of revolutionary principles and of faith in the people. The administration of Lázaro Cárdenas quite properly has been called the high-water mark of the Mexican Revolution, which he revitalized and reinvigorated. Land reform was accelerated and large-scale collective *ejidos* were created where commercial agriculture requiring extensive capital was to be carried on. Foreign petroleum holdings were expropriated; labor unions were supported and were entrusted with control of the railroads; socialist and laical education was pursued as was an indianist policy emphasizing preservation of indigenous culture.

Cárdenas recognized that what Mexico needed was internal peace and legal, non-violent succession (a view that makes his later conduct understandable), a mechanism for political accommodation under which the "people must learn that they can be governed without terror."[10] It was Cárdenas who changed the name of the official party to the Mexican Revolutionary Party (PRM) and introduced a corporatist representation by four sectors—farm, labor, military, and popular (including bureaucratic and some middle-class elements). By 1940, the military sector had been eliminated and gradually the elements incorporated in the popular sector were expanded. The collectivist and proletarian orientation was clearly a product of its times.

The Second World War served as another period of transition and as the background of a major transformation in policy and politics. Mexico shifted from agrarian revolution to industrialization in its struggle to escape from its difficulties and create a better life. The emphasis was on agricultural production through credit, capital investment, etc., and on guarantees giving security to owners rather than on land distribution. Labor was brought under control; the foreign investor was welcomed, although theoretically under control to protect Mexican interests; a *modus vivendi* with the Church was achieved; the educational program was to be democratic rather than socialist and was to stress equality, moderation, unity, and conciliation rather than class strife.

Miguel Alemán's administration, building on that of his predecessor, elaborated these ideas to such a degree that industrialization and urbanization became characteristic of the new Mexico. And the official party was reorganized once again on the eve of his inauguration. Highly suggestive was its new designation as the Institutional Revolutionary Party (PRI), a seeming contradiction in terms that was intended to convey the notion that henceforth change would be achieved in Mexico through institutional processes rather than through more forceful means.

Since then Mexico has had impressive political stability and striking economic development. No Mexican government has been overthrown since 1920. The year 1929 marks the last national armed movement against the government, while the last abortive regional movement occurred in 1937. Over the past three decades, Mexico has averaged close to 7 percent economic growth annually. Small wonder that some observers talked of the political and economic miracle of Mexico. And the official party contributed to and benefited from that sustained period of peace and progress.

It was in the late 1940s, however, when the Mexican Revolution had entered a phase which can only be called its Thermidor, that the voices of critics were heard in the land. There were those concerned about the new direction being taken, the price being paid by Mexican farmers and workers to create an industrial society, and the rampant corruption. With improved communications, rising expectations were more generalized and were subject to greater disappointment, a disappointment that may be attributed both to poor distribution of the new wealth and to the demands for improvement from a rapidly increasing population.

One of the foremost critics of the Mexican situation, both then and later, was Cosío Villegas. In the 1920s, Cosío had been filled with the desire "to do something for the new Mexico." Remembering those years, Don Daniel would write with pride of "his generation," of those intellectuals whose youth coincided with the "springtime" or the "good years" of the Mexican Revolution.[11] It was then that Cosío, employing a critical attitude, contributed to the examination and growth of national identity. Here were the beginnings of his analytical probing of the historical antecedents of the Mexican Revolution and of the institutional framework of Mexican society. In the late forties, he wrote his seminal essay on the crisis of the Mexican Revolution and initiated his "Historia Moderna de México" project.

While recognizing that the achievements of the Revolution in terms of its three major goals—political freedom, agrarian reform, and labor organization—had not been inconsiderable, Cosío found his nation in crisis: "For some years now Mexico has been suffering a crisis which gets worse day by day, but as in the case of fatal illness in a family, one either does not talk about it, or talks with tragically unrealistic optimism. The crisis springs from the fact that the goals of the Revolution have been so exhausted that the very term revolution now lacks meaning." He sadly affirmed that "all the men of the Mexican Revolution were, without a single exception, inferior to its demands." For example, he noted that Madero destroyed the Porfirian regime, but did not create democracy in Mexico. Admittedly, "to create in Mexico a democracy with clear evidences of authenticity is a task which would dismay any reasonable man." While sadly concluding that the men of the Revolution had lost their moral and political authority,

Cosío still saw a ray of hope—weak to be sure—that "from the Revolution itself may emerge a reaffirmation of principles and purification of men."[12]

A dozen years later, Don Daniel would conclude that the Revolution had not survived its crisis, that the Revolution had died and was awaiting decent interment. It was to be kept seemingly alive by the pronouncements of politicians whose words and deeds did not mesh. Nevertheless, Cosío closed his 1960 essay with the hope and the confidence that Mexico could find a way out of her dilemma.[13]

There were those who dissented, protesting that the obituaries were premature. Most agreed that the revolutionary goals had been incompletely realized, that there had been changes in approach and emphasis, and that all was not well in the revolutionary household. The protestants included old revolutionaries who emphasized the incompletely realized goals for which they had fought, intellectuals who were products of the Revolution, economists who had charted Mexico's new direction, and the aforementioned politicians.

The achievements of the Mexican Revolution have been significant. An agrarian revolution has been effected, rural productivity augmented, and both the gross national product and the per capita income increased—changes that have produced a gradual and widespread improvement in the standard of living. This is true not only in an economic sense, but in terms of health and education as well. Other far-reaching changes were inaugurated: the transformation of a semifeudal economy and the elimination of the dominant landed element; the emancipation of the Indian; the strengthening of the place of organized labor; the spread of public education; the nationalization of petroleum; the emergence of a new, expanded and dominant middle class; the creation of a national system of communication and transportation; the achievement of political stability, together with the reduction of the role of the military and the clergy; the stimulation of a wide-ranging cultural renaissance. And above all, there has been the growing Mexican sense of national achievement and the Mexican consciousness of national character, which is as clearly defined as any in the hemisphere.

Even so, the incompleteness of the Revolution's achievements and the shortcomings of some of its solutions, as well as the changed tone and direction of Mexico, have prompted some observers to question whether the historic movement has not failed, stopped, or even ceased to exist. There are many who still share incompletely, if at all, in the benefits of the Revolution.

It was in the sixties that evidences of stress and strain became apparent. What happened might well be described as the stresses of progress. As the economy progressed, demands on the political system increased, and expectations were aroused that even the rapidly growing economy could not satisfy. The Mexican situation was made difficult, if not impossible, by two elements. First, the sustained and rapid growth of population from 20 million in 1940, to 30 million in 1954, to over 63 million today cut the rate of growth of the aggregate gross national product when figured on a per capita basis in half. It put tremendous strain on the nation's educational system and social services, and aggravated the problems of urbanization. Mexico's second major handicap has been the maldistribution of the new wealth created, resulting in a greater degree of income inequality than in most Latin American countries.

Evidence of stress was reflected in a widespread voter alienation from the official party, particularly in urban areas, taking the form of votes for the opposition parties, abstentionism (despite the threat of legal sanctions) exceeding a third of the eligible voters, and the casting of blank or otherwise nullified ballots. More dramatic was the student unrest which climaxed in the tragic events of Tlatelolco in 1968. Underlying the immediate causes of the conflict was a sense that economic development had not solved all the country's social problems and that politically there was much that could and needed to be done to democratize the system.

It was perhaps inevitable that, in 1968, amid the political and moral crisis of the suppression of the student movement, when the Mexican political system was showing signs of stress and its viability in a changing world was being questioned, Cosío Villegas should again use the journalistic political essay to try to influence the direction of events by means of a critical analysis of the Mexican political process.[14] His efforts attracted public attention, but evoked very little echo from others. His essays in *Excélsior* were followed by a series of booklets[15] on the Mexican political system, President Echeverría's personal style of governing (the first judgment of a Mexican president published while he still exercised power), the process of presidential selection, and the resolution of that process in 1975. That each of these volumes went into multiple editions of 50,000 to 80,000 copies suggests that the Mexican public wanted and needed a voice like that of Don Daniel.

In a sense, both of Cosío's principal activities in his last few years—the "History of the Revolution" and the essays of political analysis and commentary—are simply different sides of the same coin. In both instances, he was trying to define the direction of the Mexican people—through a scholarly examination of the nation's recent history and by stimulating and contributing to a serious evaluation of its political system. On both fronts he worked to make intelligible Mexico's past and present in order to open the way for a better future.

Cosío recognized the profound dissatisfaction with the political life of the country and the popular desire for democratization of the political process. He identified as the key obstacle the overwhelming dominion of the president and of the official party and the hidden method of selecting candidates and particularly presidential candidates. There is no question that the official party is absolutely dominant. Indeed, one critic—urging a bi-party or multi-party system—has said that "it is not a party, but rather an electoral agency of the government."[16] Moreover, the opposition has won no governorship, only one senatorship, and never the presidency. Only at the levels of deputy or municipal president has the opposition triumphed. More recently, in an effort to maintain some semblance of a "loyal opposition," the other parties have been granted deputies of party (seats on the basis of receiving a percentage of the total vote) in addition to seats actually won. The pallid parties of opposition, however—PAN (Party of National Action) on the right, PPS (Popular Socialist Party) on the left, and PARM (Authentic Party of the Mexican Revolution) —dogging the footsteps of the official party, do not offer meaningful alternatives, even though they do serve as a legal outlet for those on the extremes as well as a means of protest for those alienated by the official party. These groupings offer no constructive alternative ideology, nor do they represent a danger to the PRI. In any event, the PRI has shown no inclination to tolerate any serious threat to its hegemony.

So, it seems unlikely that greater democracy will come to Mexico in the near future through bi-partyism despite the obvious appeal that might have to those accustomed to equating democracy with party competition or with a two-party system. The Mexican president enjoys tremendous power which affords him the ability to dominate the other branches of the government as well as the states and municipalities. There are two views of the official party: one that it effectively represents, reconciles, and protects its constituent groups, which are themselves representative of broad social interests; the other that it serves as the mechanism to control and discipline the groups and currents, co-opting the leadership of the workers and the campesinos. And there are those who, viewing the dominance of the latter function in recent decades, talk of neo-porfirianism. What the official party has done is to make the transmission of power regular, orderly, and peaceful, and to incorporate groups ignored during the Porfiriato: campesinos, workers, and small bourgeoisie.[17]

The fact remains that the structure has within itself the means of being more responsive, more democratic. And the Mexican political élite has shown itself pragmatic, resilient, and astute. It continues to enjoy a fair degree of freedom of choice and the power to exercise it. Those are not the only favorable elements. The political system, with its principle of "no-reelection" and an expanded bureaucratic structure, provides periodic access to opportunity and mobility through politics. Labor and agrarian leadership has been co-opted with rewards from above. The revolutionary regimes have conferred benefits, creating a reservoir of goodwill which has persisted. The political system still enjoys an aura of prestige as the heir of the revolutionary upheaval and its accomplishments. It inherited and to a fair degree retains massive peasant, labor, and middle-class support. It benefits from an assumption that the state is operating for the common welfare and for the satisfaction of the people's aspirations.

A survey in the mid-sixties revealed that a great number of

Mexicans maintain a strong reserve of goodwill for their political system, though paradoxically they feel alienated from its everyday operation and the officials who direct it. Cynical about political leadership and operations, they nevertheless retain an attachment to revolutionary symbols and manifest goals. Twenty-five percent thought that the goals had been attained; 61 percent believed that people were still working to attain them; and 14 percent felt that the revolutionary goals had been forgotten. In another study, it was found that 78 percent of urban respondents felt that Mexico was "better off" as a result of the Revolution and that "things are slowly improving."[18] A recent study of the politicization of Mexican children revealed that two-thirds affirm that the Revolution benefited all Mexicans, while only 15 percent denied that to have been the case, leading the researcher to conclude that "the mythification of the Mexican Revolution is an omnipresent and undeniable fact."[19]

There is another plus in the situation, namely, the assured change of leadership every six years. While the nature of the system is marked more by continuity than by change, the sexennial turnover does afford an opportunity for the new president to assess the situation and make needed adjustments. It is an opportunity for the Mexican political pendulum to swing; a chance for reappraisal of methods and direction. In 1970 Mexico was indeed ready for a change from the regime of Díaz Ordaz, which was development-oriented and provided huge public works programs, emphasized law and order rather than flexibility, and revealed itself to be extremely sensitive to criticism. In 1976, for different reasons, Mexico was again ready for a change.

Luis Echeverría was called by Cosío the most original president Mexico had had since Cárdenas.[20] Other adjectives which have been applied to him tell much about the ambivalent reactions he provoked. He has been described as well-intentioned, active, peripatetic, lacking in consistency, weak and vacillating, and given to rhetoric rather than effective action. Politically, he was tireless and insisted on the same kind of almost compulsive activity by his associates. He seemed to be responsive to demands for political progress: he encouraged criticism, released imprisoned student leaders, undertook political reforms and actions that facilitated participation by the other parties and opened up the élite to youth, and designated and backed an untraditional aide as reforming head of the official party. Jesús Reyes Heroles is an intellectual and, interestingly enough, best known for his serious studies of liberalism in nineteenth-century Mexico. At the national and state level, however, the power of the president and the PRI remained unchallenged, and in the final stage of his administration, Echeverría was much less tolerant of criticism. He showed courage in reversing his stand on population control, initiating in 1972 a national program of family planning. It is worth observing, however, that if that critical problem is to be dealt with at all, there will need to be a response that is systematic and sustained. Echeverría also focused attention on rural Mexico, with its growing millions of landless and its excess population, feeding the streams of migrants to the north and to the urban centers. It is important that effective attention be given to rural Mexico despite the political reality of an increasingly urban electorate.

There was increasing uneasiness about and criticism of the Echeverría regime during its final two years. The criticism most often focused on the divergences between word and deed, on the lack of consistency and completeness of effort. One scholarly observer called it "government by rhetoric," complete with "self-contradictory programs."[21] Concern also was expressed about a tendency to act or speak without reflection and what was viewed as a demonstrated insensitivity to specific groups or to the public in general. Finally, the administrative structure became increasingly complex and clumsy, as was illustrated by the creation of 277 inter-secretarial commissions, frequently with overlapping jurisdictions.

Economically, Echeverría called for fiscal reforms directed at redistributing wealth, but his reforms proved to be a patchwork rather than a general plan. His attacks on external dependence appeared more threatening than they proved to be in fact. His efforts to diversify Mexico's trading partners did not significantly reduce United States dominance.

While Echeverría and Mexico were victims of forces beyond their control—general economic difficulties, shortages of materials, the energy crunch, and inflation—his economic and international policies contributed to the disarray. Both at home and abroad, his pronouncements and policies caused investors first distress and then distrust and fear. Private investment dropped sharply in recent years from two-thirds of the total Mexican investment in 1970 to 50 percent in 1975, with economic growth declining to 4 percent—barely ahead of population growth—in the latter year.[22] More appealing at home, but nonetheless frightening to establishment elements there and abroad, were Echeverría's efforts to identify with and assume a leadership role in the Third World. That effort, too, appeared at times to be more rhetoric than action; for example, while proclaiming her solidarity with the OPEC nations—and occasionally voting with them in the United Nations—Mexico did not formally associate herself with the organization.

The emphasis on the Third World derived in part from conviction and in part from personal ambition. For some time, Echeverría endeavored to promote his own candidacy for the position of secretary-general of the United Nations. Included was what was reported as a twenty-million dollar, forty-four day air tour of fourteen nations. While that hope soon faded, he continued to court leftist leaders and developing nations, and displayed a tendency to see "imperialism" at every turn.

It was within that framework that Echeverría discussed Mexican democracy in his final annual message. After describing the turnout of almost eighteen million Mexicans in the presidential election as testimony that "the people once again overwhelmingly ratified their faith in democracy as a system of life for the Mexican people," the outgoing president declared: "We Mexicans have determined the forms of our coexistence: dialogue and democracy for the solution of our problems. No interventionist pressure, whether open or concealed, ever has been able or will be able to supplant our right to popular self-determination."[23]

So, it was not surprising that many Mexicans looked forward to December 1 and the possibilities of change. Echeverría conducted the process of selecting a successor in a characteristically personal manner, including describing the ideal candidate and having one of his ministers announce a list of seven ministerial "presidential possibilities." Chosen and subsequently elected was José López Portillo, the moderate finance minister.

López Portillo received from his predecessor an unhappy inheritance which can only be described as a critical situation. He has had to confront three major problems all likely to affect the immediate prospects of liberal democracy in Mexico.

First, he must develop his own personality and his own following.

Second, he must grapple with an exceedingly difficult economic situation: inflation, by official estimate, exceeding 20 percent annually; an unfavorable balance of payments which increased fourfold in three years (from $1,000,000,000 in 1973 to $3,643,000,000 in 1975); a 300 percent increase in the nation's external debt in a six-year period; high unemployment and underemployment; tourism adversely affected both by economic conditions and by postures assumed in world affairs; a bureaucracy of over 800,000 which had swollen to double its size in the previous six years; and a continuing rapid growth of population despite a modest decline in the rate of growth the past two years. In September 1976 the economic situation necessitated the first devaluation of the Mexican peso in a quarter of a century. There can be no doubt that the economic situation is bad and urgently in need of attention. The renewed prospect of large reserves of oil and gas affords the only real basis for optimism. Amid these economic problems, it is interesting to note that the president-elect declared that the fundamental challenge facing him was "to continue our development within democracy without loss of freedom and without impairment of justice."[24]

Third, he must contend with what appears to be Echeverría's desire to retain power and influence. One of his associates put it simply that Echeverría would "continue serving the country." More tangible evidence was the early and partisan selection of legislative candidates. Overwhelmingly those nominated and elected as deputies and senators were Echeverristas. Another significant signal was the acquisition by Echeverría and his associates of a television channel and thirty-seven newspapers—including *El Universal* and *El Sol de México* in the capital. That drive for influence through control of communications media could also be seen in the effort to assure control of *Excélsior* by having the workers' cooperative force out editor Julio Scherer. By mid-1977 reports were published indicating the López Portillo administration was taking steps to facilitate the return of editor Scherer and some 200 writers who had resigned from the paper when he had to leave. The premature disclosure of these moves apparently resulted in matters being left as they were.

During the final months of the outgoing administration, the government's television channel preceded the showing of the late movie with a nightly program dedicated to "President Echeverría's day." Finally, Echeverría pushed the establishment of a Center for Third World Studies in which he obviously intended to play a major role, and which would provide a potential platform for pronouncements on foreign policy. No doubt Echeverría would like to ensure that his major policies are continued and carried out, but these efforts also seem to reflect an unwillingness to surrender power. Whatever its purpose, the continuation of direct influence by the former president would be, if successful, a radical departure from Mexican political tradition.

Daniel Cosío Villegas anticipated this very problem and viewed it as quite serious. After López Portillo's nomination, Cosío expressed the view that the candidate was faced with "cohabitation with his fraternal friend and protector now President Luis Echeverría for a year and for the six following years with Citizen Luis Echeverría."[25] In an essay published posthumously, Cosío warned that "Echeverría will not yield voluntarily a whit of his present power." Characteristically, however, he closed with a ray of hope for the future because, "It must be admitted that a Mexican President has the necessary resources to demolish quickly and definitively the handsomest fellow that may get in his way."[26]

As if to answer this critic from beyond the grave—and avowedly to respond to those attacking him for his treatment of critics—Echeverría chose the occasion of the inauguration of the new building of El Colegio de México and the dedication of its library to the memory of Daniel Cosío Villegas to announce that he was arranging to have Don Daniel's remains removed to the Rotunda of the Illustrious.

López Portillo and the officials of his government have been very candid about the necessity of giving priority to the restoration of confidence and the amelioration of the economic situation. There is recognition that failure to do so could lead to even more serious social and political problems. It is reported that the Mexican president told Jimmy Carter privately that if conditions in Mexico did not improve visibly during his term, he might well prove to be the last of the post-revolutionary Mexican constitutional presidents. And he sounded a similar, if more muted, warning to the United States Congress when he remarked that "we do not want the present situation to make us lose our way by forcing us ... to extremes."[27]

As López Portillo seeks to restore confidence and to confront his legacy of unresolved problems, one must believe he is aware —as one sagacious politician observed—that "the Mexican State has an established political capacity much greater than that which is utilized."[28] Perhaps this essay might best close with the advice to a new president offered by novelist Carlos Cuevas in his 1976 political novel: "One has to be optimistic. And smile; always smile. Never feel defeated. And to perceive a blue horizon, regardless that there are some very large, black clouds. Moderation, Mr. President...."[29]

Notes

1. *Excélsior*, March 11, 1976, p. 18 A.
2. See Josefina Zoraida Vázquez, ed., *Dos revoluciones: México y los Estados Unidos* (Mexico City: Editorial Jus, Fomento Cultural Banamex, A.C., 1976).
3. The mestizo represented the blending of the European and the Indian while the Creole was a European born in the New World.
4. Jesús Reyes Heroles, *El liberalismo mexicano*, 3 vols. (Mexico City: Universidad Nacional Autónoma de México, 1961), vol. 3, p. xvii.
5. Charles A. Hale, "Scientific Politics and the Continuity of Liberalism in Mexico, 1867–1910," in *Dos revoluciones*, ed. Josefina Zoraida Vázquez, p. 148.
6. Rodney D. Anderson, *Outcasts in Their Own Land: Mexican Industrial Workers, 1906–1911* (Dekalb: Northern Illinois Press, 1976), pp. 323–325.
7. Frank Tannenbaum, *Peace by Revolution* (N.Y.: Columbia University Press, 1933), p. 166.

8. This analysis of the Constitution of 1917 is based on the following sources: Frank Tannenbaum, *Mexico: The Struggle for Peace and Bread* (N.Y.: Alfred A. Knopf, 1950), pp. 58–61; Victor V. Niemeyer, Jr., *Revolution at Querétaro: The Mexican Constitutional Convention of 1916–1917*, Institute of Latin American Studies, no. 33 (Austin: University of Texas Press, 1974).
9. Tannenbaum, *Mexico*, p. 61.
10. Ibid., p. 75.
11. See Daniel Cosío Villegas, *Ensayos y notas*, 2 vols. (Mexico City: Editorial Hermes, 1966), vol. 1, pp. 17–22; and the same author's "The Mexican Revolution Then and Now," in *Change in Latin America: The Mexican and Cuban Revolutions* (Lincoln: University of Nebraska Press, 1961), pp. 29, 33–34.
12. Cosío Villegas, "Mexico's Crisis," in *Is the Mexican Revolution Dead?* ed. S. R. Ross, 2nd ed. (Philadelphia: Temple University Press, 1975), pp. 73, 75, and 85–86.
13. Cosío Villegas, "The Mexican Revolution Then and Now," p. 37.
14. S. R. Ross, "Daniel Cosío Villegas y el ensayo político," in *Extremos de México: Homenaje a don Daniel Cosío Villegas*, Centro de Estudios Históricos, 14 (Mexico City: El Colegio de México, 1971), pp. 33–48.
15. Cosío Villegas's four *libritos* are *El sistema político mexicano*, 2nd ed. (1972), *El estilo personal de gobernar* (1974), *La sucesión presidencial* (1975), and *La sucesión: Desenlace y perspectivas* (1975). All were published by Editorial Joaquín Mortiz in Mexico City.
16. Manuel Moreno Sánchez, *La crisis política de México* (Mexico City: Editorial Extemporáneos, 1970), pp. 51–63 and 136–165.
17. Lorenzo Meyer, "Continuidades e innovaciones en la vida política mexicana del siglo xx. El antiguo y el nuevo régimen," *Foro Internacional* 16, no. 1 (1975): 57.
18. Gabriel A. Almond and Sidney Verba, *The Civic Culture* (Boston: Little, Brown and Co., 1963), p. 40; Joseph A. Kahl, *The Measurement of Modernism* (Austin: University of Texas Press, 1968), pp. 114–115.
19. Rafael Segovia, *La politización del niño mexicano*, Colección Centro de Estudios Internacionales, 14 (Mexico City: El Colegio de México, 1975), p. 96.
20. Cosío Villegas, *El sistema*, p. 8.
21. James Wilkie, "Pulling and Hauling Mexico's Land Reform," *Los Angeles Times*, December 26, 1976.
22. "Reversal of Policy: Latin America Opens the Door to Foreign Investment Again," *Business Week*, August 9, 1971.
23. "President Luis Echeverría's State of the Union Address, September 1, 1976," *The News* (Mexico City), September 2, 1976, Supplement, p. 3-B.
24. J. López Portillo, speech in Caracas, September 21, 1976, *Excélsior*, September 22, 1976, p. 1.

25. Cosío Villegas, *La sucesión*, p. 114.
26. Cosío Villegas, "Donde no estamos hoy," *Plural* 5, no. 10 (July 1976): 27.
27. John B. Oakes, "Portillo's [sic] Visit Shows Need for Changed Views," *Austin American Statesman*, March 3, 1977, p. F7.
28. Rafael Segovia, "Vocabulario político," *Vuelta* 3 (February 1977): 33–34.
29. Carlos Cuevas Paralizábal, *Sonríe, Señor Presidente* (Mexico City: Federación Editorial Mexicana, 1975), p. 93.

ROBERT E. WARD

9. Liberal Democracy in Japan

The question whether the prospects for liberal democracy in Japan are good is timely in both general and specific senses. In general there is widespread current concern with the problem that has come to be known as "the governability of democracies."[1] More specifically, the question of Japanese democracy has additional interest in the sense that the origins, periodization, and cultural setting of its democratic institutions, practices, and values differ in numerous important respects from those of their Euro-American counterparts. The obvious question is: "What difference does this make?" Allow me to elaborate briefly on these propositions.

Where the question of the governability of democracies in general is concerned, we are all sadly familiar with the underlying malaise: at the popular level a syndrome involving a strange and in part contradictory amalgam of mounting political apathy, suspicion, alienation, and outbursts of protest, occasionally violent; matched by progressive proliferation, rivalry, and assertiveness at the interest-group level and an enfeeblement of legitimacy, authority, and effectiveness on the part of democratic governments; and the entire process set in a cultural context characterized by the attrition of civility, a decline in the traditional moral and social standards, and a rising dissatisfaction with the working of the economy and the distribution of its products. This is not intended as a balanced presentation of the contemporary democratic scene. The situation is not as desperate as these shorthand characterizations imply, but reasonable men and women of all persuasions will readily agree that such problems are serious and menacing.

Professors Crozier and Huntington in their excellent contributions to the 1975 work entitled *The Crisis of Democracy*, prepared for the Trilateral Commission, share a view as to the nature of the proximate causes of these distressing phenomena. In Crozier's formulation:[2]

> The European political systems are overloaded with participants and demands, and they have increasing difficulty in mastering the very complexity which is the natural result of their economic growth and political development.
>
> The bureaucratic cohesiveness they have to sustain in order to maintain their capacity to decide and implement tends to foster irresponsibility and the breakdown of consensus, which increases in turn the difficulty of their task.

Huntington's view is similar:

> The vitality of democracy in the United States in the 1960s produced a substantial increase in governmental activity and a substantial decrease in governmental authority.[3]

A major theme running through both of these formulations is the explosion of popular participation in the political process that has occurred recently in both Western Europe and the United States and its conjunction with an access of a new moral fervor among increasing segments of an organized citizenry that is unwilling to accept compromised solutions to its political demands. The Crozier-Huntington message is clear: there is a finite limit to the capacity of democratic systems to absorb marked increases of popular participation and demands, at least in relatively brief periods of time. If exceeded, the system suffers an "overload" and falters—as it now seems to be doing.

One issue to which this paper will be directed arises from this general concern with the current ailments of democracy. Is the Crozier-Huntington analysis applicable to Japan and, if so, what does this import for the future?

The other major issue with which I shall be concerned relates to the unusual conditions in which liberal democracy developed in Japan and the consequences that follow therefrom. More specifically, I have in mind historical circumstances such as the following.

While there is doubt and controversy as to the most accurate way of characterizing the prime social, economic, and political attributes of Japanese society during the Tokugawa period (1603–1868), no well-informed scholar would think seriously of applying the terms "liberal" or "democratic" to it. Indeed, "centralized feudalism" is the label most frequently and authoritatively used. For most of the 265 years involved, the salient features of the Japanese society and polity were a rigorously enforced four-class system that segregated the population into samurai, farmer, artisan, and merchant groups, the whole capped by an hereditary emperor, shogun, and nobility; imperial rule in fiction and oligarchical rule in fact; class-based standards of access to public office and power; and a total lack of institutionalized popular participation in government at any level higher than the village.

It was not until the adoption and enforcement of the Meiji Constitution in 1889–90 that the structure and practice of governance in Japan were substantially altered, and that was less than ninety years ago—a single long lifetime. If, however, we are seeking the advent in Japan of political institutions and behavior that we today would recognize as both liberal and democratic, then we must come down to the period since 1946–47 when the present constitution was adopted. Liberal democracy in Japan is only slightly over thirty years old—not much past its majority.

Another way of putting this case is that Japan's "feudal" past is remarkably close in point of time to Japan's "democratic" present. Japanese experience has encompassed in a very brief time—at the most about ninety or at the least thirty years—a process of political change that elsewhere—to reach a comparable stage of institutional and behavioral development—has normally entailed several centuries of more gradual and organic evolution.

One must add to this unique compaction of the temporal dimension the further consideration that when Japan adopted the formal and behavioral trappings of a democratic polity in 1946–47, it did not do so of its own choice. It was pushed over the threshold by the arbitrary actions of an all-powerful foreign military occupation, whose American agents literally wrote the present constitution, translated it into rather awkward Japanese, and by a variety of none-too-subtle pressures enforced its adoption on a distinctly reluctant Japanese government.

How does one assess a phenomenon of this sort—liberal democracy in Japan—that seems, on the surface at least, totally to lack native roots; all of whose basic institutions and values have been borrowed importations from culturally and experientially alien sources; whose development in situ has been singularly brief; and whose origins were both involuntary and imposed?

One begins such an assessment by recognizing that so unqualified a characterization of the antecedents of liberal democracy in Japan is incomplete and seriously inadequate for diagnostic purposes. Far more than constitutions and formal political institutions must be taken into account. Without going into detail, it seems to me that the following considerations are also relevant and important.

First, there is considerable agreement among students of political development that durably democratic societies have certain functional prerequisites. Fairly widespread literacy is one such quality. In Japan's case our best estimate is that by the time of the Restoration of 1868 "somewhat more than forty per cent of all Japanese boys and about ten percent of Japanese girls were getting some kind of formal education outside of their homes."[4] These statistics are impressive, even by then-contemporary English and French standards.[5]

A second functional prerequisite of this sort is the existence of a professionally trained, rationally structured, and achievement-oriented bureaucracy. This was largely realized in Japan by the beginning of the eighteenth century.[6]

Against this background, political institutions that, first, provided a means of popular participation in the national political process through regular elections, second, gave to elected representatives some voice in the decision-making process, and third recognized and protected popular civil and political rights did not come into existence until the effectuation of the Meiji Constitution in 1890, and then only on carefully restricted terms. But from these scant and unpromising beginnings important developments sprang.

Political parties were first organized in the 1870s and gradually succeeded in expanding their role and influence until in the 1920 party cabinets became a normal aspect of what was then called parliamentary government in Japan. In fact, of course, partie never ruled prewar Japan, but they did become a sort of junior partner in a complex system of oligarchical rule. Since the 1870s these relatively populist and liberal elements in the Japanese polity have existed continuously and played a role of appreciable, if not critical, importance.

In the same period, moreover, the suffrage expanded continuously and rapidly so that, from an electorate of only 451,000 in 1890, universal manhood suffrage had been realized by 1925, a period of only thirty-five years. Through such means the populace gradually became habituated to at least the apparatus and the mechanics, if not the true and full substance, of a parliamentary political system. The press was also in many respects a lively and politically active force with significant democratic content and effect in prewar Japan, while the courts as well showed a surprising degree of independence and impartiality considering the political setting in which they operated.

The prewar historical record of liberal democracy in Japan is, therefore, mixed and indeterminate. The long-term trend until 1932 was definitely and continuously in the direction of more democratic form and content, but the democratic elements never gained the ascendancy. In 1932, moreover, this trend was temporarily reversed for a period of thirteen years.

The seven years of the American occupation of Japan (1945-52) in many ways deliberately built upon these pre-1932 foundations in an attempt to refashion the Japanese political system along liberal democratic lines. The tempo of occupation-stimulated change was explosive; and its scope was so sweeping that it left untouched no significant Japanese political, economic, or social institution. Its model and its goals were largely American in provenance with occasional borrowings from the British. More than an evangelistic fervor for democracy lay behind this massive American effort. Fundamentally American officials felt that democratization plus demilitarization were the most durable and reliable means of assuring that postwar Japan would remain peaceful and friendly to the interests and policies of the United States.

The combined results of these American efforts are often referred to as "the New Japan." That is quite appropriate since, with the exception of the early years of Meiji, there has been no period in Japanese history that has given rise to more numerous, more far-reaching, or potentially more seminal changes. It is far too easy, however, to overestimate the American role in effecting these changes, especially those in the political sphere. To be sure, Americans planned them in almost all instances; Americans cajoled or pressured a reluctant Japanese government into adopting them; and Americans supervised and frequently intervened in their implementation. But these undoubted facts must be seen in the light of certain Japanese influences that were also at work.

One should recall, first, the prewar history and antecedents of liberal democracy in Japan and accord due credit to the facts that there were available in postwar Japan significant elements of an experienced political leadership that had long been relatively democratic in tendency, that political parties had only to be resuscitated not created, and that professional politicians, the bureaucracy, and the citizenry were in a mechanical and operational sense long familiar with and habituated to the procedures of a parliamentary system of government.

It is also true that the Japanese people, while for the most part not active agents or instigators of this democratization, were at this particular point in their history uniquely predisposed to favor some form of political change. The country was faced with a completely unprecedented disaster—crushing defeat, unconditional surrender, and a foreign military occupation. Never before had Japan suffered defeat, let alone occupation. No people, unless it be Americans, were less prepared psychologically or by prior experience to cope with such an ordeal.

Circumstances such as these are calculated to produce widespread suffering and physical deprivation linked with a psychic distress that leads naturally to questions that in more normal or tolerable circumstances are seldom raised by major portions of a population: "Why have these disasters occurred?" "Who is responsible?" "How can we best get out of this mess and prevent its recurrence?" The assessment of guilt, or more accurately the assignment of blame, is an important and probably an inescapable part of the mass psychic catharsis that is involved. The all-too obvious and probable target for blame is the government and, if the circumstances are sufficiently bad, the entire political system. "If the old institutions are to blame, then they should b changed" is the sort of explicit or implicit reasoning that emerges in many quarters that normally would be ignorant of and indifferent to such issues.

This is what occurred in the early years of postwar Japan. Widespread physical and psychic distress produced attitudes of this sort on a scale sufficient to legitimize the types of changes that the occupation authorities, with the support and assistance of some Japanese, were pressing upon the Japanese government.

In this sense one may claim that this was perhaps Japan's most plastic moment, that the people, or at least a critical mass of the people, were favorably disposed toward changes in the old institutions and not averse to the refurbishing and reinvigorating of the institutions of party governance with which they were already partially familiar. Actually, so negative a formulation probably understates the real degree of popular support and positive approval for democratic innovations that existed in postwar Japan.

Moving beyond the occupation period, one should also keep several more recent developments in mind. In a rough sort of way people tend to evaluate both particular governments and entire political systems by their fruits, especially those that relate to such basic matters as standards of living, physical well-being, and the provision of national security. It is not irrelevant, therefore, that postwar Japanese governments in general have presided over explosive economic growth and mounting general prosperity unprecedented in Japanese experience, and probably in world history as well. At the same time, and however fortuitous the consequences, they have also held office during a period of unbroken peace so far as Japan's own foreign relations are concerned, even though the world in general during that time has been continuously beset by stress and strife.

Naturally, both the governments in power and the liberal democratic political system on which these governments are based gain considerable, if less than total, credit and acceptability from this record.

This retrospective assessment of the origins and development of liberal democracy in Japan suggests several conclusions that are relevant to our next concern—the present and future status of liberal democracy. First, liberal democratic institutions and beliefs are not new in Japan. They have foundations that extend back to at least the late seventeenth and early eighteenth centuries and institutionalized forms that date back to 1890. They have existed continuously since that date and, in a long-term sense, have developed progressively with only occasional setbacks. Second, the fact that the present institutional forms of liberal democracy in Japan are of American, not indigenous, authorship may not be of critical importance. There was a substantial and favorable disposition toward political change in postwar Japan and many felt that change should be along liberal democratic lines. When after 1952 Japan progressively regained a truly independent and sovereign status, the Japanese government, while altering materially a number of the occupation's reform programs, has shown no serious disposition to abandon any of the essential institutions or practices of a democratic society. Third, Japan's national experience since the end of the occupation in 1952 has confirmed in the popular mind the impression that this new system of government is on balance effective and productive of important values to an extent that argues for its acceptance if not for its enthusiastic support.

These findings lead to the further conclusion that the unique cultural and historical circumstances that have attended the advent of liberal democracy in Japan may in fact prove not to be critical in determining its future. The facts that it is now established, that it has gained general acceptance, that it is producing goods that its public values, and that it benefits from the inertia and the accumulation of supportive interests that accompany any established and functioning system are probably considerations of greater importance for the present and the future than are the adverse cultural and political circumstances of the past.

These conclusions, although relevant and important, assert a negative rather than a positive hypothesis about the future of liberal democracy in Japan. They simply argue that, in the light of offsetting factors, peculiarities of past experience will not necessarily have a determining effect on its survival. This is not to say that its future is either assured or free from other serious perils. Let us turn now to this question, which is to say, to a discussion of where Japan stands with respect to the threats to its governability that are apprehended by Professors Crozier and

Huntington in their treatments of Western European and American democratic institutions.

In his chapter on Japan in the Trilateral Commission's report entitled *The Crisis of Democracy* Professor Joji Watanuki concludes that "Japanese democracy is not in a serious crisis at the present moment."[7] In a semantic sense I agree with him. The turning point, the decisive moment is not yet—or, at least, not quite yet. But allow me to sketch some grounds for concern with so unadorned a conclusion.

A most significant factor in facilitating the general degree of popular acceptance accorded liberal democratic forms of government in postwar Japan has been the dramatic expansion of the economy and its products. The story is well known. Beginning in 1952 and accelerating with amazing rapidity after 1960, domestic production, consumption, and prosperity have boomed on a scale unprecedented among major states in recent times. Annual and real increases of 10 percent or more in gross national product became the rule not the exception. Despite sectoral inequities and particular grievances, the populace on the whole benefited materially in a quite spectacular fashion—real wages nearly doubled between 1960 and 1972. Under these circumstances politics was not for most people a subject of urgent concern, while a tendency to assign some measure of credit to the party in power and to the underlying political system was quite widespread. Prosperity bred political passivity, if not positive dedication to the system.

The oil crisis of October 1973 changed these happy economic circumstances. In Japan as elsewhere the ramifying effects of the energy crisis coincided with other factors to produce the worst recession in many years. The economic growth statistics went negative in 1974 by a factor of 1.8 percent. In 1975 GNP grew only by an estimated 1.5 percent, a far cry from the customary 10 percent. Even the official statistics indicated more than a million unemployed—a startling figure for a society long habituated to a job surplus—while companies struggled with increasing difficulty to retain on their payrolls another three million or so laborers who were actually surplus to their needs and capacities to support, but whom the practice of lifelong employment obligated them to retain.

Several years later it was not yet possible to say with assurance that the Japanese economy had overcome these difficulties and was on the road back. Predictions were mixed and even the optimistic were concluding that full recovery implied something like a 5 or 6 percent annual growth rate rather than the 9 or 10 percent of yesteryear.

Even relative economic deprivation of this sort is bound to have political consequences. There is no doubt that popular impatience with what is seen as the government's failure to deal effectively with this prolonged economic crisis is steadily mounting. Some ascribe it to inefficiency, some to corruption, some to the inequities and inherent weaknesses of a capitalist system. In any event the circumstances are adverse to the reputation and the fortunes of the party in power and, by extension, to the political system with which that party is strongly identified.

Taken by themselves and viewed solely as a product of several years of relative economic adversity, such developments might not be serious in a long-term sense. What several years of recession had wrought might quite plausibly be remedied by several years of prosperity. But there are added factors that must be taken into account—some economic, some political, some psychological. Let us look briefly at the more important ones.

First, on the economic side it seems probable that Japan had reached by 1973, somewhat later than all of her rivals, the end of a truly remarkable spurt of postwar economic growth. In the most analogous case, that of West Germany, the period of dramatic increases in gross national product had tapered off before the end of the 1960s and, even so, Germany by no means equaled the Japanese performance—Japan's GNP increased at an average annual rate of 9.6 percent over the sixteen years from 1953 to 1968 whereas the comparable German rate was 5.8 percent (measured at market prices). For the sake of comparison, the other major rates for that period were 5.0 for France, 3.5 for the United States, and 3.0 for the United Kingdom.[8] But in Japan's case the average annual increase remained very high, 9.6 percent, through 1972, and it fell only to 6.1 percent in 1973, the year of the oil crisis. In other major western states comparable points of decline in average growth rates had been reached far earlier—usually about 1965–67.

There are a number of persuasive reasons for assuming that this decline is of more than passing significance for the Japanese economy. For example, ready and relatively cheap access to the fruits of foreign, largely American, research and development have become a thing of the past. In recent years potential foreign licensers, fearing Japanese competition, have become much more hesitant to sell technology to the Japanese. When they do, joint ventures are apt to be required, or the price is higher, or restrictions limiting use to Japanese domestic markets only, or to Japan plus Southeast Asia, are apt to be attached. The Japanese are trying to compensate by increases in domestic R&D expenditures which reached 1.6 percent of GNP in 1972.[9] But even so, it will not be easy for Japan to compensate for the disadvantages involved in these new circumstances.

The problem of access to raw materials is, of course, especially crucial for Japan. Oil is only the most acute and dramatic of a series of such problems. More than 99 percent of Japan's oil is imported, and this oil in turn accounts for more than 80 percent of Japan's energy needs. In 1972 Japan was already taking about 10 percent of the world's total available oil supply and the prime minister was warning that this demand could be expected to triple in five or six years. Practically speaking, any such expectation was nonsensical. No country in Japan's circumstances at a time of generally increased needs and competition for limited supplies could realistically hope to purchase 20 to 30 percent of the world supply of a commodity as critical as oil. In less dramatic terms Japan was experiencing similar difficulties of access to adequate supplies of iron ore, copper, lumber, and a variety of other natural resources as well as foodstuffs. The terms of trade have been becoming more difficult from Japan's standpoint. The overall cost of the country's essential imports is escalating at a rate which is increasingly more difficult to compensate for by added volume or price rises on the export side.

A further factor of rising importance in this connection is the adverse shifts that have been occurring in the relation between productivity and wages. During the 1955–65 decade productivity rose at a faster pace than wages. This facilitated the steady increase in real wage rates that has been so notable in Japan. During the second half of the 1960s, however, wage increases began routinely to surpass productivity increases, an imbalance that was exacerbated by the drastic inflation of 1973–75 which witnessed increases for unionized labor on the order of 20 and 30 percent. While Japan's performance in this respect is still notably superior to that of the United States, Great Britain, West Germany, France, or Italy, its margin of competitive advantage is steadily eroding, and thus another of the factors that have underlain the sustained "economic miracle" of Japan's recent growth is suffering attrition.[10]

It is a hallmark of the modern condition that problems of this sort seldom occur alone. They come in complexly interrelated clusters. It should be no surprise, therefore, to discover that, as the productivity of labor begins to decline vis-à-vis wage increases, the pressures for shorter working hours begin to mount. That is exactly what has been happening since the mid-1960s. The six-day week is still normal in Japan and the actual number of working hours per week in manufacturing industries is two to six hours longer than in the West (4 to 13 percent).[11] Still, the trend is definitely downward, and more and more of the larger enterprises in particular are shifting to five- or five-and-a-half day weeks.

Noteworthy also are the rapidly mounting pressures in almost all quarters in Japan to catch up with the West in terms of social infrastructure. It is not generally realized how far Japan lags behind its peers in this aspect of modernization. Let us look at a few figures.[12]

	Japan	Italy	France	U.K.	West Germany	U.S.A.
Social insurance expenditure per person ($)	73.8	222.7	—	235.9	413.2	359.4
Percentage households with running water	17.1	—	53.2	98.2	83.3	89.7
Percentage households with sewage disposal	N.A., but very small	71	—	63	40	90
Urban park area per person (m²)	1.2	—	5.8	22.8	26.9	19.2
Telephone for home use per 1,000 persons	61.4	93.6	—	122.4	—	405.1

If relatively high rates of performance on indicators such as these are felt to be characteristic of modernized societies or partial measures of the good life, Japan shows to very poor advantage. Recently the Japanese people have become much more aware of this sort of lag in their society, and increasing political pressures are being brought to bear on the government to do something about it.

These few samples of the current state, problems, and prospects of the Japanese economy are not intended as a message of unrelieved gloom. They are simply the other side of the "economic miracle." All major social changes have their costs. Sometimes it takes a while to appreciate the size and particulars of the bill. That has been so in Japan. A people and a government, long dazzled by the immediate benefits of growth and unprecedented affluence, are now, as the period of explosive development draws to a close, beginning to contemplate the longer-term consequences and costs of the entire process, to assess these in the light of new values and their now far higher levels of expectation, and to ask hard questions and make insistent demands about the future—demands that will be difficult for any government to cope with satisfactorily.

It is no different elsewhere in the developed world. Japan has just reached this point at a slightly later date and from quite a different background than have her peers. She is now beginning to share fully in the problems and frustrations as well as in the accomplishments of modern societies.

Our particular concern at the moment, however, is to inquire how these economic developments and problems relate to the future of liberal democracy in Japan. The brief answer is that they constitute acute and serious challenges to the capacity of both government and the underlying political system to cope with a complex of problems that would in the best of circumstances be extraordinarily difficult but which now must be faced under circumstances of growing adversity and complexity. The question is, of course: "What are the prospects that government will be able to cope with them effectively?"

In answering such a question popular perceptions and attitudes are almost as important as actual governmental responses to the problems. How do the Japanese people perceive their government? How much credit does it enjoy in the popular mind?

In general all of the polling data agree that there is strong popular support for the 1947 Constitution and the basic democratic principles on which it rests. Such positive views are even more strongly held among the younger cohorts of the population—an encouraging sign for the future. But when one shifts attention from the system of government to the people who govern, a dramatic change of opinion is apparent. National political leaders from the prime minister to parliamentary and party leaders are generally held in low repute. The *Mainichi Newspaper*'s regular assessments of the degree of popular support for the five men who served as prime minister between 1950 and 1972 are representative. Their overall average was only 37 percent, with a range extending from a brief high of 54 to a low of 19 percent. During the same period the American popular support for the president averaged 57 percent—20 points higher—with a range of 87 to 23 percent. Only the premiers of France seem to have enjoyed less popularity.[13]

It is interesting also that these initial views appear to be shared even by Japanese schoolchildren. Massey's data show a steady decline in most indices of schoolchildren's confidence, liking, or approval of the personnel or performance of the Japanese national government, a decline that intensifies with advancing grade levels. The degree of this negative affect is unusual by international standards.

Linked with this predominantly negative assessment of the leading figures in their government—a view based on suspicions of inefficiency, dishonesty, irresponsibility, and corruption in office—one finds another development that promises problems for the future, namely an increase of popular participation in Japanese politics. In the abstract that increase is seen in sources such as the National Character Studies of the Institute of Statistical Mathematics conducted regularly every five years since 1953. For example, on five separate occasions between 1953 and 1973 a random and stratified sample of the Japanese people was asked if they agreed or disagreed with the statement that: "Some people say that if we get good political leaders, the best way to improve the country is for the people to leave everything to them, rather than for the people to discuss things among themselves." The extent of disagreement with this anti-participation sort of question rose steadily from 38 percent in 1953 to 51 percent in 1973. Significantly, among the 20–24-year-old cohort it rose from 54 percent to 67 percent.[14]

In the harder currency of political action, one sees this trend toward a greater degree of popular participation in the proliferation of "citizens' movements" that has been so salient an aspect of the recent Japanese scene, especially at the level of local and, in particular, municipal politics. This is doubtless in part a manifestation of the growing disrepute in which most of the formally organized political parties are held. Citizens' movements established on an ad hoc basis for the accomplishment of specific goals represent a way of bypassing the parties as a means of representing, aggregating, and pressing for popular interests and causes; they afford a more direct, focused, and participatory way of accomplishing those particular ends. Such movements, however—unless they end by becoming political parties themselves—pose serious problems for the viability of government; in a democratic system at least, government requires some regularized instrument for organizing popular support and consent and for representing public views and interests, an instrument that is possessed of more than a temporary and highly specific mandate from its constituents.

Finally, one cannot very well ignore a curious and worrisome aspect of the liberal democratic condition in present-day Japan, that is, the relative absence of a serious and professional literature of advocacy. The literary scene abounds in reasoned expositions and ardent polemics on behalf of every conceivable variant of socialism and communism. There is a small but serious group that supports the classic tenets of anarchism. There are even a few supporters of the sorts of views and causes that flourished in Japan during the late 1930s. But where are the advocates of liberal democracy? One seldom encounters in Japan a serious and committed philosophical or theoretical statement or analysis of the democratic persuasion in politics.

This is the more curious and worrisome because the Japanese by no means lack a capacity for passionate commitment to intellectual causes. It is doubtful if any modern society supports a larger number of journals of opinion, many with serious intellectual pretensions, and many dedicated to particular political and social views. Behind such journals lies a sizable body of scholarly monographs, but very few of these represent serious efforts by Japanese intellectuals to explicate in original terms or to adapt to Japanese circumstances the corpus of available democratic thought.

One can argue of course that the genius of the Japanese people is not philosophical and that they have not in modern times produced an innovative theoretical literature of great note in any nonscientific field. But even if that is so, the sheer disproportion between the scale of advocacy for liberal democracy and that for other political theories and causes is bound to be disturbing to many Western observers.

In the light of these considerations, several intermediate conclusions suggest themselves. First, the Japanese government faces a series of interlinked economic and social problems of a degree of difficulty and complexity that would severely test the utmost capacities of any modern democratic political system. Second, it does so under economic circumstances that are themselves increasingly unfavorable and constraining to the capacities of government to act effectively. Third, its hold on popular affection and support is already tenuous and attributable more to inertia and a lack of persuasive alternatives than to positive loyalty. At the same time, however, the public-opinion polls indicate general support for the basic institutions and values of the present democratic political system—as distinguished from the government in office—although a good deal of literary evidence suggests a greater variety of views among the intellectual class.

Against this rather ominous background, let us turn now to the performance characteristics of the Japanese government itself. In one sense the task is simplified by the fact that the present Liberal-Democratic Party or its immediate progenitors have been in power for practically all of the postwar period. In another sense the task of political prognosis is rendered far more uncertain and difficult by the almost complete lack of data as to the competency or probable performance of any alternative form of party government in Japan. There is nothing to go on but the records established by such parties in opposition or in coalition, and these leave a great deal to be desired.

What is one to say about the record of Liberal-Democratic Party governance in Japan? Most obvious is the fact that it has presided successfully over the re-emergence of the Japanese state from an unprecedented and disastrous defeat followed by almost seven years of foreign military occupation. Then, unless one considers the American occupation a sort of *deus ex machina* gifted with superhuman visions and skills, it is also true that the Liberal Democrats, their predecessors, and the governmental apparatus that they directed ultimately had more to do—albeit sometimes reluctantly and under duress—with fashioning the current forms, practices, and performance levels of liberal democracy than did any other agency foreign or domestic. Beyond this, they have presided over the period of greatest and most rewarding economic growth in the history of Japan. While not distributed with absolute equity among all sectors of the population, the benefits of this new-found affluence have been generally and massively felt and have resulted in real and large improvements in the national standards of health and physical well-being, of life expectancy, of diet, of access to education, of remunerative employment, of the physical amenities of life, of justice and personal security, and, on the whole, of effective and responsive government. These are most impressive accomplishments by any criterion and while, to be sure, the credit does not belong entirely to the party in power, it is certainly more than a coincidence that these changes occurred and were sustained and expanded solely under its régime.

There is, of course, another side to this coin and, for better or worse, it is the other side that seems to bulk ever larger in the public consciousness. The Liberal Democrats have not solved all of Japan's problems, and, in solving some, they have created others. A cruel inflation has beset Japan as well as many other nations; its effects, though diminishing, are still widely felt and earn the government criticism for not dealing with it sooner and more effectively. The hectic pace of urbanization in Japan has brought with it the full panoply of urban problems—overcrowding, poor and expensive housing, traffic congestion, long and exhausting travel to work, increasing prices and costs, pollution, anomie, and a spreading sense of social malaise, a decay of traditional morality, and widespread psychological stress or unease. The countryside has been stripped of population and the farms and villages—long the mainstay of traditional Japanese virtues and values—have been left to the elderly or to part-time labor. In such ways as these the quality of Japanese life has suffered as well as benefited, and the blame is inevitably assigned to the government, both for the incidence of such evils and for a prolonged failure to confront them squarely and do something effective about them.

Unfortunately, the political style of the Liberal-Democratic Party lends added credence and force to such critics. Not since Yoshida has it produced a leader possessed of even modest charisma and mass appeal. It is internally divided into warring factions, conspicuously competing for intraparty position and power, and obviously neglectful of their public image or responsibilities. It is corrupt in its electoral campaigns, strategies, and finances, although the degree of such corruption is not remarkable by real-world standards. Its relations with the leaders of big business are close and, in the popular view, strongly suspect of secret influence and dealings contrary to the public interest. Above all, it conveys an impression of indecisiveness, of lacking any firm policies or commitments beyond maintaining its hold on power, of endless delay and compromise in the hope that pressing problems will somehow solve themselves or simply disappear if given sufficient time. Finally, all of these traits are ceaselessly spotlighted, dramatized, and magnified for one of the world's most literate and attentive audiences—the Japanese public—by an almost uniformly critical press, by an intelligentsia largely committed to hostile political allegiances, and by a group of opposition parties noted for the uncompromising ardor of their public onslaughts on the party in power.

It is an unresolved question as to how long any government, whatever its record of past accomplishments, can withstand cumulating adversities and attacks on such a scale. Electorates are forgetful; in the long term, electorates are demanding, not grateful; above all, electorates are present- and future-oriented. The classic question "What have you done for me lately?" is all too characteristic of Japanese politics. This is documented by the recent electoral performance of the Liberal-Democratic Party. Prior to the thirty-first general election of 1967, the Liberal-Democratic Party or its predecessors had on the average captured 60.8 percent of the popular vote in postwar competition. In 1967 this shrank to 48.8 percent, in 1969 to 47.6 percent, in 1972 to 46.8 percent, and in 1976 to 41.8 percent. The decline has been gradual and, because of superior campaigning skills and additional independent support, it has not yet resulted in a proportional loss of power in the lower house of the Diet, where the LDP still controls about 51 percent of the seats. But the implications for the future are ominous for the party in power. Japan seems to be edging closer to the point at which either the parties will reconstitute themselves along somewhat different lines or a coalition government becomes necessary.

What does all this portend for the future of liberal democracy in Japan?—this combination of mounting public dissatisfactions, indecisive policy responses thereto, and the possible loss of power by the party that has ruled without interruption since the Second World War? One can only speculate. My own views are as follows.

The greatest strength of the Liberal-Democratic Party is the lack of any generally acceptable or attractive alternative to its continued rule. The opposition parties are hopelessly fragmented, quarrelsome, and lacking individually in the capacity to attract majority support at a general election. In some cases the extraordinarily doctrinaire quality of their commitments, in others very real and deep-seated elements of mutual distrust, rivalry, and real programmatic differences, make it highly improbable that the opposition parties collectively could piece together a viable coalition government.

Under these circumstances either the Liberal Democrats will retain a tenuous hold on power or, should they, in the course of the next few elections, lose control of either house of the National Diet (their hold on the upper house is also tenuous), it would seem probable that the first consequence would be an attempt to form a coalition government in which the Liberal Democrats would continue to play the dominant role but in association with either or both of the Democratic Socialist or Komeito parties. This in turn in the longer run might well give rise to a move to reconstitute major elements of this coalition, and perhaps some others as well, into a single new majority party.

The advent of either such a coalition or such a new party would doubtless assure the continuance in power of individuals and the persistence of policies not very different from those that presently prevail under the Liberal Democrats. Under these circumstances it is likely that the groups remaining in opposition would adopt two principal strategies.

First, at the national level the creation of a new ruling coalition that excluded them would have a strong adverse effect on the remaining opposition parties. There would be heightened incentives and new pressures inducing them to explore afresh the possibility of themselves coalescing into some more formidable political grouping. Since the principal elements involved would be the Japan Socialist and Communist parties, it is hard to see how the new group could be based on anything other than Marxist grounds. In such a combination it also seems probable that the communist tactics of gradualism, nationalism, and change achieved by peaceful, parliamentary means would prevail over the more doctrinaire and less compromising stands of the dominant left wing in the Japanese Socialist Party. Under such circumstances the erstwhile Socialist Party elements could look forward with some certainty to a dwindling role in the councils of such a new combined opposition party.

Second, the remaining opposition forces, however constituted, would surely explore and develop further the potentialities of a strategy of political struggle at the local as well as at the national level. It is not generally realized that by 1975 over 20 percent of Japan's 642 mayoral positions and 10 of the 47 prefectural governorships were held by so-called progressive candidates, i.e., those elected with primary support from either or both of the Japan Socialist and Communist parties. The jurisdictions involved included Tokyo, Osaka, Kyoto, Yokohama, Nagoya, Kobe, and Kawasaki—practically all of the nation's major cities. Those régimes, while not without their problems, have proven quite resilient and have gained strong support for their relative honesty, their openness, and their solicitude for the citizenry and for local interests and problems. The resulting situation is very reminiscent of the Italian experience in recent years and the general strategy involved would seem to be similar. If your party is debarred, at least temporarily, from making significant progress at the level of national politics, then shift a portion of your efforts to the local scene; cultivate a firm base there, especially in the largest metropolitan areas; and in so doing strive to disarm popular suspicions and to acquire new followers who may ultimately support you at the national as well as the local level.

If this is a reasonable scenario for Japan's near political future, what does it portend for the fate of liberal democracy in Japan?

Unfortunately, it argues for more of the same. Developments along the lines that seem most probable are not calculated to provide a fresh infusion of leadership or policy into the current political scene. By themselves, they solve none of the underlying problems. Either an essentially unchanged Liberal-Democratic Party clings to power or, by bringing new elements and opinions from other parties into coalition, it simply multiplies the occasions for dissensus and the obstacles to decisive policy formation and action.

Under these circumstances it seems probable that what Messrs. Crozier and Huntington are pleased to call "the crisis of democracy" will not in Japan's case be brief.

There seems to be small prospect that the efficacy or the authority of governance at the national level will increase appreciably in view of its internal liabilities and the unprecedented complexity and difficulty of the domestic and international problems that confront it. On the other hand, there seems every probability that public demands and dissatisfactions will gradually mount, both because of objective circumstances and because the media, the intelligentsia, and the opposition parties will carefully cultivate them. These are conditions that make probable continuing increases in popular participation in politics through the expansion of what the Japanese call "citizens' movements" (*jūmin undō*). Under such circumstances the possibilities of an intensifying and interactive spiral of governmental lag and ineffectuality, coupled with rising popular participation and demands, the whole leading to some sort of denouement adverse to the interests of liberal democracy, are unhappily evident.

Against such a scenario one can posit only arguments and considerations that, while powerful, are even more difficult to assess in probabilistic terms. They would include such things as the patience, discipline, and good sense of a people who are certainly among the world's most notable in these respects; the undoubted talents and truly remarkable record of a system of government that, however lacking in personalized leadership and political flair, has successfully met and coped with all major challenges to date; the changing and basically unpredictable effects on domestic politics of external developments on the international scene; and finally, that ultimate unknown, the capacity of the system to respond along inventive and innovative lines when confronted with truly serious threats.

These countervailing forces should not be undervalued. There are good reasons for optimism about the prospects of liberal democracy in Japan, but one must in honesty admit that accepting them as persuasive is as much an act of faith as the product of dispassionate scholarly analysis.

Notes

1. See, for example, Michel Crozier, Samuel P. Huntington, and Joji Watanuki, *The Crisis of Democracy* (New York: New York University Press for the Trilateral Commission, 1975), or the Fall 1975 issue (no. 41) of *The Public Interest*, which was devoted to the same subject.
2. Crozier et al., *Crisis of Democracy*, p. 12.
3. Ibid., p. 64.
4. R. P. Dore, *Education in Tokugawa, Japan* (Berkeley: University of California Press, 1965), p. 254.
5. Ibid., p. 291.
6. John W. Hall, "Feudalism in Japan—a Reassessment," *Comparative Studies in Society and History* 5, no. 1 (October 1962): 47–48.
7. *Crisis of Democracy*, p. 152.
8. OECD, *National Accounts Statistics, 1950–1968* (Paris, 1970), pp. 366–415.
9. This is still well below the rates in Japan's principal competitors—2.6 percent in the United States, 3.0 percent in the USSR, 2.0 percent in

West Germany, 2.1 percent in the United Kingdom, and 1.7 percent in France (all in 1971). Ed McGaffigan and Paul Langer, *Science and Technology in Japan—a Brief Analytic Survey*, a report for Defense Advanced Research Projects Agency (R-1736-ARPA, November 1975) by Rand, pp. 4–5 and 51.
10. Japan Institute of International Affairs, *White Papers of Japan, 1972–73* (Tokyo, 1974), pp. 114–115.
11. Ibid., p. 116.
12. Ibid., pp. 104–105.
13. Joseph A. Massey, "The Missing Leader: Japanese Youths' View of Political Authority," *American Political Science Review* 69 (1975): 38.
14. Quoted in Herbert Passin, "Changing Values: Work and Growth in Japan," *Asian Survey* 15, no. 10 (October 1975): 837.

10. Liberal Democracy in Israel

The existence of Israel is a fact of life from which the world cannot escape. It is a permanent attribute of the history of mankind. Nothing strengthens it more than the effort to suppress it. The capacity to translate external hostility into inner strength is as old as Israel itself. This indeed was the first judgment ever passed by a foreign potentate about ancient Israel: the more this people is afflicted, the greater and the stronger does it become.

For three thousand years, the Jewish people has marched across history, bearing its message of order and progress in the universal design. Its road falls and rises between deep valleys of grief and high peaks of fulfillment. But nothing since its original redemption from servitude thousands of years ago can compare in exaltation with its recent ascent. The establishment of a sovereign, democratic republic in 1948 marks a turning point in that historic journey. For many centuries, after all, Jewish history consisted very largely of what Jews suffered, resisted, endured, overcame; but not of what Jews themselves fashioned, created, and determined. All of a sudden, from that summer day onwards, Jewish decisions could levy taxes, build a society, assemble kinsmen, and compel the reaction of others near and far. Destiny had given this people not only a pride of equality within the international concert, but also a renewed sense of its collective creativity. From that point forward, the Jewish people had to some degree become not simply the victim, but the architect and the agent of its own history. Its career had entered upon a new phase of autonomy.

It is, however, neither realistic nor rewarding to contemplate the domestic predicaments of liberal democracy in Israel without reference to the unique setting in which that drama is enacted. Alas, the setting is still one of conflict. There is nothing in modern international relations quite like the Arab-Israeli dispute. It is not like the conflict between India and Pakistan about boundaries, between Turkey and Greece about the fate of an eastern Mediterranean island, between the United States and the Soviet Union about spheres of influence or the respective merits of their social systems, or between China and Russia concerning the form and direction to be given to a common ideology. For in all of those conflicts, no matter how virulent and explosive, there is after all an agreed principle, a common point of departure. The agreed principle is, of course, the statehood of the parties, their peoplehood, their juridical status. Russia and China and America and Turkey and Greece and Pakistan and India have no doubt whatever of each other's sovereign capacity, and it is from the starting point of respect for that principle that they contend and maneuver for interest and advantage. The Arab-Israeli dispute is one of those rare instances in which one of the parties frankly takes its stand on the total denial of the very legitimacy of the other, of its statehood, of its sovereignty, of its very place in history and in the world. It is this that gives to the Middle Eastern conflict its implacable character. And that is why, even after years of ostensible tranquility, it has erupted again and again into flames. It is fundamentally a conflict between historic images, passionately and sincerely held on each side. We are here face to face with a conflict between two contradictory visions of the Middle East in history.

On the one hand, there is an Arab vision that sees the Middle East as the Arab world, so that everything in it that is not Arab or Moslem tends to be reflected in the Arab imagination as unauthentic, inorganic, alien, external, artificial—and being artificial, destined one day to be covered over by the shifting desert sands. It is a monolithic, unifying vision of the Middle East. It does not make provision for sovereignty or independence for anyone else. In the name of this unifying, monolithic vision of the Middle East, an attempt is made to smooth—to iron out—all the wrinkles of diversity. This lies at the root of the attempt to eliminate by violence the Kurdish National Movement in Iraq. Another expression of it is the attempt to blot out the specific Christian vocation of Lebanon. And if the same has not been done to Israel's Jewish particularity, it is only because we are strong. Let there be no illusion: if we were not strong, there would be happening to Jews in Israel today that which so tragically happened to the Christians in Lebanon.

Against this conception of the Middle East as a region whose history and meaning are largely exhausted by Islam and Arab nationalism, we suggest a different conception, a truer one, one that rests upon an appreciation of comparative justice. We see our region enriched in the spectacle of its diversity. It is not the home or the arena or the cradle of Islam and Arab nationalism alone. The older Middle Eastern civilizations of Judaism and Christianity are a permanent part of its historic memory and cannot be eliminated from its future. We therefore reject as heresy the contention that an Israeli society is somehow artificial, inorganic, external to the Middle East. Israel is a part of the Middle East—of its past glory, of its present reality, of its future destiny. This then is our central truth: there has not been, there is not, and there can never be a Middle East without the sovereign state of Israel at the very heart and center of its life. In our vision, the Middle East is not a monolith of one color, but a tapestry of many colors of which the salient thread was woven by Jewish experience thousands of years ago.

In proclaiming this as our axiom, we must be rigidly formal in the historic and juridical sense. Israel's separate Jewish statehood is not something to be argued about, but something to be proclaimed. We must never ask anybody to recognize Israel's right to exist, because Israel's right to exist is independent of anybody's recognition of it. When the world comes to analyze the international reality, it must be understood that some propositions are axiomatic. In saying this, we do no injury to Arab nationalism. In this era of its triumph, the Arab nation is 100,000,000 strong, 3 percent of the human race. Yes, 3 percent of the human race, but 16 percent of the votes in the United Nations. And there the political reality is even more striking, for the 16 percent represent only the inner circle of Arab states. If one adds the outer circle of Moslem solidarity and of communist support, the Arab voting strength comes closer to 50 percent. Three percent of the human race, but 15 percent of the inhabited land surface of the globe. Three percent of the human race, but 60 percent of the world's oil reserve. Three percent of the human race, but a vast proportion of the unemployed currency reserves that flow in and out of the international monetary system. And with all this glut of privilege and advantage, the Arabs present themselves to the world as the underdogs, the aggrieved victims of historic destiny. With all respect, we do not regard them as the underdogs at all. History has not done badly for Arab nationalism in this generation. No other people has gained with such little sacrifice so large a measure of its total ambition in so short a time. And when, out of this abundance of resources and opportunities, it casts a grudging and rancorous eye on Israel's small and parched domain of sovereignty, is it not the story of Naboth's vineyard all over again? But Israel is not Naboth and is not likely to die or to disappear or to be swallowed up into something else, or to renounce its name or its flag or its faith or its tongue or its Jewish particularity. It will do none of these things.

Now this conviction of Israel's Jewish particularity causes trouble in some places. I know not why it should. Whenever the flag of any other new nation goes up on its mast—in Oman or Bahrain or Qatar or Belize or Equatorial Guinea or the Maldive Islands— you can hear the chorus of applause throughout the liberal world, acclaiming another stage in the onward progress of national freedom. It is only when it happens to be Jewish national freedom that we hear murmurings about exclusivism, parochialism, chauvinism. It appears that that quality of love of country and devotion to heritage, which men call patriotism when they possess it themselves, is called chauvinism when they observe it in others. Israel is nothing but the decision of the Jewish people to be itself, and to live renewed within its own memories, within its own patrimony, within its own social visions, within its own tongue and faith, and to make the special shape of its mind its contribution to the universal human legacy.

This then is the second truth that rests upon a comparative justice. If the world can get used to the existence of twenty Arab states, it had better get used to the existence of one Jewish state as well. It is the least debt that history owes us, for this planet passed from barbarism to civilization at that moment in antiquity when it was touched in Israel by the lucidity of the Hebrew mind. That is why it is a salutary thought and experience throughout the democratic world that equates anti-Semitism with anti-Zionism. There is no difference at all. Classical anti-Semitism proclaimed the equality of rights for all individuals within society—unless they happen to be Jews. Anti-Zionism proclaims the right of every state, every recognizable national unit in the world, to its own domain of sovereign freedom—unless it happens to be a Jewish domain of freedom. Mark well that the unifying principle here is the principle of discrimination. All that has happened is that the discriminatory principle has been transferred from the realm of individual rights to the domain of collective identity.

Therefore, my conclusion is that the conflict is rooted in historic memories. It is an ideological conflict very hard to assimilate to the general pattern of international disputes. It must be viewed as a virtually unique event in its own special historical setting. At this time, the special setting seems to be one of alleviated tension. In recent years the Arab-Israeli conflict has not been in the central focus of regional and international preoccupation. There has been a diplomatic lull since September, 1975, when the Egyptian-Israeli disengagement agreement was concluded. But I must warn everyone who wishes well to the Middle East not to rely upon the permanence of this lull. It is neither enduring nor profound. Insofar as there is a period of relative quiescence, it rests upon realities outside the matrix of Middle Eastern-Israeli relations. It derives in part from the Lebanese drama and in part from the American reality.

First the Lebanese drama. As we look across the border, we become intensely aware of its human dimensions—more than 40,000 dead in three years. That is more than five times the total sacrifice that Israel has had to bear in all of its four wars and in the frontier tensions in between. For our part, we know how heavy the weight of that anguish has been. Think of that multiplied by five and spread not across three decades but over thirty months; the gravity of Lebanon's travail is measured by that intensity.

One lesson to be drawn from that experience is that we do no live in a world organized for initiative, intervention, responsibility. The slaughter went on week by week and month by month, with no serious attempt by the powers or international agencies even to concert a stable cease-fire. Not a hand was raised in reinforcement, and few voices in consolation. As a result of the Vietnam trauma and the weakness of the United Nations, those involved in regional conflicts must understand that they are very largely alone, and that the outcome will be determined by the indigenous balance of strength on the ground.

Another lesson lies in the fragility of external assurances, declarations, and guarantees. Was not Lebanon, perhaps more than any other state in the eastern Mediterranean, theoretically defended by a protective rhetoric—from Paris, from Rome, from the western world—Lebanon, the special charge and protégé of the Christian West? And yet in the ordeal and the trial, this rhetoric melted away into the empty air. When Israel hears it proposed that it should regard external declarations, guarantees, statements, as a substitute for a viable balance of strength on the ground, it must remember the Lebanese fate.

Another lesson lies in the daily manifestation on our northern frontier of a humane vocation, a spectacle enacted between the martyred villagers who cross over day by day, and the Israelis who afford them care and succor, health and social services. I know not how long that policy will last or whether any gratitude will ensue, but it seems to us, throughout the whole of our democracy, to be a valid and a liberal policy, and a purposeful investment in our common human fate.

The other factor that has brought about a relative quiescence in the Middle East is the American factor. Perhaps the Americans do not always understand that when their diplomacy is immobile, the immobility becomes contagious. It certainly commands the Middle East. There is no substitute for the American role in serving as a focus for dialogue and encounter in the Middle East. Everybody else has ruled himself out. The Soviet Union has ruled itself out by its breaking of relations with Israel and the consequent imbalance of its diplomatic structure in the Middle East. The United Nations has ruled itself out by the imbalance in its composition as well as by the virulent extremism of some of its recent majority resolutions. Europe rules itself out by its own decision to renounce its traditional strategic and political role and devote itself exclusively to economic recovery and the construction of a community. That leaves the United States alone in the field in simultaneous and parallel communication with the parties on both sides of the conflict in a general atmosphere of mutual confidence. Now this parallelism of contact and dialogue has been skillfully used. But as a result of conditions that obtained in America for two years or more, at least as familiar to you as to me, the American presence has been in abeyance.

But neither the Lebanese war nor the factors that brought about the suspension of American initiative were permanent factors. The Carter administration has resumed an American initiative in the region, and the Lebanese war is ending. Israelis would do well not to draw too immediate an optimism from the renewal of the American presence, and to draw no consolation at all from the internecine character of Arab relations. These are very easily and very quickly transcended. The history of the Middle East in the past few decades tells us something about the speed and the volatility with which coalitions arise, with which they fall, and with which new combinations develop. There is often a transition from the embrace to the dagger, from hostility to reconciliation, almost overnight. Therefore, we should not regard these two factors as in any sense alleviating, or even postponing, the necessity for a serious exploration of the vistas of an Arab-Israeli peace.

Peace is the issue, not only for the survival of a liberal and democratic Israel but for the survival of Israel itself. The conflict continues not because of an Israeli refusal to evacuate territory, but because of an Arab difficulty about making peace. There is a consensus, indeed there is a policy, in Israel for massive territorial concessions in the framework of peace. Is there yet a consensus throughout the Arab world in favor of that revolutionary transition from hostility to regional cooperation? Implicit in the abandonment of hostility is the abandonment of the old attitudes and slogans and historic visions. It is a revolutionary transition. It may take some time for it to be realized. Yet I believe that change may be under way. Whereas 1976 was a year of immobilism, 1977 was a year of increasing political activism, and 1978–79 years of re newed initiatives on both sides. Everything comes to an end sometime, and the circumstances that contributed to American passivity as well as the regional conditions that have shifted the focus away from Israel are inevitably coming to an end.

One of the questions that haunts the Israeli democracy is this question of the regional balance. Now what is the trouble? The trouble is, of course, that the assets that the Arabs can put on their scale in the balance are very concrete, tangible, visible. You can see them on the map: the territory, the population, the money, the oil, the multiplicity of states, the consequent capacity for pressure on the scales of international strategy. What is it that Israel can put on its side of the scale in order to create a viable equilibrium? It is manifest that in territory, population, money, oil, multiplicity of states—in these not only is there no equivalence between ourselves and our neighbors, there is no prospect that this imbalance will ever be corrected. Yet there are qualities which, if they can be identified and put to work, have proved themselves capable in the past three decades of securing a balance of survival, security, and creativity. But it is very hard to put them on the map or on the balance sheet. How does one portray in terms so concrete and precise such qualities as vitality, social cohesion, democratic responsibility, scientific dynamism, technological resourcefulness, a capacity for sacrificing the present in the name of the future, and of course the strong links of worldwide Jewish solidarity. But unless you believe that matter and quantity can sometimes be transcended by mind and quality—unless you believe this, you have no explanation for Israel's career or experience since 1948, indeed little explanation for the persistence of the Jewish people across the centuries, always outnumbered by vast empires that exceeded it in military strength and economic power, in the sophistication and refinement of their arts. But so many of those empires have crumbled in ruin, while the small voice of Israel comes down across the centuries with undiminished strength.

Certainly, the most potent influence in stabilizing and sustaining the Israeli democracy is the special relation between Israel and America, developed and nurtured within the context of our common fidelity to the cause of liberal democracy. Judging by the declarations and speeches on both sides of this partnership, America and Israel are intensely preoccupied with each other. It is one of the most surprising associations in modern international life. What makes it incongruous at first sight is, of course, the enormous disparity between the size, the power, and the influence of the parties. But apart from the disparity in size, everything else is in harmony: harmony of memory, harmony of values, and a deep, underlying, and universally recognized harmony of interests.

Harmony of memories. What is it after all that Israel means to America and America to Israel? Israel to America means first the cradle in which its own model values were born. Israel means to America the memory or the premonition of its own past, the days when it was morning and felt good to be alive, the days when pioneers and immigrants two hundred years ago converged on a new continent to build a new civilization. So too in this century, out of an anomalous variety of origins and backgrounds, in Israel, has a similar drama been enacted—a drama of immigrants and pioneers constituting a new union and a new culture out of an even wider variety—almost to the point of anarchy—of origins, of cultures, of economic outlooks, and of social visions. And Israel means to America a communication of democracy, a working example of it, the more important to America because she does not have many Israels at her side. There are not many countries that vindicate democracy by their exertion and by their example.

A former American diplomat, Ambassador Moynihan, has said that there are only thirty-one democracies in the world. He didn't say exactly who they were—an unusual exercise of reticence and discretion on his part. It might perhaps have been wise to give some of them the benefit of the doubt. But let it be understood that parliamentary liberal democracy is a minority cause. It is embattled. It is not in a state of advancement, but it surges and recedes, and the balance of force is very delicate. In the very recent past we have seen the democratic cause suffer a vast defeat in the world's largest democracy in India, and then recover from it. Democracy has gained ground in the Mediterranean: in Greece, in Portugal, and in Spain. The central disappointment for the adherents of parliamentary democracy is the fact that most of the developing nations, after making an initial attempt to apply its

Liberal Democracy in Israel 193

procedures and principles, have generally abandoned parliamentary liberal democracy in favor of charismatic presidencies with an increasingly centralized form of government and of authority.

Israel's democratic structure can be taken for granted. It arises from the circumstances of its history, from the immense individualism of its people—a people that has never bowed the knee to despotism, a people that has got into much trouble throughout the centuries by an almost excessive skepticism about the claims of authority. Indeed there are many friends of democracy who are disquieted by what they seem to think is an excessive application of democratic freedom in Israel—a vast contentiousness. This should not cause concern. Underneath the external surface of turbulence, there are some unifying features that make for coherence. But it is true that Israeli democracy is commanded by a very great skepticism about authority. I often feel that it was very wise on the part of our ancestor, Moses, to obtain divine ratification for the Decalogue. If the Israelites could be made to believe that the Ten Commandments were written by the Almighty, there was some chance that they would pay attention to them. If they merely believed that they had been written by another Israelite, they would at best have become the basis for argument, amendment, and counter-proposal.

The strains upon parliamentary democracy in Israel are similar to those in many other countries, but they are very much enlarged by the variety of origins. After all, the population is composed of two main elements within the Jewish sector: those who came bearing with them the industrial and the scientific revolutions, and those who came from countries in which the industrial revolution and the French revolution and the scientific revolution had had no impact, in which technology and social democracy had been either unknown or unavailable to the Jewish communities who were cut off from the application of them. But what we call the social gap within Israeli democracy is not created by Israel. It is created by Diaspora history, that history which upon the Jews of Yemen and North Africa had one set of influences, and upon those emigrating from eastern and central Europe and the West another set of influences. And thus the gap was imported ready-made into Israel. All one can say about the Israeli process is that it tends to narrow the gap—through the educational system; through the unifying effects of a linguistic, cultural, and religious tradition; through the exigencies of a military service which performs a socially unifying role beyond its immediate functional purpose; and through a sense of belonging to that small, embattled, but solid group of liberal democratic nations.

There is, of course, the economic dilemma: how within a free-market society to impose even temporary measures of austerity? I cannot say we have resolved that dilemma, but I can say we are grappling with it. In my view it will be the events in the economic arena that will decide both the fate of Israeli democracy and perhaps ultimately the Arab-Israeli dispute.

I knew that Israel was not likely to win many medals at the Montreal Olympic Games. So I looked around for some respects in which we could hope to win some world record. Is there anything at which Israel is better than others? I think we are better than others in understanding and combatting international terrorism. Israel bears the burden of the attack of terrorism, as it bears the burden of freedom's cause against the dangers of aggression and tyranny in the Middle East. Many people talk about resistance to tyranny, aggression, terrorism. But there is one nation—Israel—that is the carrier of a vast burden in that resistance.

According to the *United Nations Yearbook*, we are better than anybody else at living long. Israel is now first or second in the list of longevity and expectation of life. I find this very surprising in the light of our politics, our climate, and our telephone system. And then just a couple of years ago we were told that, as a result of a free competition, we now held the record in feminine beauty. Anyone who has gone around our country with his eyes open in recent years need not be surprised at that.

But there is another record which we would easily renounce. We hold the record for a deficit in the balance of payments. Not only a per capita, average record, but an absolute record. It is a rare thing indeed for any political society, however small or great, to have a deficit in the balance of payments of 4 billion dollars a year! Now if that is not to bring our democracy unto challenge, if it is not to lead either to a weakening of defense, or to social disorder or turbulence, or to a collapse of the welfare-state system, to disillusion—I won't say to hunger and dearth—this gap must be bridged. And it is at present bridged by American aid, which makes partial provision for the military burden (2.3 billion dollars a year). But on the occasion of the American bicentennial, I read the Declaration of Independence carefully, and I found there no engagement whatever to make 2.5 billion dollars a year available to Israel until the end of time.

Thus the urgency of the economic predicament is extreme. It is indeed the key to the future of liberal democracy in all the developing world. Across Asia and Africa and parts of the American continent, we have seen nations emerge into the exhilaration of freedom. The flags and the stamps and the parliaments and the constitutions and the embassies—all the outer symbols of institutional freedom excite the dignity of these peoples and elevate their spirit. This is a moving spectacle. But the flags are not enough: behind all the emblems of institutional equality, the old inequalities continue, unaffected by the transition from tutelage to independence, sometimes even aggravated by that very transition. Men awaken to learn that they can be free in every institutional sense, and yet lose the essence of their freedom in the throes of famine and hunger and want. For the old squalor, the old illiteracy, the old backwardness, the old exploitation very often linger on behind the glittering externalities of sovereign independence. National independence has not gone hand in hand with a similar progress toward equality in the economic and social and cultural sphere. It is in the gap of disillusion between institutional liberation and economic servitude that liberal democracy has fallen into decline.

But Israel, despite this deficit, does have something to show to other developing nations—in two respects. First of all, it has shown a capacity to emerge quickly from a subsistence economy into one solidly based on a technological, scientific infrastructure. Our exports in 1948 were $48,000,000; they now exceed $4,000,000,000. That is a rate of growth in exportable productivity for which I do not think there are any parallels in modern economic history. Second, we have tried to prove that the scientific revolution is not the monopoly of a few advanced nations in the western and northern part of the globe. Any country, however small, that develops its own indigenous scientific tradition can hope to enter the new world of opportunity opened up by scientific research and its technological application. The spectacle of a small country in western Asia of 3,000,000 souls, with its research institutes, with its capacity to mend jet planes or advanced ships, with its reactors, with its accelerators, with its integration into the world's scientific community, should sustain the pride (and perhaps challenge the effort) of other small countries, which need not feel themselves excluded from this inheritance.

Subject then to a disciplined effort to overcome the economic tensions and to maintain a democratic form of government even within the circle of regional tension, Israel can say that the prospects for its democratic stability are strong. Of course, they would become stronger in peace, which would remove some of the tensions within Israeli society, between citizens of Jewish and of Arab origin. There is no use blinking the fact that these tensions do exist. One must bear in mind that Israel is a dual state, embracing both Arab and Jewish peoples. Given the circumstances of its birth and growth, and the environing pressures of its geographical and political setting, it is not surprising that there should be tensions between its Arab and its Jewish citizens.

It is important to say, however, that those tensions are not matters of law or administration, but of psychology and political participation. The problem is not one of rights, because on the level of rights, everything is satisfactory. There is no such thing as a Jew or an Arab in the eyes of the court. There is only a citizen, his rights, and his obligations. And therefore the executive branch cannot with impunity carry out any action of coercion or restraint against Arabs that could not be applied against Jews. But it would be wrong to say that there isn't a problem. There is a psychological problem. There is also a problem beginning some thirty year ago. The Jewish and the Arab communities were at different level: in their educational and social services. We can say that the gap has been narrowed; it would be quite wrong to say that it ha been transcended. And there are of course the pervasive effect of the conflict upon the minds of the Arab citizens of Israel. A Israeli Arab must awaken every morning to say, "My people is a war with my state." That is a predicament. Within the framewor of that predicament, I think a great deal has been achieved to insure a civic tranquility. It would be unrealistic to say there will be a perfect harmony until peace with our neighboring world is achieved, but it is quite realistic to say that Israel, despite its travail, is a liberal democratic state and will remain so. One does not need a very extensive poll to predict that a decade from now, Israel—whatever its fortune and whatever its mood—will face that mood and that fortune within the framework of a liberal, democratic ethic.

For this the United States can take a measure of credit because of the consistency with which it has supported the balance of strength in the Middle East. In the past few years, America has supplied to Israel more military support than in all the previous twenty-five years put together, more economic support, more assistance in diplomatic attempts at conciliation, and a more frequent defense of her basic juridical interests, very often in conditions of solitude. But this proceeds, in my judgment, from a national consensus in the United States. It is the result of a policy pursued by both the administration and the Congress, and by both political parties, with a great mutual stimulation of each by the other.

The present stage in American policy begins in 1967 with the enunciation by President Johnson of two principles: first, that there should be no return to the previous explosiveness; and, second, that there should be a balance of power in the area, a declaration that involved the attempt by the United States to overcome its inhibitions about defensive arms. Those foundations have been maintained by various administrations ever since.

I do not mean by this that America and Israel have always agreed with each other. If America were always to agree with Israel, it would have to be right 100 percent of the time. And we have never expected such total rectitude from anybody. When we signed the Syrian-Israeli disengagement agreement in Jerusalem a few years ago, Secretary Kissinger invited me to explain what I meant by "objectivity" when I suggested that as the theme of our relations. I had no answer then other than the one I have now: by "objectivity" of course I mean the uncritical acceptance of all my views. I do not believe that anybody else has a different definition of objectivity—he certainly didn't. But even if the two countries cannot celebrate a complete identity of views, there has been enough community of principle to enable us to pursue a common course and to afford some hope that in the near future we shall be actively exploring the possibilities of an overall settlement in the Middle East, or if that does not prove immediately feasible, then at least some further steps leading toward it.

As the democratic world looks upon Israel, as an example, an exponent, an advocate of democracy, it can, I think, be filled with proper pride about what we have achieved. The mark of imperfection is written on all human performance, and it is written on the achievement of Israeli democracy as well. There are defects and faults in Israel—and we have no lack of friendly advisers to point out exactly what they are—but when everything is said and recorded and remembered, it is in an affirmative spirit that we look back upon these decades. The society that we have built, the enterprise that we have created, the assets that we have assembled, the kinsmen that we have redeemed, the graves that we have dug, the tears that we have shed because of them, the passions that have been roused, the griefs that have been suffered, the inexpressible hopes that have been kindled—all these are part of our common memory. There are some in Israel who gained special renown in sacrifice or in action, but in a deeper sense it is a people's victory, won by countless men and women caught up in an agonizing alternation of courage and disappointment, of despair and renewed hope. And now this state of Israel belongs to world democracy. Israel is everyone's possession. Out of its hope and travail, there is a new tomorrow, a new tomorrow waiting to be born.

GIOVANNI SARTORI

11. Liberal Democracy in Western Europe

Western Europe is a large and highly diversified political arena. It contains sixteen major independent states (including Ireland and the United Kingdom) whose liberal democratic practices arise from very different historical hinterlands, and which are now at very different stages of democratic development.[1] Portugal and Spain are just born, or re-born, to liberal democracy. Greece has a discontinuous and retarded record, and returned to civilian constitutional rule only a few years ago. Under Mussolini, Italy suffered a twenty-year interruption and is again in deep water. Germany became a democracy only after the First World War, and the Weimar experiment (1918-33) ended with Hitler's dictatorship—by far the most ruthless one ever to materialize on European soil. As for France, currently in its Fifth Republic, its revolutionary record (including coups) since 1789 is not only impressive but also disconcerting for a country that stands out, together with the United States, as being the ancestor and the model of present-day democracies. That is not to disparage the United Kingdom, but only to note that England's transition from constitutional rule to democracy was slower and more cautious. Historically, England was a latecomer and has not been a pacesetter for democratic institutions.

On the continent, it happens that Belgium is the oldest, continuous European liberal democracy, for it still abides by its 1831 Constitution.[2] After more than a century of successful democratic development, however, Belgium has become, during the last decade, the most troubled member of the family of the small democracies. In spite of being a small country, it is now torn by an intense linguistic and ethnic conflict between the Walloons and the Flemish. And the interesting, or puzzling, thing is that Belgium, with all its difficulties, still displays, at least on the surface, a stable three-party pattern, while the Netherlands and Denmark are effective working democracies (though less stable and less effective than they were some ten years ago) in spite of possessing fragmented party systems, each affording five to six active and meaningful political parties.

We come next to the Nordic group of countries: Norway, Sweden, and Finland. But even they are not a "group." Norway and Sweden are quite similar—in their performance, in the range and spectrum of political opinions, and in the structure of their party systems. Finland, however, displays a pattern that more closely resembles that of the Italians and French than of its Scandinavian neighbors. Last but not least, we find the southern belt of the small democracies: Switzerland and Austria. Both countries are, so to speak, Alpine islands, yet they have hardly anything in common. Switzerland has a highly fragmented party system and is a polyethnic, multilingual, and multireligious state, while Austria provides the only continental instance of two-partyism.[3] Interestingly, it is Switzerland that stands out as the most stable and peaceful of the European democracies, whereas Austria with its two parties is a highly compartmentalized, sharply divided, two-camp polity.

This sweeping enumeration reminds us that Europe consists of a complex and uneven constellation both of institutional arrangements and of performances that defy simple generalizations and even more simple explanations. If one says that democracy needs time to operate successfully, France and Belgium are "old" democracies, while the German Federal Republic is a "new" democracy; but the latter is currently in far better shape than the former. If one says that too many parties, that is, party fragmentation, make for inefficient democracy, the assertion seemingly holds true for Italy and France, but hardly for the Netherlands. If one says that religious and linguistic cleavages are unmanageable, Switzerland stands out as clear evidence to the contrary. If one says that poverty breeds hostility to democracy, whereas prosperity cures political extremism, the assertion has never withstood serious testing and appears increasingly disconfirmed by the frequency with which extremism is embraced by well-to-do university students. And so on.

That does not mean that we are unable to explain why some democracies "work" while other democracies are non-working, unstable, or eventually doomed. But while we cannot here afford to probe in any detail the question "How and why does a democracy succeed?" this much can be pointed out right away: the experience of Europe forcefully attests both to the inherent fragility of liberal democracy, and to its very great plasticity and adaptability. Countries that seemingly afford favorable objective conditions suddenly and unexpectedly enter serious crises, while countries seemingly faced with adverse objective conditions perform remarkably well. The point can be illuminated by an economic analogy: the two countries that have boomed most during the last twenty years—Germany and Japan—are both overpopulated and remarkably lacking in natural resources. Thus, on the basis of all the facilitating natural conditions they are economic miracles. On similar grounds we can well speak of democratic miracles—and also, be it added, of democratic delusions.

Of course, in the real world miracles do not happen: nothing is obtained for nothing. If a people enjoy the benefits of that brief miracle—historically speaking—that goes under the name of liberal democracy, this is first and foremost because a people have earned it. This obvious remark brings me to the central, unifying clue to any and all democratic experiments, namely, to their belief element, a clue well known and yet recently neglected or mistreated.

While Europe is indeed the major testing ground of how diverse democracies can be—both in success and failure—one can still speak of Europe in general, or generalize about Europe, as I shall here attempt to do, by focusing on the distinctive democratic mind (*forma mentis*) that was nurtured by the French Revolution of 1789. That distinctiveness can be seen most clearly if 1789 is compared with 1776, that is, if the French Revolution is contrasted with the American Revolution—or, in this contrast, with the American non-revolution.

Present-day liberal democracies throughout the world can be said to draw—in very different proportions, to be sure—from four major sources of belief inspiration: the Greek and Latin classics, the English rule of law and constitutionalism, the *Federalist Papers*, and the French or Rousseau-type democracy. But if one looks at democracy in the real world, that is, as a successful blending of theory and practice, of ideals and implementation, then there is no doubt in my mind that 1776 and the *Federalist Papers* have been, and remain, the fundamental and most creative breakthrough.

The message of the classics was not, let it be recalled, in favor of "democracy" (a derogatory word for well over two thousand years) but in favor of a "republic" that rested on a balanced "mixed government" (the kind of thing that the Americans—not the British—translated into the constitutional division of power). On the other hand, at the time the American colonies seceded, the major British political thinker was Edmund Burke. Burke vehemently denounced the principles and the excesses of the French Revolution. Yet he was by no means a reactionary or an admirer of the past. Burke understood and accepted both modern parties and modern representation. But he typically represented the distinctively British path to liberty: the constitutional rather than the "people's power" path.

We are thus brought back to the distinctively European, and basically French, component of present-day democracies. People often speak of Rousseau-type democracy. Yet Rousseau admired Romans and Spartans (not the demagogic and fickle Athenians); he believed that no democracy was possible over a large territory; and he was equally future blind in most other respects. But there was a major force behind Rousseau: *la raison*, reason, that is to say, the rationalistic tradition symbolized by the clear and distinct ideas of Descartes and epitomized by the Age of Enlightenment. The 1789 French Revolution was a child of the Enlightenment; and the rationalistic catalyst of the French Revolution remained the characteristic propellent of "rational democracy," of democracy conceived as a rational society and constructed as a matter of rational deduction from the "will of equal people" principle.

Now, such a rational democracy is a far cry from what the American founding fathers had in mind and actually fabricated. Their professed intent was to establish a republic (not a democacy) in which the periphery (the states of the Union) remained free vis-à-vis the Union, and the freedom of the individual and of any lesser power was protected against abuses by any superior power. The will of the people entered the overall construction merely as one of its checks and balances. Nonetheless, when Tocqueville visited the United States some fifty years later he found it (and masterfully interpreted it in 1834) already a democracy. And it does not detract from the stature of the founding fathers—unquestionably the most inventive and skillful constitutional engineers of modern times—to note, first, that this development was neither desired nor foreseen, and second, that it was enhanced by two major facilitating conditions (as compared with Europe), namely, the absence of feudal encroachments and open frontiers. Those facilitating conditions, however, do not explain the difference between the European "rational democracy" and the American "empirical democracy."[4] That difference ultimately rests on two basic cultural orientations: the rationalistic versus the empirical mind.

It is always true that things are more easily said than done. But the rationalist is largely satisfied by the saying, by the design; the doing, or the how, is his very last concern. In the rationalistic approach, when the practice does not conform to the theory, it is the practice, not the theory, that must be wrong.[5] Conversely, in the empirical or pragmatic orientation if a theory fails in practice something must be wrong with the theory. Thus the rational mind ranks principles and consistency above experience and results, while the empirical mind proceeds through trial and error and can be described as reasonable rather than rational. The implications of these two fundamentally different ways of confronting the real world are—at least in the search for the good society—far-reaching, as we shall see.

But let me pause and explain—since the stage of the exposition now allows me to do so—the thread of my argument and where I propose to end. I first intend to follow up the European developments, thus qualifying, at the same time, the notion of rational democracy. I will then argue that it is only in the last twenty years that the European and American notions of democracy have really been interacting, and that we are currently confronted, in my view, more with a Europeanization of the American type of democracy than with the Americanization of the European type.

Let us begin by swiftly following up the European developments. It was the combined and counterpoised effects of the French Revolution and of the Napoleonic conquest that established across Europe the French influence and the primacy of the French model. Thus, Europe developed its own theory of liberal constitutionalism (with Benjamin Constant as a leading advocate, to mention one name only) during the Restoration, that is, between 1815 and 1830; it began to practice liberal constitutionalism in 1830; and the subsequent step, liberal democracy, was inaugurated with the 1848 revolutions. Clearly in 1815 Europe was lagging far behind the United States and England in terms of both the doctrine[6] and the practice of liberal democracy. By 1848, however, Marx had promulgated the *Communist Manifesto* and Tocqueville had perceived "socialism" (both the term and the thing) as the major driving force—and menace—of the future. One may thus say—under the optics of progress—that in just about thirty years the European doctrine (not the practice) had leaped far ahead of that in the English-speaking countries. There were many reasons for this startling speed. One was the far greater variety of contributions afforded by the very polycentricity and diversity of Europe. For instance, Marx stems from, and belongs to, the dissolution of Hegelian philosophy; and this means, in turn, that European rationalism currently plays on two keyboards, drawing either from the "mathematician philosophers" (from Descartes to Leibniz) or from the German post-romantic "dialectics" codified by Hegel and converted by Marx into a powerful revolutionary logic.

A more important explanation for the European acceleration however, is that it is part and parcel of a rationalistic impulse The deduction of consequences from premises can be done very rapidly if one glosses over the practical implementation. In turn this acceleration helps explain, on the one hand, the fear that led some countries to prolonged delays, and on the other hand, why the liberal democratic performance of the major European continental countries has often been suicidal. In France the 184 revolution was dismantled (as had been that of 1789) by the Sec ond Empire, which lasted until 1871 and was actually overthrown by military defeat. The German-speaking countries remained up until 1918 very much at the stage of the French Restoration; and the case of Spain was not very different. Thus the first German experiment with democracy, the Weimar Republic (whose constitution, be it noted, was a model of rational construction), succumbed after fourteen troubled years to the joint impact of inexperience, excessive ambitions, devastating inflation, mass unemployment and the failure to command the loyalties of the key elites. As for Spain, it plunged into democracy even later (in 1931) and even less cautiously; and the rapidity of the change quickly backfired, in 1936, into the cruelest and bloodiest European civil war since the wars of religion. On the other hand, Italy, which had moved toward liberal democracy by a series of stages from 1848 until 1922, could not withstand the post–World War difficulties created by universal suffrage and proportional representation.[7]

Until 1976 it could be said that at no single point in time has the whole of Western Europe been democratic. (Let it be stressed that the reference is only to Western, not Eastern, Europe. If the whole of Europe were counted, the gain of Portugal and Spain in 1975–76 would not balance the losses of 1944.) Nonetheless one can surely speak of a distinctively European pattern of liberal democracy. Whenever a European democracy emerges, or reemerges, it differs markedly in at least three major respects from the American-type democracy. For one thing, since the nineteenth-century beginnings no European country has adopted the American presidential model (though that model has been followed, if seldom successfully, by many Latin American constitutions) until France in 1958; but even the Gaullist constitution can hardly be considered American-inspired (it was tailored by De Gaulle for De Gaulle, and it actually combines a parliamentary with a presidential system).[8] Furthermore, as of the turn of the century two additional characterizing ingredients were clearly emerging, albeit with different intensity and proportion, throughout most of the European scene: class politics and socialism.

That no European constitution has borrowed from the American is easy to explain: until the end of the Second World War the American constitutional experience had virtually no influence on European soil. The French looked, at most, to the British; and the other Europeans sought inspiration from France or England (with the difference that France was imitated and England admired). However, as the new postwar constitutions were adopted, one American imprint did occur: Italy and Germany imported the American Supreme Court.[9] But that was about it (at least for Italy; Germany also adopted—or adapted—the principles and practice of American federalism).

It is more complicated to explain, instead, why class politics and socialism were born in Europe; and also why both ingredients have since travelled across the entire world, with one major exception—the United States. But that would divert us from our major concern. What matters at this point is to explain how Europe and the United States interacted when they finally began to interact, that is, in the period before and after the Second World War.

That explanation is facilitated by taking a brief step back. When we say "liberal democracy" we are correctly reminded that modern democracies are very different from the ancient ones in that modern democracy is made up of two constituent elements, namely, liberalism *plus* democracy. (Incidentally, this point is obfuscated when "liberal" is taken to mean "radical," for that meaning is far removed from the "liberalism" that has been, and remains, the historical component of modern democracy.) The liberal and democratic elements of liberal democracy are not, however, of equal force or of equal attractiveness. The contribution of liberalism to the composition is, in essence, the rule of law and the constitutional protection of individual freedom. The contribution of democracy per se to the composition is equality and the principle of the "power of the people."

Now, the general feeling currently is that liberal democracies have reached a stage of development at which more remains to be done on the equality side than on the liberty side.[10] Nonetheless, liberal democracy cannot be all democracy and no liberalism. Hence the problem is to maximize the democratic element without jeopardizing the liberty element. And here one encounters again the distinction between empirical democracies and rational democracies. Among the former, the United States has thus far succeeded in blending and in balancing equality with liberty, affirmative action, and individual rights. Contrariwise, rational democracies are easily led to maximize equality to the detriment of liberty, and thus quickly become unbalanced liberal democracies—a tendency that goes a long way toward explaining the greater fragility and more frequent breakdowns of continental European democracies.

In summing up, if an American looks today at the European democratic scene he will be struck by these differences.

First, a lesser belief in the constitution, which attests to an erosion of confidence, and ultimately to a marked imbalance between the liberty and equality elements of liberal democracy.

Second, a far greater degree of "extremism," defined here as going to the extreme of repudiating (for whatever reasons) liberal democracy itself.

Third, even *within* the ambit of liberal democracy, a far broader spectrum of political aspirations and options. Since the European scene is characterized by class politics and socialism, the spectrum of democratic politics is far more extended—on both left and right—than the American. Thus Europe displays not only socialist parties allied with communist parties, but non-communist social democratic parties that are still well to the "left" of the American Democratic Party. Likewise, Europe breeds parties that are farther to the "right" than the American Republicans. The point can be restated by saying that Europe is characterized by ideological politics, for it is the ideological element that produces the wider left-to-right spectrum.[11] And all of this adds up to saying that the breadth of consensus—consensus not only on fundamentals, but also on policies—is far greater in the United States than in almost any European country.

The question now is: with respect to the European pattern, is the United States remaining as it is, that is, unexposed? Or is the United States listening more and more to European messages? In the late 1970s, the weight of two centuries of remarkable achievements does keep the United States on the path of its own tradition. At the level of the political system one may thus advance the contention that Europe is not affecting the American polity. Yet we do live in a highly interactive and intercommunicating world in which "the medium is the message," and in which it is hard to believe that even a continent, no matter how towering and self-sufficient, can remain impermeable. And if the focus is shifted from the political system to the learning institutions, intellectuals, media personnel—that is, to the sites in which the seeds of the future are grown—one can indeed detect significant changes between the fifties and the seventies. Unquestionably the absolute number, if not the proportion, of intellectual liberals has been steadily on the increase; and an American liberal is nowadays very similar to a European radical or progressive. "Law" and "order" have become (I dare say unfortunately and unjustly) conservative slogans. European extremism appears thrilling. Marx and Marxism enter most curricula, often expounded by believers. And the American dream is slowly, but perceptibly, assimilating to the rationalistic type of democratic perfectionism. It would be surprising if all of this were not to reverberate on the American political scene. That is not my hope. If anything, it is my warning. The European vocation is toward the unbalancing of liberal democracy. If the United States leans in the same direction, this may well tip the balance for all of us on both sides of the Atlantic.

Clearly my key terms here are "balance" and "unbalanced." I realize that these notions may be considered outmoded, or that they may not impress the reader as being of prime significance. So let me take up that challenge and attempt to assess the future prospects of liberal democracy, interpreting it in the light cast by the concept (and label) of the "unbalanced society."

Let us ask ourselves: what makes a society a free society? The belief in, and desire for, individual liberty? Surely. A *garantiste* constitution that emphasizes the protection of liberties? That is of great help. A capable, democratic-minded leadership? Yes, that is important. But when all of this is said and done, we must reckon with the *structural conditions* that allow for a free society, and with the mechanisms that enable such a society to function and to change. Briefly put, a society is all the more free—structurally—the more it is capable of self-regulation, and the more it entrusts its development to internal countervailing forces and feedbacks. In the technical jargon of my profession, a free social system is a self-steering, self-repairing, and self-sustaining system in a state of homeostatic equilibrium (and therefore, over time, a system of equilibria that are ever changing, but not in disequilibrium). In more familiar terms, that means that the power structure of a free society must be such as to neutralize any overwhelming power. At each point in time we shall obtain different global equilibria resulting from different agglutinations of the disequilibrating and re-equilibrating factors. But at no time can any single force (whether a class, a party, an army, a union, a church, or any organized group) be overpowering if the other forces join to resist it. In practice that is tantamount to saying that if a society develops within its ambit an overwhelming, irresistible power, then that society can scarcely expect to survive as a free society.

Thus an unbalanced society is hardly a viable free society. And the crucial question is: are liberal democratic societies—or western-type societies in general—still capable of self-regulation? Or is this capacity being steadily undermined?

If that is the question, or if the question is so phrased, then there is little doubt that the re-equilibrating automatisms of the free societies are everywhere increasingly eroded, and in some places already clogged. There are at least three reasons for this trend. One is that the visible hand—seeking rationalization, planning, and distributive justice—is increasingly replacing the invisible hand. (We also seem more and more to need the visible hand for repairing the damages—the external diseconomies and ecological disruptions—that we are increasingly producing.) The second reason is that bigger government is growing apace with overloaded and inefficient government. Democratic governments are —sometimes more, sometimes less—overburdened and nearing paralysis. And governments that are increasingly unable to satisfy and process the demands arising from the revolution of rising expectations end by tossing back into the society heightened conflicts that are no longer amenable to "natural" market-type processing, no longer susceptible to automatic re-equilibration. The third causal factor—in some ways the most menacing of all—is technology itself. Technological progress affects the automatic conflict-resolving capacities of a social system in two major, and consequentially related, respects: first, in that it generates enormously complex interdependencies that interact almost instantaneously, that is, just like chain reactions; and second, in that it increases at an exponential rate the vulnerability of the whole society, both to social forces and to the breakdown of any one element of the technology.

Again this is not a novel discovery. But remember that the issue is whether non-rebalanceable forces are in fact emerging in our societies, and whether such forces may not be destructive of the ultimate conditions that permit a free society. And if that is the issue, then we must pay careful attention to the fact that technology is creating, among and between social groups, formidable and indeed unprecedented inequalities. I am not concerned here, clearly, with inequalities in wealth (they can be easily corrected), or with inequalities in talents and expertise. By "technological inequalities" I mean that technology in and by itself affords to special, and indeed very small, groups a hugely disproportionate leverage, and consequently an immense blackmailing power vis-à-vis the other groups in society and the society as a whole.

Think of one extreme but telling and hardly futuristic instance, namely, the role of computer personnel, that is, the people who actually sit at the computer, if only to switch the on and off buttons. Computer personnel exist for the very simple, inevitable reason that the machine not only has been invented but increasingly serves (and controls) all the ganglia of the advanced industrial and post-industrial society. The computer people do not add up to a profession or to a vocational class, for the group is largely composed of easily trained, and therefore easily replaceable, individuals. Thus no problem or harm is threatened unless or until the computer personnel become unionized. But if that should happen, it immediately creates a professional class and, as the people involved catch on, closed-shop practices result. At that point an automated society (or a "technetronic" society, as Brzezinski has baptized it) can be blackmailed in piecemeal fashion, and almost endlessly, by say one-thousandth of its population. Blackmailed almost totally, for no wild stretch of imagination is required to understand the disruptive, if not unbearable, damage resulting from computer stoppages, that is, from computer personnel strikes

I could expand this example in greater detail and also ente

many other examples of the kind; but my purpose is only to expound the notion of vulnerability. Vulnerability means that the means of attack outweigh the means of defense, that the attack is easy, the defense difficult. Vulnerability is thus a disproportion, or better, it presupposes a disproportion. And the vulnerability of the highly technological societies is that they are exposed to a fantastic exaggeration of the damage that can be done. There is no comparability, that is, between the enormous damage that can be inflicted and the slight cost and risk for those who inflict it. Note that what is envisaged here is not the goods-producing or manufacturing society, but rather the "service society." A service society is not merely a society of tertiary and service employments but—and this is far more important—a "service-needing" society, one in which a number of services (electricity, water, and all that is connected with their supply and distribution) are indispensable, and cannot be withheld without endangering—in a matter of days or hours—the very survival of the inhabitants of the megalopolis, of the huge, technology-based city exemplified by Manhattan.

The issue is compounded by asking: vulnerability of what, to whom, how? The answer to the question "of what?" is clear enough. It is the consumers, the citizens as a whole, those to whom the services of a service-needing society are indispensable. As for the question vulnerable "to whom?" the answer can be stated in general terms as follows: our societies are endangered in their conflict-regulating capacities by the emergence of a single, crushing power resource, that is, by the overwhelming power, or leverage, of the groups in charge of the society's daily technological sustenance. This power resource adds up to being the "power of labor." But that is only an abstraction whose concrete potentialities can be detected far better in Europe than in the United States. So let me focus on the two countries where the process under consideration is most advanced, namely, Italy and France (in that order). It is there that we can best examine the third question, "how?"

Europe, as I have said, is characterized by class politics, socialism, eventually by extremism, and surely more by ideology than is the United States. The point now is how these characteristics are reflected in, and embodied by, organized labor. Both Italy and

France display highly politicized, ideologically committed unions with a high degree of centralized organization; and in both countries the largest federations of labor are communist-controlled. Under such circumstances labor becomes by far the major mobilizable force in the society, and its mobilizational leverage is such that organized labor becomes untouchable. Its numbers, strength, and ideological commitment constitute a virtual sanctuary. Under such circumstances not only are the political authorities and the courts largely impotent, but the nation's consumers, as a collectivity, are utterly defenseless.

To be sure, consumers are always dispersed, difficult to organize, and tend to be on the losing side. But I am implying here that we should revisit the well-known argument that since producers (labor) are also consumers, there is a built-in, self-restraining factor by which the balance is ultimately restored. That ancient argument, I fear, will not hold up. We live in highly diversified, cushioned, and redundant societies in which the producer and the consumer roles are not automatically and quickly converted into one another. He who inflicts the damage is necessarily hurt as consumer only by an enduring general strike. That is precisely the reason why the general strike theorized by Georges Sorel is by now, in Europe, only a symbolic, brief demonstration, and never really "general." Labor's tactics and the weapons of its arsenal are by now far more subtle and selective: they consist of piecemeal, stop-and-go, and similar striking practices (whose names are not as yet established in English—and that is very telling) whose costs and discomforts are generally discharged on third parties. Clearly, in the final analysis, all of this means that our societies are more and more entering a gigantic minus-sum game in which each and all are destined in the end to lose. But no effective consumer reaction can be mobilized on such a basis.

Let us now conclude. The major reason for having focused on the "power of labor" as the principal unbalancing pressure that impairs the self-regulating capacity of the free society is precisely that it is with respect to union practices, organization, and overall structure that Europe (Britain included) differs most from the United States. The United States appears at the moment to be hardly aware of this menace. And that seems a good reason, indeed a very good reason, for dwelling on it. In the United States the alarm can still be sounded in time.

On the other hand, it is important to stress that if, in some European countries, organized labor is already displaying a virtually irresistible power, that power does not result from technology alone; for technology, like science and knowledge in general, is a Janus-faced instrument that can be used both to help or to harm. The power that clogs the self-balancing mechanisms of western societies also stems from class politics, from socialism, from ideology, and from heated or overheated politics. And here I revert again to my earlier remarks about the Europeanization of the intellectual atmosphere and youth culture in the United States. If more politicization, more ideological passion, more European-type parties, the so-called "more responsible party system," more mobilization, and, in the aggregate, a "rational democracy," appear to be the good things that America needs, then she should also expect the "unbalanced society," with all its perils for liberal democracy, to cross the Atlantic. It bears repetition that this is not my hope, but my fear. As Hölderlin wrote after the French Revolution: "What has always made the State into a hell on earth has been man's attempt to make it into his heaven." This has not been, and need not become, the genius of American politics.

Notes

1. The total would be twenty-four if we were to count Iceland and the very small units: Luxembourg, Malta, San Marino, Monte Carlo, Andorra, Lichtenstein, and the Vatican City. For an all-inclusive comparative coverage, see Gordon Smith, *Politics in Western Europe*, 2nd ed. (London: Heinemann, 1976).
2. Sweden is actually older than Belgium, for its constitutional monarchy goes back to its first constitution of 1809. That was hardly a liberal constitution, however, for it was based on the medieval-type system of representation of the estates (nobility, clergy, burghers, and farmers). Sweden caught up with the Belgian constitution only in 1866. Similarly, the liberal constitutional development in the Netherlands can hardly be traced back to 1814; it is more appropriately assigned to 1848.
3. Malta, independent since 1964, is another instance, but hardly a significant one.

4. I have labored at length over this distinction in my *Democratic Theory*, 2nd rev. ed. (Indianapolis, Ind.: Liberty Press, 1977), ch. 11.
5. Marxism is currently the major and most potent illustration of the rationalistic habit of blaming the practice when it does not conform to the theory. Stalin is explained away as a "practical degeneration," and the inability of the communist regimes (in the Soviet Union after sixty years) to achieve their fundamental goals (think of the withering away of the state and of the "true liberty" that would follow from the elimination of classes) is incessantly attributed, when reluctantly admitted, to "wrong practices." That is also to say that Marxism is characteristically rationalistic in being all ends and no means.
6. Montesquieu is the only major exception to this statement, but he received little attention in his own time. Montesquieu eclipsed Rousseau only among the authors of the Restoration.
7. The smaller democracies (Austria excepted) seemingly lived outside these major perils. Even though the relation between size and democracy is difficult to assess—as one can infer from R. A. Dahl and E. Tufte, *Size and Democracy* (Palo Alto, Cal.: Stanford University Press, 1973)—the larger European countries seemingly display less controllable, multiplying factors of both acceleration and disintegration.
8. Perhaps one should also mention the first Austrian Republic (1918–33), whose constitution was amended in 1929 in order to provide for a directly elected president. In 1933, however, Chancellor Dollfuss suppressed the constitution and shortly afterwards established an authoritarian regime that brought Austria (in 1938) to the *Anschluss* with Hitler's Germany.
9. I exclude France, for the French Constitutional Council of the Fifth Republic is *sui generis*, and surely not derived from the American model. Furthermore, the French Council of State is in substance more powerful, in spite of being an administrative body, than the Constitutional Council. Austria also has a Constitutional Court, but it is not of post–Second World War vintage; it follows from the re-enactment of the 1920 constitution (as amended in 1925 and 1929), and finds its autochthonous predecessor in the Imperial 1867 *Reichsgericht*.
10. This liberty-versus-equality dissection of liberal democracy goes back to Tocqueville and was convincingly restated by, among others, Guido De Ruggiero in his classic *History of European Liberalism* (London, 1927).
11. The end-of-ideology prophecy relates to the intensity of ideology, not to ideology as embedded in, or as the source of, the left-right perception of politics.

SAMUEL H. BEER

12. The Strengths of Liberal Democracy

This essay will deal mainly with the origins of liberal democracy, and will say only a little about its current prospects. I turn to the history, however, because I believe we can learn from it a great deal about the strengths and weaknesses of liberal democracy and therefore its prospects. Indeed, what I wish to stress is a certain source of strength that has helped free government survive in the long competition with unfree government in modern times. That source of strength is free speech. I want to emphasize the role of free speech as an instrument of self-government. Free speech has other aspects—for instance, its function in promoting the private concerns or personal growth of the individual. In this present inquiry, however, I am thinking of its public function as the way in which liberal democracy enlists the intelligence of its citizens in solving common problems. I am concerned, in short, not with the moral value of liberal democracy nor with the individual's right of free expression, but rather with the utility to the modern democratic state of government by discussion.

In modern political thought this public function of free speech and free discussion has been perceived and appraised with favor by men of many different schools. All share in some degree the great tradition of modern rationalism. I can suggest the thrust of the basic analysis and the spread of its advocacy over time by mentioning the work of a few of the more notable. This body of thought includes—indeed, I should say, it starts with—John Milton's immortal rhetoric in defense of freedom of the press in *Areopagitica* (1644). It includes Burke's portrait of the eighteenth-century Parliament as "a *deliberative* assembly" guided by "the general reason of the whole";[1] and Walter Bagehot's analysis, a hundred years later, of the long-run survival value of what he first termed "government by discussion."[2] On the American side the case was made by Thomas Jefferson in the confident plea for political toleration in his first inaugural; and by Mr. Justice Holmes in the defense of "free trade in ideas" put forward in his famous dissent in the Abrams case.[3] More recently, the essentials of the analysis have been restated and put to use by political scientists who have shown how in democratic systems policy making can be a process of "social learning" in which outcomes are determined not by "the bumping of impenetrable billiard balls of power, but by men who could learn and whose viewpoints could change."[4]

Even today the best statement of the case for government by discussion—the fullest and clearest articulation of the model—is found in the writings of John Stuart Mill, principally his two works *On Liberty* (1859) and *Representative Government* (1861). In order to know what we are looking for in our historical inquiry, it will be helpful to summarize what Mill had to say.

He bases his argument upon what he terms "a quality of the human mind, the source of everything respectable in man, either as an intellectual or moral being, namely, that his errors are corrigible." Because of this quality of mind, Mill continues, man "is capable of rectifying his mistakes by discussion and experience. Not by experience alone. There must be discussion to show how experience is to be interpreted. Wrong opinions and practices gradually yield to fact and argument; but facts and arguments, to produce any effect on the mind must be brought before it."[5]

Mill's hypothesis is that truth will prevail over error, when both can be freely tested by investigation and discussion. That sounds innocent enough. But in stating this view, he is rejecting another view, indeed a major tenet of the western tradition, that truth is unlikely to prevail, unless the opinion of the many is authoritatively controlled by the few, specifically the wiser sort of men, such as kings, priests, or philosophers. He could reject this older hierarchical view because of his belief in the capacity of the individual for rational self-correction. But his hypothesis also includes the proposition that this capacity will be rendered far more efficacious —more productive, I am tempted to say—if individuals freely and rationally exchange ideas with one another.

Mill did not let his brave hypothesis stand without qualification. He was aware that representative democracy is not "practicable or eligible in all states of civilization"[6] and that if free discussion were to bear the fruit he expected of it, certain preconditions must exist.[7] Nor did he expect that even in those communities which met these moral and material prerequisites every individual would make an equal contribution. Some people would know more than others and therefore would probably make a larger contribution to the consideration of public policy. Yet he did not give these people a particularly honorific title, usually calling them simply "the instructed minority,"[8] and conceived their influence as proceeding not from coercion, or manipulation, or status, but essentially from rational persuasion.

His earnest and central concern was to make the greatest possible use of the intellectual and moral resources of all citizens. Rather like the economist who looks for that economic system in which the material resources of a society will be so allocated as to maximize the national product, Mill sought that political system which would so utilize these less tangible resources as to elicit the greatest possible enlightenment regarding public policy. He criticized authoritarian government for "not bringing into sufficient exercise the individual faculties, moral, intellectual and active, of the people."[9] He saw in representative democracy the means by which these faculties would be utilized by opening office-holding to all classes of private citizens, but "above all, by the utmost possible publicity and liberty of discussion, whereby not merely a few individuals in succession, but the whole public, are made, to a certain extent, participants in the government."[10]

As a child of Benthamite utilitarianism, Mill could not overlook the function of democratic government as a means by which individuals and groups protect and promote their interests, using their political power to put forward and make good their demands on the polity. In his view, however, the discussion that takes place under liberal democracy is not merely a process in which demands are made and the will of the people is asserted. It is also a process in which the truth about public policy is examined, criticized, and improved—a process in which something is discovered or invented or learned. Free government consists not only of an organization of will, but also of an organization of thought. For that reason it has access to a source of power denied to unfree government.

If we ask when government by discussion began, we cannot fail to think of the Greek city-state and especially Athens, at any rate of Athens as Pericles described it in the words reported by Thucydides. He said: "Our constitution is named a democracy, because it is in the hands not of the few but of the many.... Our citizens attend both to public and private duties, and do not allow absorption in their own various affairs to interfere with their knowledge of the city's.... we decide or debate, carefully and in person, all matters of policy, holding, not that words and deeds go ill together, but that acts are foredoomed to failure when undertaken undiscussed. For we are noted for being at once most adventurous in action and most reflective beforehand."[11]

This is surely what is meant by government by discussion. It may also be found in Rome during the heyday of the Republic—in the Senate and perhaps in the other assemblies.

These classical examples did have influence on the champions of free government in modern times. We recall Shelley's words: "Liberty said, let there be light, and like a sunrise on the sea, Athens arose." We think of Montesquieu's admiration of Roman liberty and Rousseau's elaborate concern with the popular assemblies of the Roman Republic. Still, as historical evidence, these examples are not likely to change the mind of anyone who contends that free government is a short-lived and exceptional form of polity. In the classical world, monarchy, empire, and other authoritarian forms predominated. Moreover, such free government as we find there was separated from our own age by centuries of medievalism.

The medieval polity did make important contributions to the theory and practice of free government in later times. Chief among these are constitutionalism and representation. The principle that authority should not be exercised arbitrarily, but rather according to a norm that limits and regularizes it, is fundamental to medieval political thought. The rigidity and particularism of the norms that were legitimated by that mode of thought, however, radically differentiate medieval from modern constitutionalism, and as representation arose, they ensured that it would function in such a way as to narrow prohibitively the opportunity for government by discussion.

Throughout Europe from the twelfth century on, feudal monarchy was modified by the addition of representative bodies which gave a share in power to the various estates, primarily the clergy, the nobility, and the commons. Within this "polity of estates,"[12] the members of these bodies might "parley" with the king over grievances and grants, as the English term "parliament" suggests. Yet the specific ways these institutions functioned and the general spirit they served were a whole world distant from the lawmaking, problem-solving, innovating régimes of modern times with their wide-ranging controversies over policy and their ideological challenges to the form of the régime. Feudalism looked to a fundamental custom as the security for its right and, even after the rise of the polity of estates, tradition was pervasive. In England, for instance, the Parliament was called the "high court of parliament"[13] and, while grievances were sometimes remedied by statute, its proceedings were essentially regarded as the application of an existing and traditional law to particular needs and cases.

To a modern mind one of the peculiarities of that age must be its poverty of political imagination in comparison with its wealth of opportunity. Rebellion against authority was endemic and kings were from time to time resisted, deposed, and even killed. Yet, monotonously, once the old king had been gotten rid of, a new king was put in his place. A change to a non-monarchic régime was almost never attempted or even discussed. The traditionalism of the medieval mind was so strong as to extinguish any sense of alternative political worlds.

Medieval constitutionalism extended the rule of law to the protection of the liberty of the individual. "Liberties" rather than "liberty" would be the appropriate word. For medieval liberty was not one and the same for all, but, on the contrary, a different sort of liberty, depending upon one's rank and order in society. The *Magna Carta*, that great emblem of medieval constitutionalism, was entitled not *Magna Carta Libertatis*, but *Magna Carta Libertatum*. And the liberties it proposed to guarantee to churchmen, to earls and knights, to free men, to the merchants of London, to the villeins, depended upon the function—one can use the Latin term, *servitium*—each order performed in a hierarchic and corporate scheme that was at once natural and divine. Liberty so differentiated and restricted could hardly be the liberty to innovate, to strike out on a new course, to launch, in John Stuart Mill's approving words, "different experiments in living."[14]

If external conduct was so hemmed in by authoritative guidance, thought and belief were even more narrowly circumscribed. Liberty of conscience, which for us is perhaps the sphere least restrained by legal and social sanctions, was in terms of the medieval ideal the sphere where orthodoxy was most fully articulated and enforced. Error in belief could lead to eternal damnation, and the first duty of any ruler, spiritual or temporal, was to defend the faith. St. Thomas Aquinas was only uttering the most conventional wisdom of his time when he wrote: "Heresy is a sin which merits not only excommunication but also death, for it is worse to corrupt the Faith which is the life of the soul than to issue counterfeit coins which minister to the secular life. Since counterfeiters are justly killed by princes as enemies to the common good, so heretics also deserve the same punishment."[15]

In this view nothing could be more threatening to survival—the kind of survival that counted—than a free and open competition among ideas.

Medieval beginnings, I am trying to say, were by no means a promising foundation for government by discussion. The transformation of the representative constitutionalism of the Middle Ages into free government on modern lines was intrinsically a very unlikely happening. That transformation must appear even more improbable when we consider the setting in which it took place. For the modern age in European politics began, not with a liberalizing of the medieval polity, but on the contrary with the elimination or subjection of these institutions by princely absolutism and expert officialdom.

By the latter part of the seventeenth century absolute monarchs held sway over most of Europe from the France of Louis XIV in the West to the Russia of Peter the Great in the East. For the student of the modern state, however, the more interesting feature of these new polities is not so much their powerful personal sovereigns as the new instruments through which they exercised their sovereign wills, that quintessentially modern type of administrative organization, the bureaucracy. In the medieval polity the administrative staff derived from a feudal regime that dispersed power under the legitimation of baronial and corporate right. In contrast, the members of the modern bureaucracy have no personal rights in the means of administration and presumably achieve their positions of authority because of specialized training and professional competence. The ability of bureaucracy to get things done derives on the one hand from rational and systematic organization and on the other hand from the technical knowledge mobilized and managed by this structure.

Thanks to its stress on technical knowledge, bureaucratic organization is specially well fitted to use the power over nature and society made accessible by the advance of modern science and technology. The exaggeration is tolerable when Max Weber writes: ". . . the bureaucratic type of administrative organization . . . is, from the purely technical point of view, capable of attaining the highest degree of efficiency and is in this sense formally the most rational known means for carrying out imperative control over human beings."[16] If we are interested in assessing the sources of the survival power of the modern state—its ability to act effectively, solve problems, and get things done in civilian and in military affairs—we must give great weight to the contribution of this very modern component of the polity. To be a bit fanciful, the transition to political modernity might be seen as occurring when those experts in transcendental survival, the prophet and the priest, were superseded by the new experts in secular survival, the scientist and the bureaucrat.

The rise of bureaucracy was a central event—perhaps, as Weber implied, *the* central event—in the political modernization of Europe. Already during the sixteenth century, according to Weber, in what he calls "the more advanced countries," expert officialdom, based on the division of labor, was triumphant in the three critical areas of the modern state: finance, war, and law.[17] As bureaucratic absolutism spread in the next century, the France of Louis XIV provided the model for Prussia, Spain, Austria, Russia, and the lesser principalities of continental Europe. In the eighteenth century "enlightened despotism" came into style, and improvements on the French model were made by such countries as Sweden and Prussia.

If you will imagine yourself a friend of free government in some

European country at almost any time in these years and look abroad to gauge the future, you may well feel discouraged. During the struggle with the Stuarts in the seventeenth century, Englishmen were apprehensively aware that representative institutions were coming to an end all over Europe. "England," said Sir Robert Phelips, an MP from Dorset and one of the leading opponents of the king during the 1620s, "is the last monarchy that retains her liberties." In the next century, one important motive for the agitation in the American colonies was the fear of a far-flung plot to extinguish their liberties—a fear shared by many in England. If in looking back we find these fears a bit paranoid, we can perhaps put them in better perspective by considering the lesson a contemporary might draw from what was happening elsewhere—say, in the early 1770s: the renewed subjection of the Riksdag in Sweden, the rising power of Frederick the Great's Prussia, the economic and military decline of the Dutch Republic, the partition of Poland. In these first centuries of the modern era, the general trend of political development was against free government.

There were exceptions, the three principal ones being England, Switzerland, and the Netherlands. The vigorous direct democracies of Switzerland were greatly admired, but little imitated. The looseness of the Dutch confederation meant that the real seat of government was in the assemblies of the seven quite small provinces. In the course of time, it was the English example that provided the basic model for the free governments of Europe and America. To put the main point plainly: it was in England during the seventeenth century that the essential mechanisms of government by discussion were invented, mechanisms that provided the basic model for diffusion and further development.

In the background of this momentous instance of social invention was an explosion of political imagination that took place during these first generations of the modern era. This sudden emergence of a sense of alternative political worlds was the fundamental cultural premise of government by discussion. It did not by any means make inevitable the rise of government by discussion, but it did immensely widen the opportunity. Now the greater range of possibility in public action invited a clash of opinions at a higher level of generality and intensity. At the same time, the chance of radically new departures in public action made more urgent a thorough and informed canvassing of alternatives.

In England we know the ensuing conflict as the struggle of Parliament against the Stuarts and rightly think of it as a major step in the rise of free government not only in England, but also in the West generally. But if the Parliament that engaged in this contest with the rising bureaucratic absolutism of the Tudor-Stuart polity had been the Parliament of the fifteenth century, or even the Parliament of Henry VIII's day, it could not have won—and would not have deserved to win. Its transformation into a modern legislature at once precipitated the contest and enabled the Parliament to win it.

The crucial change was the change in the meaning and function of freedom of speech in the House of Commons. The old system of petitioning for a redress of grievances in exchange for a grant of supply inherently involved an appropriate degree of freedom of speech. Freedom to raise and present grievances was a necessary condition for that process of political exchange. Beginning in 1541, at the opening of every session of Parliament, the Speaker of the House of Commons asked that its privilege of freedom of speech be respected by the monarch, who routinely assented. But in the eyes of the monarch this privilege was confined at its widest to medieval dimensions. As the Lord Keeper, speaking for the queen, warned the Commons in 1571: "They should do well to meddle with no matters of state but such as should be proponed unto them and to occupy themselves in other matters concerning the Commonwealth."

Those "matters of state" on which the Commons were forbidden to initiate discussion included all topics of foreign policy, the royal succession, the religious settlement, and exchequer questions, including even grants of monopoly by royal patent. The "other matters" with which members might independently occupy themselves were still questions of local right or interest, not general policy, foreign or domestic. In the still thriving medieval imagery of the day the "matters of state" were reserved for the "head" of the body politic, the principal organ of thought and will. As Elizabeth said when warning off the Commons from one of those matters: "Who is so simple that doubts whether a prince that is head of all the body may not command the feet not to stray when they would slip?"

In these same years, however, a politics of principle on a grand scale was being introduced into the House of Commons, as its members, especially those who were coming to be called Puritans, began to put forward their own ideas regarding precisely these "matters of state." In asserting this new right of free discussion during the ensuing contest with the Stuarts, the House developed appropriate new machinery for combat and deliberation. This new mode of production of public policy, if I may call it that, consisted mainly of a system of committees: select committees to investigate problems and formulate legislation, which might have the power to compel the attendance of witnesses and the production of papers; and committees of the whole House for deliberation and decision, which removed the Speaker, a royal nominee, from the chair, and proceeded under more relaxed rules permitting greater freedom of debate and amendment.

No American can fail to be fascinated by this first effort at what we call "Congressional government": the use of the power of the purse to control the executive; the use of the power of impeachment to reach members of the executive directly; the use of specially appointed committees to investigate problems and frame bills; and especially the use of those great deliberative mechanisms, the committees of the whole house, for the discussion and determination of the main issues of public policy. As the structure of power was changed, the imagery of political discourse also changed radically. John Pym, leader of the House, declared on the eve of civil war, "The powers of parliament are to the body politic as the rational faculties are to the individual man."

The victory over the Stuarts destroyed the beginnings of bureaucratic absolutism in England and created the balanced constitution of the eighteenth century. In that century, compared with its despotic neighbors, England was a free country and English liberty was a model for admiring intellectuals from the continent, such as Montesquieu and Voltaire. This regime, of course, was by no means democratic, but on the contrary, narrowly oligarchic, only a tiny percentage of the people having the vote and a still smaller fraction enjoying real political power. Yet the crucial advance had been made. Although on a small scale, government by discussion had now been invented; it was institutionalized in the Parliament and joined to a vigorous life of debate and controversy outside its walls.

In later years, as the electorate was enlarged toward a democratic standard, the norms fashioned in this smaller forum were transferred to wider arenas of participation. Surely, the most important of these norms was that protecting the right of opposition. Redlich has remarked that because of its historical origin in a struggle against the monarch, the procedure of the House of Commons "was worked out as the *procedure of an opposition*."[18] This had two consequences. First, forces of popular protest and reform, even when aimed at the oligarchic constitution itself, were able to win a hearing in Parliament. Second, as political discussion spread to wider and wider circles of the public the old parliamentary norm protecting criticism was further embodied in the developing rights of the ordinary citizen. Freedom of the press grew up as the right to do in public what was already being done in Parliament under the protection of its by now ancient privilege. By the time Mill wrote his treatises, the need for opposition—he called it "the antagonism of influences"[19]—was fully recognized, and not for the sake of opposition, but for the sake of government. "The citizens of any country, in this view," as Robert Dahl has observed, "need dissenters and oppositions in order to act wisely, to explore alternatives, to understand the advantages and disadvantages of different alternatives, to know what they want and how to go about getting it."[20]

Looking back on the rise of free government in England and its diffusion to other countries, one may be tempted to think of this development as constituting some sort of inevitable historical process. Certain pre-conditions are necessary if there is to be a chance for free government. But one lesson of the history we have reviewed is that free government is not a mere automatic reflex of some other change, cultural or material. As these centuries demonstrate, economic development is quite compatible with authoritarian and bureaucratic rule. In the first generations of the modern era there was a quickening of economic life. Indeed, the vigorous intervention of the new bureaucratic states was one reason for this surge forward of their national economies. Under the system later called mercantilism, the new states promoted economic development by measures that directly and indirectly led to the creation of nation-wide markets, the spread of a money economy, the extension of trade to distant parts of the world, and so on.

One is reminded of parallels today. Developing countries then, as now, commonly used highly authoritarian means to shape their economies along lines determined by the state. With the spread of free government, capitalist economies did arise and their record of productive advance was undoubtedly better than that of the mercantilist regimes. But looking broadly at the record, past and present, one must be struck by the high degree of compatibility of economic development in both its pre-industrial and its industrial phases with authoritarian bureaucracy.

If free government was not a by-product of capitalism, neither was it the consequence, intended or unintended, of the cultural change brought about by the Reformation. The fundamental beliefs of the Protestant reformers—the doctrine of justification by faith, not works; the denial of transubstantiation; the assertion of the priesthood of every believer—directly attacked the old hierarchic order in the church itself. They did not, however, convey a clear and unambiguous message as to the proper form of secular rule, and during the sixteenth and seventeenth centuries were cited as justifications by advocates of a great variety of régimes, ranging from the anarchism of the Anabaptists to the absolutism of the Hohenzollerns. Accordingly, in the comparative history of that time, the old and the new in religious faith do not co-vary with authoritarian and liberal regimes. Catholics as well as Protestants fought for Swiss liberty, while in Brandenburg-Prussia both Calvinists and Lutherans dutifully supported a sternly authoritarian polity. In the English civil wars, all factions, whether for king or Parliament, whether of left, right, or center, consisted of Protestants. Neither in theory nor in practice did free government appear as the necessary offspring of the new religious culture.

The rise and spread of free government were not deposits of nonpolitical events, but products of political development. A glance back over that history of choices taken and refused, of dubious ventures and close calls, reveals the frailty of any hypothesis of inevitability. During the crucial struggle in the seventeenth century, one can readily imagine the Stuarts making certain changes in policy—and not necessarily great changes—that would have given the victory to bureaucratic absolutism. The personal rule without Parliament on which Charles I embarked in 1629 went very well for some time and by the late 1630s seemed secure. One can see it succeeding in England much as a similar effort was succeeding in France after the Estates General ceased meeting in 1614.

The habit of free government, once established in England, was then diffused to other countries of Europe. The major step was the conversion of the French intellectuals early in the eighteenth century. "It was after Bolingbroke's peace," Bertrand de Jouvenel has written, "that my compatriots suddenly came to admire the governance of England and its praise was carried throughout Europe in the French language."[21] The hard lessons of power reinforced this attraction to English ways. Bolingbroke's peace of 1713 had sealed a major victory over France in a war lasting more than a decade. Further repeated defeats of the premier bureaucratic power by the leading free government followed. The external victories of English arms were, so to speak, supplemented by internal subversion of the Bourbon régime as English thought and practice provided the principal models for its antagonists and for the men who launched the great Revolution of 1789. I am not interested in making odious comparisons but merely in pointing out how 1789, with all its consequences for the spread of free government, was itself crucially dependent upon the prior and very chancy victory of free government in England in the seventeenth century.

If its origins owed much to accident, free government survived thanks in no small part to its own demonstrated strength. It won its victories in peace as well as war. In the nineteenth century during the great age of reform, the English polity showed a capacity for adaptation and innovation that was unprecedented. The pressures of the industrial revolution had created acute dangers of violent revolution and authoritarian reaction. But through the medium of prolonged agitation and debate, the old constitution proved capable of that most difficult political task, the surrender of power to new participants; and in a series of new departures in public policy, which were not only peaceful but successful, the economy was rendered more productive and the society more solidary.

The instance of diffusion most interesting to us is, of course, the adaptation of government by discussion to American circumstances by the founders of the Republic. Already by their time the English had begun to shape that version of the original model which was ultimately embodied in cabinet and party government. Our presidential and congressional version remained in many respects closer to the original structure developed in seventeenth-century England. Both versions were widely imitated. By 1872 Walter Bagehot could conclude: "The practical choice of first-rate nations is between the Presidential government and the Parliamentary; no State can be first-rate which has not a government by discussion, and those are the only two existing species of that government." [22]

Bagehot did not regard bureaucratic absolutism as a serious rival. So short a distance did he see into the future.

Today we find liberal democracy in perhaps two dozen of the 159 governments of the world. In the light of the history of the modern state, this depressing statistic should not surprise us. In the West itself the rise of free government was, as Wellington said of the battle of Waterloo, "the nearest run thing you ever saw in your life."

Yet there are distinctly hopeful signs. Greece, Portugal, and Spain have emerged from dictatorship. India has again become "the world's largest democracy." Nor is this the first evidence that power as well as right may well be on the side of free government. Accident or not, once the seventeenth-century model was put to the test, it showed great survival value. Not every state that tried the experiment has been able to sustain it. But for those states that have succeeded in doing so, government by discussion has added to their strength. In this sense, freedom is power and on its own an important force in history.

Notes

1. In his address to the electors of Bristol, November 3, 1774, *Works* (Boston: Little, Brown and Co., 1865–7), vol. 2, pp. 89–98.

2. Walter Bagehot, *Physics and Politics*, with an Introduction by Jacques Barzun (New York: Knopf, 1948), ch. 5, "The Age of Discussion." First published 1872.
3. Abrams v. United States, 250 U.S. 616, 627–28, 629–31 (1919).
4. Hugh Heclo, *Modern Social Politics in Britain and Sweden* (New Haven: Yale University Press, 1974), p. 321.
5. *On Liberty* in the collection titled *Utilitarianism, On Liberty, and Representative Government*, with an Introduction by A. D. Lindsay (London: Everyman's Library, 1910), p. 82.
6. *Representative Government*, in ibid., p. 208.
7. Ibid., pp. 177–180, 197–202.
8. Ibid., p. 266.
9. Ibid., p. 243.
10. Ibid., p. 243.
11. Zimmern's translation in Alfred Zimmern, *The Greek Commonwealth* (New York: Modern Library, 1956), pp. 204 and 206.
12. So Max Weber's term, *Ständestaat*, is translated in Max Weber, *Economy and Society: An Outline of Interpretive Sociology*, ed. Guenther Roth and Claus Wittich, 3 vols. (New York: Bedminster Press, 1968), p. 1086.
13. The classic study is Charles Howard McIlwain, *The High Court of Parliament and Its Supremacy* (New Haven: Yale University Press, 1910).
14. *On Liberty*, p. 115.
15. Quoted and translated in Richard W. Southern, *Western Society and the Church in the Middle Ages* (London: Penguin Books, 1970), p. 17.
16. Max Weber, *The Theory of Social and Economic Organization*, trans. A. M. Henderson and Talcott Parsons, with an Introduction by Talcott Parsons (New York: Oxford University Press, 1947), p. 337.
17. "Politics as a Vocation," in *From Max Weber: Essays in Sociology*, trans., ed., and with an Introduction by H. H. Gerth and C. Wright Mills (New York: Oxford University Press, 1946), p. 88.
18. Josef Redlich, *The Procedure of the House of Commons*, trans. A. Ernest Steinthal, with an Introduction and Supplementary Chapter by Sir Courtenay Ilbert, 3 vols. (London: Constable, 1908), vol. 1, p. 56.
19. *Representative Government*, p. 201.
20. Robert A. Dahl, ed., *Political Oppositions in Western Democracies* (New Haven: Yale University Press, 1966), p. 391.
21. "The British Parliament," *Government and Opposition* 1, no. 1 (October 1965): 135.
22. In his Introduction to the second edition of *The English Constitution*, 1872. See World's Classics edition (London: Oxford University Press, 1928), p. 311.

LIBRARY OF DAVIDSON COLLEGE